The Man

Who Lived Twice

Edward Sheldon

PHOTOGRAPH BY
Pirie MacDonald

THE MAN
WHO LIVED TWICE

The Biography

of EDWARD SHELDON

BY ERIC WOLLENCOTT BARNES

WITH AN INTRODUCTORY CHAPTER

by

ANNE MORROW LINDBERGH

Charles Scribner's Sons NEW YORK

The Introductory Chapter by Anne Morrow Lindbergh is reprinted here with the kind permission of Mrs. Lindbergh and *The Reader's Digest* wherein it first appeared under the title, "The Most Unforgettable Character I've Met." Copyright 1946 by The Reader's Digest Association, Inc.

The lines from T. S. Eliot's "East Coker" appearing on pages 10 and 11 are reprinted by permission of Harcourt, Brace and Company, Inc. from *Four Quartets*, copyright 1943 by T. S. Eliot.

The lines from John Hall Wheelock's "Departure" appearing on page 174, and his poem, "Silence," appearing on pages 355 and 356 are reprinted by permission of Charles Scribner's Sons from *Poems 1911–1936*, copyright 1936 by Charles Scribner's Sons.

The selection appearing on page 228 is reprinted by permission of Appleton-Century-Crofts, Inc. from *We Barrymores* by Lionel Barrymore as told to Cameron Shipp, copyright 1951 by Appleton-Century-Crofts, Inc.

TO MY MOTHER

ACKNOWLEDGMENTS

SHORTLY after Edward Sheldon's death an old and close friend, Marion Meigs Hyde (now Mrs. William Woods), began to collect information on his life and career. Aided by Sheldon's mother, who died in 1949, Mrs. Woods worked indefatigably for several years. It is largely due to her preliminary effort that this biography has been possible. In stating my indebtedness to Mrs. Woods, I wish to make clear that without her promptness and foresight in rescuing material that would otherwise have disappeared with the people in whose memories it resided, no reasonably complete life of Sheldon could have been written. My obligation to Mrs. Woods goes still further. In my own research and during the writing of the book, her intimate knowledge of the subject, so generously shared with me, has been invaluable.

The text of the book itself will make clear, I think, the extent of my obligations to dozens of other friends of Sheldon's who have contributed details of his career, personal recollections and letters. To all these individuals I offer my gratitude.

I wish particularly to acknowledge my indebtedness and to express my appreciation to the following: Mrs. Charles A. Lindbergh for her kindness in supplying the Introductory Chapter to this volume, and to *The Reader's Digest* for permission to reprint the material which it contains; Mrs. Alfred MacArthur and Mr. Theodore Sheldon for their generosity in making available their brother's papers and for their continued cooperation throughout the project; Mr. John Hall Wheelock for important suggestions, active assistance and many kindnesses through the whole course of the work; Mr. Van Wyck Brooks, Mrs. Henrietta A. Metcalf, Mr. Addison M. Metcalf, Dr. and Mrs. Carl Binger for friendly advice and many useful details; the Theatre Collection, Houghton Library, Harvard University, for permission to use material from its archives—and to the Curator of the Collection, Dr. William van Lennep and his assistant Miss Mary Reardon for their kind offices. Finally, as always, I record my thanks to my wife for her editorial assistance and willing servitude to the mechanics of authorship.

For permission to quote from copyrighted works I wish to thank Messrs. Charles Scribner's Sons for selections from *Poems 1911–1936* by John Hall Wheelock; Harcourt, Brace and Company, Inc. for the lines from T. S. Eliot's "East Coker" appearing in the Introductory Chapter by Anne Morrow Lindbergh; the Estate of the late Constance Collier for the passage from *Harlequinade* (1930 John Lane); the Estate of the late Lionel Barrymore for the excerpt from *We Barrymores* (1951 Appleton-Century-Crofts, Inc.), copyright 1951 by Lionel Barrymore and Cameron Shipp.

E. W. B.

South Harwich, Mass.
January 18, 1956

CONTENTS

Page

Contents

ILLUSTRATIONS

The Man

Who Lived Twice

INTRODUCTORY CHAPTER

The Most Unforgettable Character
I've Met*

BY ANNE MORROW LINDBERGH

I REMEMBER lying in bed in the hospital, after the birth of a child, on an autumn morning crisp as an apple, rosy on one side, chilled on the other. The sun was pouring in my window and, outside, every yellow leaf, touched by frost the night before, stood still in the golden air. The nurse brought me a telegram from Edward Sheldon which read:

THIS IS A BEAUTIFUL MORNING. I AM SURE YOU AND YOUR DAUGHTER ARE HAPPY.

I felt full of joy at such a swift and magical sharing of my mood. Then suddenly I thought, shocked almost to tears, "But how does he know it is a beautiful morning? The man who sent that telegram is blind. He has not seen a tree for twenty years."

I remember very well the first time I met him. I felt rather shy as I rode up on the elevator to his penthouse and I wondered nervously whether I would say the right thing,

* Copyright, 1946, by The Reader's Digest Association, Inc., reprinted by permission.

how I should be able to talk to such a man. A nurse met me and ushered me into the long room with windows on two sides opening out onto the roof. On one side of the room, in front of the windows, there was an enormous table, piled high with books, stacks of them, seven or eight deep, current books which he was "reading." At the end of the room was a high bed, rather like a bier ("Like the last act of *Tristan*," someone once described it), with a thronelike canopy towering over it. The man lying in the shadow of this velvet canopy was covered with a Persian shawl, intricately patterned in soft reds and browns. Only his head and shoulders were visible. He was immaculately dressed as if he were lying down for a few minutes only. His eyes were bandaged. He greeted you with a rather breathless whisper.

I mention these details because the first time one entered the room they pricked at one sharply and uncomfortably. After five minutes one never noticed them again. They were not even a barrier to be leapt across; they simply ceased to exist, so overshadowed were they by the personality of the man one went to see.

The nurse directed me to the comfortable chair and low table by the side of the bed where tea or lunch was always laid for his guests, even though he did not partake of it. But before I could sit down, Edward Sheldon had thrown a verbal life line to me, across that gulf of shyness that exists between two people meeting for the first time.

"Tell me, Mrs. Lindbergh," he said, referring to a line in a book of mine he had read, "did you ever get that crust of French bread and that piece of runny cheese you were thinking about over the Alps?"

I laughed; the life line fell neatly; the gulf had been bridged; we talked all afternoon.

As I have said, one went shyly the first time, on faith,

perhaps because one had been asked to go, or even out of kindness. After that, one went for oneself, to fill a need. One talked to him as to an old friend, on all subjects; daily life, literature, politics or problems of morality—how to live the good life. On one occasion we had a long discussion, suggested by a quotation of Pascal's about men "of the middle." We were alike in our sympathy with the man in the middle, the moderate who will not be classified with this or that extreme group, who is never violent in his judgment or his praise, who has humility about his opinions, who sees the world and most of his fellow human beings as neither black nor white but gray. I ventured the opinion that, in one's critical judgment, the ideal attitude would be "black and white about oneself but gray about the rest of the world."

"Oh, no," Ned Sheldon corrected me quickly. "Oh, no, you must be gray about yourself, too; you must forgive yourself, too. That is the hardest thing of all."

He gave abundantly, advice, encouragement, stimulus, criticism. But he also allowed you to give to him (most subtle form of giving). He knew how to receive so graciously that the gift was enhanced by its reception. It was the rarest pleasure to bring things to him, books one had found, passages of poetry or philosophy, a seventeenth-century mystic or a modern poet, comments on life by a soldier one had met in a train, or by a child in a school bus. He took them all in eagerly. Warmed by his welcome, how beautiful became the things that one brought him. So often one has the opposite experience, gifts shrivel under the critical gaze of the recipient. One is like a child running in from the beach with a jewel found in the retreating rim of the tide, only to have it fade to an ordinary stone on the dry palm of another. With Edward Sheldon everything became more beautiful in the light of his appreciation. Seen through those transluccnt depths, sea shells became pearls; ordinary stones were jewels.

No, I should not have worried about having nothing to say to this man. One always talked too much and stayed too long. One went away refreshed and stimulated, with a hundred new paths shooting off in the mind, and the quiet certainty that there was infinite time in which to follow them. The world opened up from those four closed walls.

Why did one feel this way about him? How explain this extraordinary influence over other people? In what resided his power? The question is not answered by any listing of his qualities, saintlike though they were. Of course, all who knew him were fired by his sustained gallantry, were quickened by the unquenchable flame of his spirit, were overcome by his princely prodigality of heart. And you had only to walk into his room to be won by his chivalrous courtesy. Courtesy is generally considered a social value only, but in this case it passed the bounds of ordinary courtesy and took its place in the scale of moral values. It was, in fact, a combination of courage and extreme consideration.

He never mentioned his infirmities or referred to them in any way, even by implication or negatively. And he took the greatest pains to create and preserve in the minds of others the delicate illusion that he was just like everyone else. So perfect was the spell he cast over his bedroom that you ceased to think of him as an invalid. You had almost the impression, as a small boy once expressed it after a first visit, that he was "a prince under an enchantment." He spoke of "reading" books, "seeing" friends, and "meeting" people in a way that was physically impossible for him. But he spoke like this not out of any vanity, I am sure, but simply not to burden his friends with the constant awareness of his difficulties. Such an awareness might have stood between him and them, as a barrier—or a bridge. Either would have been distasteful to him. He would have abhorred the thought that people came to him *because* of his invalidism or even in *spite* of it. And they did neither.

If you should ask them why they came, what was the compelling force that drew them, I believe many would say, in one form or another, "He understood me; nobody understood me so well." This was true; in anything which he apprehended directly he had the most uncanny powers of perception. Not only had he developed his hearing to an extraordinary degree (he often guessed the height of a newcomer from the position of a voice), but he seemed to have developed other senses of apprehension unknown to the normally endowed individual. The minute you walked into his room he knew all about you, inwardly and outwardly. He saw you whole, and in his presence you felt whole. The beautiful prayer from the *Phaedrus* was answered: "The outward and the inward man were at one."

This is not to say there was for him no "outward man." For Edward Sheldon did not belittle the material world. He was alive to its beauties and its richness. He delighted in any descriptions you gave him of the changing seasons. The last golden wasps of autumn and the first purple heads of the skunk cabbages were important items of news to him. Once, in answer to a letter of mine describing a spring day in the country, he wired back enthusiastically:

SO GLAD YOU COULD LIE UNDER A TREE!

And if he was still aware of the beauty of the outward world, he did not overlook its ugliness, its complications, and its troubles. If one went to him with problems, spoken or unspoken, one left with many solved—or, rather, dissolved in his presence. For it was not necessary always to mention them. In front of him they were likely to fall into proper proportion. False worries he might prick with his dry humor; actual problems, though so much less than his own, he never belittled. Sometimes, with his acute perception, he would put his finger—very gently—on the sensitive point, as if to say, like the doctor, "It is here that it hurts the most." And he would be quite wise and practical about the cure. He could be stern, too, in his admonitions. "That's your Puritan conscience again," he would chide me sometimes. "A conscience is fine if it stimulates you to action; terrible, if it keeps you from your true work. Like worry: worry is wonderful if it moves you to do things; corroding, if it doesn't. The wonderful thing about the Puritans was their energy."

No, he saw the outward active man, in his outward activities.

"But he saw us in too beautiful a light," someone once protested. "Suppose his eyes had been opened and he had really seen us for what we were—would he not have been terribly disillusioned?"

I do not believe so; his genius was for seeing *through* the outer man to the inner one. It was his understanding of the inner man that was the most miraculous and for which one was most grateful. After all, as Saint-Exupéry's *Little Prince* says, "The eyes are blind; one can only see with the heart." Edward Sheldon saw with the heart. He saw people with love, all of them, even the newcomers like myself. He saw them, therefore, creatively; not only as they were, but as they strove to be, as they were meant to be. He became for many people the creative observer in their lives.

The creative observer is a familiar but usually under-valued character in life. We have all known him and been grateful to him, but we are inclined to take him for granted. There is usually one, sometimes more, in the circle of one's friends. He stands a little removed from the daily round, but near enough to watch. He never interferes; he observes. He is perceptive, kind, appreciative, sometimes critical, but always detached. Even though he is not actively involved in one's life, he has a direct effect on it. When he is on the side lines, one's task immediately takes on new meaning and dignity. It is easier to go on when he is standing there.

A creative observer mirrors back your own life—yes—but your life seen in order, in form, in pattern, even—actually—in beauty. In this capacity, he attains the stature of a creative artist. He performs the function of an artist as analyzed once by the poet Auden. He "finds the order latent in the apparent chaos" of your life. He finds the pattern already there but unaccented. He reveals the beauty existing but unrecognized. This is not a process of deception but of discovery. It is also a process of creation. Edward Sheldon, who had been forced to abandon being a creative artist with stage figures, became one with living people. The brilliant career he left behind in the medium of drama was fulfilled in the medium of life itself.

Have I come back then to the oversimplified conclusion that Edward Sheldon was a saint? Many of us shrink before a word so dazzlingly bright in its connotations of perfection; an image, so lacking in shadows that it is almost invisible to the human eye; a term, too abstract to fit an ordinary mortal in the world today. But if the word *saint* be taken as a symbol for an ordinary man who had overcome superhuman difficulties in his own life; who, after overcoming them, still had ardor enough left to give to those he came in contact with; whose vision was so sharpened by suffering and illuminated by love that he saw everyone as they were meant to be; and, finally, a man who lived a large proportion of his life in a world of eternal values, free of the pressures of time and fear, greed and passion—yes, then it might be said that Edward Sheldon filled the symbol of sainthood.

The last time I went to see him I read to him from T. S. Eliot's *Four Quartets*. "Read that again," I can hear his breathless whisper. I think I read him three times the stanzas from Eliot's poem, *East Coker*, so concerned with eternity and eternal living:

> Home is where one starts from. As we grow older
> The world becomes stranger, the pattern more complicated
> Of dead and living. Not the intense moment
> Isolated, with no before and after,
> But a lifetime burning in every moment. . . .
>
> Love is most nearly itself
> When here and now cease to matter.
> Old men ought to be explorers
> Here and there does not matter
> We must be still and still moving
> Into another intensity
> For a further union, a deeper communion
> Through the dark cold and the empty desolation,
> The wave cry, the wind cry, the vast waters
> Of the petrel and the porpoise. In my end is my beginning.

On this note I left him, promising, as always, to come back very soon. But I was not to see him again.

Those of us who knew him—even I who had known him for so short a time—had mixed emotions when we heard of his sudden and peaceful death. First, the instinctive selfish wrench of pain to lose such a friend and companion. (Hereafter we would have to be the creative observer for ourselves.) And then, perhaps, a sense of wonder at the personality of the man we had known, the image illuminated more sharply, as always, at the moment of loss. And consequently a feeling of responsibility at having known such a person. Public responsibility to let more people know about him, to let more of the world into his quiet room. Private responsibility, which is more difficult for it involves trying to remain the person one was in that room. And this means living in that timeless atmosphere which Edward Sheldon created around him. It demands from one that nearly impossible task of living in the present moment as if it were eternity.

For "eternity," according to Boethius, "is the complete and perfect possession of unlimited life all at once." Paradoxically, this "unlimited life all at once" is what one felt in the presence of this man who had almost no life at all in the worldly or physical meaning of the word. Seated beside him, in the heart of the world's most hurried and high-pressured city, no one ever had a feeling of hurry or pressure. The sense of eternity in which he lived was passed over to the people who sat with him. There, one was able to live for a few minutes—as he lived always.

For Edward Sheldon himself, so far advanced in this difficult task of living eternally, one had no fear, only the certainty that for him the Eliot lines were now being enacted, were coming true. The flesh had become word:

> We must be still and still moving
> Into another intensity
> For a further union, a deeper communion. . . .
> In my end is my beginning.

CHAPTER I

Prelude to Fame

AT TWENTY Edward Sheldon was already a marked man—
marked, that is, by all the gifts and graces, the attitudes, the
vigor, and the habit of accomplishment that make success
inevitable. To his classmates and intimates at Harvard there
was no doubt that Ned would have his way with the world.
By the middle of his sophomore year he had established an
enviable record for scholarship, was one of the college's
leading literary lights, and was active in half a dozen organizations ranging from the very intellectual Stylus to the
purely convivial O.K. Club. Whatever he did was well
done. Furthermore, he was a favorite with everybody, for
in addition to intelligence and imagination he had a charm
that was irresistible.

This was thoroughly demonstrated the afternoon in January, 1906, when Mrs. Fiske came to tea. The reigning personality of the American stage had been playing a prosperous
season in Boston and as a gesture of good will to her Harvard
following had come over to Cambridge to lecture. Her talk
was pitched in a key of high seriousness. It was entitled
"The Ethics of the Theatre," and the student body in one
mighty ethical impulse had packed the auditorium to over-
flowing.

Afterward an informal gathering was held in the rooms

of the Stylus Club, so that the great lady might savor the
cultural tone of the College in a more relaxed atmosphere.
For the first half hour all had gone well. The members of
the club in starched collars and high-buttoned shoes plied
their guest with tea and cookies. They gathered round to
tell her singly and collectively how wonderful she had been
in *Leah Kleschna*. They expressed the hope that she liked
Cambridge. They noted the condition of the weather—and
with that the conversational resources were exhausted. For
a while Mrs. Fiske carried on alone. But she had already
talked for an hour at the Sanders Theatre and she had a
performance ahead of her that night. Soon her remarks were
punctuated by silences, and then she began to tap her foot.
A feeling of panic descended on the young gentlemen, and
the one thought in every mind was what in the name of
Heaven had happened to Ned Sheldon? The success of the
whole enterprise had been premised on the idea that Sheldon
with his knowledge of the world, of the theatre, of stage
personalities, and most particularly of Mrs. Fiske herself,
would keep the guest of honor suitably entertained. Frantically the club president dispatched a messenger to comb the
Yard for the missing Sheldon.

There followed ten minutes of agonized waiting. Then
as matters reached their unbearable climax, with Mrs. Fiske
making preliminary motions of gathering up her furs, her
handbag, her gloves, the door burst open and Sheldon, the
perspiring messenger at his heels, appeared.

Instantly—almost electrically, as those present recalled the
moment—the whole atmosphere changed. The tall, dark-
haired youth, with his high color and clear brown eyes, gave
a glance about the room and went straight to Mrs. Fiske.
He hardly waited for the president to introduce him, barely

murmured apologies for his lateness before he plunged, taking Mrs. Fiske with him, into a flood of talk, about the theatre, about stage people—and about Mrs. Fiske. There were also pertinent and knowing comments on the subject of kindness to animals, which if all else had fallen on deaf ears would have roused Mrs. Fiske to instant alertness. For the lady was passionately devoted to all dumb creatures, and had written a pamphlet on antivivisection.

But nothing Sheldon said fell on deaf ears. For an hour the Stylus rooms echoed to the lively duologue between the Harvard sophomore and Minnie Maddern Fiske, while the other members of the club sat by in happy relief, like a grand opera chorus which has discharged all responsibility in furthering the plot.

Talk flowed from Ned Sheldon like a bubbling fountain. And Mrs. Fiske, stimulated not only by the subject of the talk, which was largely herself, but by the sheer exuberance of this youth who seemed to know so many things, gave as good as she took.

At the height of the conversation the quiet of the Yard was shattered by a series of explosions, metallic clankings, and other alien sounds. At the door of Grey's Hall a glittering motorcar quivered to a halt. Sheldon glanced out the window, and without further ceremony whisked the celebrated guest off for a drive. Everybody knew now why he had been late. He had been arranging this final touch to the afternoon's entertainment; and if there was something high-handed in his preëmption of the guest of honor, nobody minded. One never did with Ned. Besides, the others knew they would all shine in reflected glory when people saw Ned Sheldon rolling through the streets of Cambridge with Mrs. Fiske at his side.

When the pair returned an hour later they were still talking. And this might have continued till evening had not a note arrived from Professor Copeland—the beloved "Copey" of English Composition fame—who was an old friend of the actress and felt he had some rights in her visit:

Dear Minnie:
When you are finished talking with Ned Sheldon, may I see you?

C. T. COPELAND

The conquest of Mrs. Fiske, memorable though it was because of the special glamor surrounding her personality, did not really surprise Ned's friends. In all the range of his accomplishments, nothing so distinguished him in their youthful eyes as his way with people. It was not only that he had so much to talk about. He had a wonderful knack of directing whatever he said so that it cast a glow of new importance over the other person. Even with celebrities like Mrs. Fiske, certainly no stranger to flattering attention, this was completely disarming because it was so manifestly sincere. And the reason for this lay in the simple but nonetheless remarkable fact that at twenty Edward Sheldon was more interested in others than in himself.

To anyone familiar with his background it was astonishing that this should have been so. The world into which Sheldon was born, back in Chicago on February 4, 1886, was so compact, so tightly hedged about by wealth and family loyalty, that one would have expected a boy's horizons to be distinctly limited.

It was not only that life was well cushioned against the outside by a considerable fortune in Chicago real estate. Within the family circle itself the currents of affection were so strong that neither parents nor children required much of society beyond the walls of the big house in Bellevue Place. Ned's favorite playmate was his brother Theodore, two years his senior, and both boys were devoted to their sister Mary, five years younger than Ned.

The elder Theodore Sheldon was a man of quiet habits and high principles. He had distinguished himself in the Chicago real estate world by inaugurating important reforms in the transfer of property titles, and also by his unswerving adherence to an ethical code inherited from his Covenanting New England ancestors. In his home he was the final authority on any question of moral doubt. Otherwise he played his part unobtrusively, content to leave domestic affairs largely in the hands of his wife.

Mary Strong Sheldon was an unusual woman by any standards. By those of late nineteenth-century Chicago she was quite extraordinary. Under conditions which would have made stodginess almost inevitable, she contrived to inject excitement into the lives of everyone around her. Besides possessing inexhaustible vitality, a firm will, and a quick grasp of practical details, she was highly imaginative. In her attitude toward human relations she was a thoroughgoing romantic, and she could endow the dullest event with high drama. Dorothy Donnelly, the charming actress who later figured in Ned's life, once said to her in wholehearted admiration, "Dear Mrs. Sheldon, you could dramatize a muffin!"

Had she been less of an individualist at heart (externally she was a rather conventional woman) and less intelligent, Mary Sheldon might have devoted herself to the pursuits then considered proper for young women of "artistic" leanings—wood-burning, or interior decoration in the spirit of

William Morris and Burne-Jones. But her vision extended beyond such trivialities. It was by and through her children, and most particularly her younger son who had inherited so much of her temperament, that she found expression for her idealistic and aesthetic impulses.

Among other things she was unusually articulate. From wide reading and a lively interest in ideas she had developed a rich vocabulary and a fine sense of word values. By the simple process of association these were transmitted to Ned, and accounted for his mature literary tastes and facility with language.

It is not surprising that a woman of Mrs. Sheldon's disposition should have been drawn to the theatre. She was not only stirred by the romance and color of the stage; she looked upon great drama as a valuable educational device. How better could one impress upon the young mind the meaning of character than through the noble and heroic actions depicted in great plays? It was easy enough for her imaginative younger son to share this taste, as he did his mother's love for books and pictures and music. When the taste soon became a passion, which might have given some mothers cause for alarm, Mrs. Sheldon was delighted. She was always an enthusiastic audience for Ned's productions on the toy stage which was the central feature of the playroom in Bellevue Place; and she saw to it that he had tickets for everything worthwhile in the real flesh-and-blood theatre.

Once when Ned was ten years old he slipped out of the house at daybreak to stand in line for tickets to Maude Adams' production of *Romeo and Juliet*. He did not return home for breakfast but went straight on to school. When he came in that afternoon his mother had not the heart to scold him. There was such triumph in his eyes as he proudly held out the tickets and told her, "Please remember you have an engagement with me for Thursday evening, and please be dressed." It was certainly an event. No one could forget the childlike quality of Maude Adams' Juliet; but the picture fixed in Mrs. Sheldon's mind was of the little boy sitting on his rolled-up reefer so that he could see over the heads in front of him, eyes glowing with excitement, responding with uninhibited delight to everything that happened on the stage.

From his earliest childhood Ned's imagination was fed by the plays he saw. If his mother exercised a certain amount of censorship over what might be considered absolutely unsuitable for a tender mind (he was not allowed, for instance, to see *Tess of the D'Urbervilles* with Mrs. Fiske), there was plenty of wholesome fare at the Chicago theatres of those days to satisfy an alert youngster's growing curiosity about life and people. More than anything else, Ned got from this early theatre-going a sense of the infinite variety, the potentialities for excitement in human nature. No one he met was without some dramatic interest for him, and the ripening of an acquaintanceship took on the same fascination he felt in watching the development of a character on the stage.

Outside his immediate family the most striking figure in Ned's childhood was his maternal grandfather, Henry Strong. He was called "General" by courtesy, a title appropriate not only to his position but to his commanding temperament. Like his son-in-law, but on a more spectacular scale, "General" Strong had achieved eminence as a real estate operator. Originally a New Englander, he had prepared for the ministry, then switched to the law. This had taken him into railroading, and from attorney he had risen to the presidency of the Atchison, Topeka and Santa Fe. In this position he had been well placed to observe Chicago's growing importance as the railroad center of the nation, to foresee and to take advantage of the rise in land values in that booming metropolis. By the time Ned was born Henry Strong had become a power in the Chicago business and financial world. He had made his way through native shrewdness, immense vitality, and a perfectly inflexible will; and though now retired from active business he continued to make all three qualities felt on those around him.

His grandchildren were most aware of him during the summer, when the family migrated to Henry Strong's country place on Lake Geneva, Wisconsin. Here the Sheldons were joined by other grandchildren from Denver, the Denisons. Elsa Denison, who was about Ned's age, was his favorite cousin. Not only was she an enthusiastic participant in the theatricals which Ned was constantly arranging; she was a sworn ally in the perpetual secret warfare the children waged against their grandfather. For at Lake Geneva, with his daughters and grandchildren directly under his eye, Henry Strong played the role of family dictator to the hilt. Much of the children's energy—when they were not swimming, or boating, or tramping the woods, or acting plays—was devoted to thwarting the edicts and ultimatums of their grandfather. To his face they called him "G–pa," but in private he was referred to as The Holy Terror. In the unfolding drama of Ned's childhood "G–pa" was a very satisfactory villain, a part he continued to play for some years. With maturity and perspective Ned came to appreciate Henry Strong for what he really was: an immensely colorful, vital figure, whose iron will, transmuted into more flexible but equally enduring metal, was part of Ned's own character.

There were neighbors, too, at Lake Geneva. Ned was

a frequent visitor at the home of fellow Chicagoans, the McCreas, whose property adjoined that of his grandfather. Ned was especially attracted by Mrs. McCrea with whom he had long, grown-up conversations. One summer her little stepdaughter, Henrietta, arrived from France where she had spent most of her life. To Ned the twelve-year-old girl, with her romantic European background, was a glamorous figure. But he sensed too her forlornness at finding herself in a new and strange world; and he immediately took it upon himself to introduce her to the other children and to make a place for her in their varied activities. The next summer Ned made friends with another little girl whose parents were likewise Chicago acquaintances of the Sheldons. In Margaret Ayer he found a kindred spirit who not only liked to see plays but even enjoyed reading them. They discovered Rostand together, and spent hours under a gnarled old apple tree down near the edge of the lake reading *L'Aiglon* aloud. They saw each other often during the next two or three years. Then their ways parted to join again twenty years later, and with unexpected consequences.

There was another summer when the Sheldon and Denison children had as their tutor-companion a young woman destined for a brilliant career as a scientist. With Florence Sabin the children had their first lessons in nature lore and learned something of the wonderful laws behind the stones and water and growing things that hitherto had been merely a background for their play. On Ned this had a lasting effect. Under the inspired young teacher he developed a reverence for the principle of life that eventually became a passion.

At fourteen, Ned went East to the Hill School in Pottstown, Pennsylvania, where his brother Ted had preceded him. For a sensitive lad whose life had been so sheltered, boarding school might have proved a dislocating experience. But any emotional wrench at being separated from home and parents was fully offset by the excitement of finding himself in new surroundings, by studies that challenged his expanding curiosity—above all by the scores of new friends he soon made. Even in 1901 the Hill was not a small school; but Ned soon knew everybody. He made friends of masters as well as boys; and for the forthright headmaster, Dr. John Meigs, of whom most of the boys stood in healthy awe, he quickly developed a warm admiration. And for the headmaster's wife he had a special tenderness which remained with him always. Years later when he was blind and bedridden, he could still evoke his first bright impression of "Mrs. John as she came up the aisle between the rows of boys at evening prayers, in white, with a blue sash that matched her eyes, the evening sun on her chestnut hair." And in that aftertime when his bedside became a mecca for half the celebrities of New York, he would say that there were two people who, when they came, left "a definite spiritual entity behind them." One of these was the young Indian mystic Krishnamurti and the other was "Mrs. John".

Ned was seventeen when he graduated from the Hill— too young, his parents felt, for him to enter Harvard. So it was decided he should have a year of postgraduate work at Milton Academy. Since Milton was not far from Cambridge, where his brother Ted was now a student, he would have a chance to sample the cultural climate of New England and to see something of Harvard before he actually entered as a freshman.

This was not a happy choice. For the first time in his life, Ned's gift for friendship met no response. He found Milton a cliquey place, and there seemed to be no niche for a one-year senior. The other boys, bound together by longer associations, were not interested in an outsider. Ned struggled hard to make a place for himself, doing everything possible to be a "good mixer." But the ingredients of his nature did not lend themselves to the Milton formula. He reported faithfully for football practice, but he was a dud at the game; and this did not raise him in the minds of the Miltonians. His passion for the theatre which took him to Boston on every possible occasion was incomprehensible to his adolescent comrades; and his tastes in reading (he discovered Ibsen at Milton) put him definitely outside the pale.

For the first time, Ned experienced loneliness, and the effect on a nature which needed constantly to share itself was depressing. Curiously enough, it was not his ego that suffered from his rejection by the other boys, but his moral sense. In January, 1904, he wrote desperately to his mother:

> I don't suppose you know, but sometimes I am horrified to see what a monster of selfishness I am! Every now and then it comes to me like a lightning flash; between times I put it out of my mind. I say, "Oh well, you'll come out all right." But if I don't change radically I won't come out all right; I'll be a disgrace to the family. So I must change. My whole character must undergo a revolution before I can attain the vague, shadowy, but lofty ambitions I have within me. . . .

He did not find much intellectual stimulus in his studies— which were mainly a retracing of familiar ground—and in his isolation this weighed on him. It was as though he had a premonition that time was pressing, that there would be little enough opportunity to accomplish the grand designs he felt stirring within him.

> Do you know [again he was writing to his mother], I am practically eighteen years old? That many men begin their

struggles of life long before that age? that as I stand I am
absolutely unfit for doing anything in life?

There was no mistaking the urgency of his tone; and after
a little deliberation, his parents yielded to his plea to come
home. In February, 1904, he was withdrawn from the school.

Back in Chicago, Ned swiftly recovered his buoyant
optimism. As a gesture of good will to his grandfather he
had a brief try at the real estate business. It was soon clear,
however, that this was not the channel to the realization of
those "vague but lofty ambitions," and that he would do
better if he used his time to work for the Harvard entrance
examinations in history and French.

When he went to his old teacher at the Chicago Latin
School to ask her to coach him in history, that overburdened
lady demurred at the thought of giving private lessons. But
history had always been one of Ned's keen enthusiasms, and
Miss Vickery could not resist his persuasive: "You won't
have to teach me. All you'll have to do is listen, while I *tell*
you about history."

Two evenings a week he spent at French with Madame
Marie de la Mare, a brilliant and stimulating French-
American, granddaughter of the painter George P. A. Healy,
who introduced Ned to the French drama, a world of new
delight into which he plunged with all the ardor of his stage-
struck soul.

When he set out for Cambridge in the fall of 1904, the
bleak months at Milton Academy were forgotten. He went
back East with a sense of high adventure, tingling at the
prospect of at last moving out into the current.

Ned was enthralled from the outset by the atmosphere of
Harvard. He sensed deeply the force of New England's
social and cultural tradition, concentrated in the College and

University. The moment he walked through the Harvard gate he felt that this was where he belonged; and one of the first actions by which he proclaimed his identification with the New England background was to adopt the middle name of Brewster, which had figured in his family some generations back. Throughout his Harvard career and for a few years thereafter he firmly held on to this. But when fame caught up with him, the Brewster somehow got lost by the way. Then he was content to be again what the world would have him—simply Edward Sheldon.

There is no doubt that Ned was of a different stripe from the average freshman entering Harvard. He not only knew why he had come to college; he knew exactly what he wanted to study and with whom. During the months at Milton when he had visited his brother Ted, then in his second year at Harvard, he had collected detailed information on courses and faculty members. He was thoroughly familiar with the personalities of the men on the teaching staff, and he was minutely informed as to their scholarly reputations.

This was Harvard's Golden Age, and the roster of the faculty had an Olympian cast. President Eliot, benign and unassailable, was still guiding the University's destiny; and in Ned's chosen field there were half a dozen figures slated for immortality. Charles Townsend Copeland, Dean Briggs, Bliss Perry, Barrett Wendell, George Lyman Kittredge— Ned knew about them all, and they would soon know all about him. There was also a younger professor who had created a good deal of a stir with a very unorthodox course —in playwriting. George Pierce Baker had braved the immemorial tradition of the liberal arts with his experimental work in dramatic technique, and his departure was not viewed with favor in all camps, even though some of his students were already achieving remarkable results. President Eliot in particular was affronted by the innovation and he had told Baker with Jovian condescension, "You may teach drama, but you are hired to teach English." (This attitude eventually cost Harvard the services of Professor Baker. He went to Yale which was happy to hire him to teach drama, and there, as head of the Yale Drama School, he produced not only playwrights, but directors and theatre technicians as well. Ned had his eye on this course above all others; but it was not until his second semester that he was able to persuade Baker to let him take it.

Under Harvard's liberal elective system Sheldon was allowed to follow pretty much his own inclinations in making out his academic program. But a kind of intellectual conscience forced him to explore fields outside his special interests. He enrolled in Professor Lowell's course in Constitutional Government because, as he wrote his grandfather, "every man should have a clear idea of his own and England's system of government." In something of the same spirit he enrolled in Philosophy I, offered jointly by William James, Josiah Royce, and Hugo Münsterberg. However, he was no slave to his conscience, academic or otherwise, and when at the beginning of the second semester he was admitted to "Baker's Dozen," as the playwriting course was known, he dropped Constitutional Government.

Whatever distinction these men enjoyed in their special fields, their classes were important to Ned because of the flavor of human personality they injected into their teaching. In turn, there were few of Ned's professors who were not struck by the eager dark-haired youth with the warm infectious laugh, whose presence somehow gave spark to the most pedestrian group of students.

Faculty and classmates alike were impressed by what

seemed a phenomenal store of information which Sheldon brought to bear on his work. His roommate and close friend, John Hall Wheelock, remembered that "Ned was avid for courses; yet from the time he came to college he covered ground already familiar to him. It might be the period of the French Revolution, or of Victor Hugo or of the modern French poets, Verlaine and Baudelaire—he had a perfect picture of the period, down to the art, the clothing, the customs, all the minutiae of life. He could *live* in the time of Julius Caesar or of Congreve."

It was this gift for projecting himself imaginatively into whatever he studied that made Ned's mind something more than a storehouse of miscellaneous details picked up through precocious reading. Beneath the bare statements of fact—which then as now made college texts such dreary reading—he seemed to grasp meanings and relationships, so that what he read appeared part of his personal experience. Obviously, at eighteen or nineteen this could not have been the case. What Ned did possess were unusual powers of observation and a deeply intuitive nature. The combination produced something which to both his teachers and his fellow students seemed very like wisdom. Years after he had left Harvard, this was still remembered. In the late thirties, someone spoke to Copeland of Ned's enduring affection for his old professor. The dim eyes grew misty and Copey murmured, "Dear Ned! I never taught him anything—he knew better than any of us."

But the happiest fruits of Ned's Harvard years were the friendships of those with whom he discovered life. By the end of his freshman year he had found a place for himself among a sizable group of boys with literary and artistic aspirations. The closest of these friendships were with John

Hall Wheelock and Van Wyck Brooks. All through their college years these three were inseparable—bound together by common tastes, by dreams of future literary fame, and by that affection special to youth—before life has built up the wall of reserve which keeps one individual from easily sharing himself with others.

Even so, in Sheldon's case there was already, if not reserve, at least an inner core of reticence which his most constant companions could not penetrate. Even with Brooks and Wheelock, there were moments when Ned seemed to slip behind a veil of remoteness. In the midst of some passionate discussion of life or poetry or love they would note that Ned was no longer taking active part but seemed rather to be listening with an air of amused watchfulness. It was as though he had threshed out that particular point long ago and were waiting for the others to catch up with him.

Perhaps he had already discovered that final point of loneliness at the heart of all personality. If so, this only heightened his need to be with others and to take part in whatever interested his friends at the moment. Though no hail-fellow-well-met, Ned could always be counted on in anything that promised fun and excitement. He had a distaste for horseplay because it affronted his sense of human dignity, and the usual undergraduate experiments with alcohol he found dreary. But he was no teetotaler, and he was always ready for a party, particularly if it promised good talk.

Saturday night sorties in Boston with Brooks and Wheelock were almost ritualistic. These began generally with the theatre and ended at the Touraine with champagne and oysters, or if it were toward the end of the month, with a few beers and a sandwich. Frequently the three looked in at the Old Howard, whose earthy offerings were Ned's special delight. Burlesque was of course already but shreds and patches of its original self; but the days of the bumps and grinds had not yet arrived, and the friends, from the height of their college sophistication, found much mirth in the hoary jokes of hayseed comics or the efforts of tarnished blondes struggling to be seductive in numbers like "I'll Go Down to Maxim's" or "Vilia." At the Howard, Ned always insisted on sitting in the gallery, even when the student budget permitted better seats—because this brought one into closer contact with a section of society one did not normally meet, and also because Ned took a sadistic delight in the dis-comfiture of Jack Wheelock who was squeamish about fleas.

Anything with a touch of the theatrical was sure to win Sheldon's instant and wholehearted co-operation. He could even enjoy a practical joke, for which he usually had a strong aversion, if an element of play-acting was involved. Once he and a friend were traveling to Boston on a streetcar to see a play. At Central Square the car was boarded by three females of uncertain age, strongly virginal cast, and militant respectability. Sheldon glanced at the newcomers from the corner of his eye and saw they were taking up positions near where he and his friend were seated. The car was very crowded but Ned nudged the other boy, and, instead of rising as was obviously expected, pushed his hat on the back of his head and launched into a noisy tirade with a low Bowery accent, in which his companion promptly joined. For several minutes the two held forth in a manner which the ladies found most objectionable, as their glances plainly showed. But the boys pretended not to notice either the ladies or their disapproval, chewing away at imaginary cuds of tobacco and bellowing at the top of their lungs, remain-ing firmly in their seats while the ladies stood with mounting indignation. When the car reached the middle of the bridge over the Charles, the boys looked up and noted the ladies, apparently for the first time. Instantly they straightened their hats, rose, bowed, and offered their seats. Then, in the most polished accents and choice vocabulary, they spent the rest of the journey discussing the relative merits of Shaw and Maeterlinck, discreetly enjoying the looks of utter bewilderment on the faces of the three females.

Girls too were naturally a part of Ned's Harvard life. Through his freshman roommate, Rae Whidden, he met the latter's charming young cousin, Eleanor Whidden, who lived with her parents in Brookline. Eleanor was not only pretty and fun-loving. She was an ardent theatre fan, and this made a special tie between her and Ned. Throughout his freshman and sophomore years Sheldon's devotion steadily deepened. If Eleanor was sometimes out of his sight she was never far from his thoughts. On vacations in Chicago, and in Europe—of which Ned had his first taste in the summer of 1905—he wrote constantly. Sometimes she was "Countess," sometimes "Princess" or "Elaine," and Ned poured into her sympathetic ear details of his daily life, using her as a sounding board for literary experiments, and occasionally revealing glimpses of the inner solitude which his reticence concealed from his men friends. When he had his first encounter with tragedy in the death of his father the spring of 1905, it was only in letters to Eleanor that he tried to find words for his grief.

Perhaps this idyl would have taken a more serious turn had not Eleanor gone away to college. Separation and many fresh interests on both sides tempered and finally cooled the relation, though its essence remained intact in the continued lifelong friendship between Ned and his college sweetheart.

One distraction which was to assume major proportions for Sheldon came from the theatre. It was probably during the winter of 1906 while Ned was a sophomore that he first met Doris Keane, the actress who was to become the lasting focus of his deepest feelings. Miss Keane, young and then comparatively unknown, was playing an engagement in Boston with John Drew. In the company, serving as understudy and traveling companion to Doris Keane, was a cousin of Eleanor Whidden's, Alice Putnam. During the Boston engagement of the Drew company, Miss Putnam was a frequent visitor at the Whidden house, and once or twice brought Doris Keane with her. Although Eleanor was away at college, Ned, who was very fond of her parents, still came often to the house. Very likely the Whiddens, knowing Ned's lively interest in the stage and its people, would have made a point of introducing him to the charming young actress.

The story of Doris Keane and Edward Sheldon has now become a part of Broadway legend, and the legend has had it always that, so far as Ned was concerned, it was a case of love at first sight. On this—as on any subject touching his inmost self—Sheldon never spoke. But if it is true that he lost his heart to Doris Keane at their first meeting, there is gentle irony in the fact that the meeting probably took place under the very roof where his first romance had flowered.

Whatever feelings Doris Keane may have aroused in him during her stay in Boston the winter of 1906, Sheldon could for the moment only worship from a distance. Miss Keane soon moved on from Boston with her company, giving way to other and greater (at least in the eyes of the world) divinities of the stage. Mrs. Fiske's presence that year was a highlight already noted. But the climax of Boston's 1906 dramatic season came with the appearance of Sarah Bernhardt in February. "I am going six times," Ned wrote his mother, "and expect to pass away when she moves on."

It was not only the prospect of seeing the divine Sarah in person that sent thrills of expectation through Ned. For her opening performance in Sardou's *La Sorcière*, Madame Bernhardt had invited Harvard's entire Cercle Français, of which Ned was a member, to "supe." This practice of enlisting the services of various French-speaking organizations wherever she went was one of the great lady's gestures toward international good will. It also made for economies in her running expenses. By using local talent wherever she went, Bernhardt avoided the cost of salaries and transportation for a large company. Naturally this idea never crossed the minds of those privileged to take part in the productions, certainly not the mind of young Ned Sheldon. After the first rehearsal of the "supes" he reported, "I was quite wild at being behind the scenes, and rushed around examining everything."

Nothing in Ned's already considerable experience of the theatre could compare with these enchanted hours spent within speaking and touching distance of Sarah Bernhardt. He wrote it all in loving detail to his mother, how Bernhardt first appeared at rehearsals "hanging lissomely on the arm of her secretary, in a long chinchilla coat, a truly Parisian hat, lovely peroxide golden hair, a face without a line, and an alluring smile . . . I would never have thought her a day over thirty!" (She was then sixty-one.) And how during a performance, while Ned watched crouching in the wings, even close at hand the effect was magical, hypnotic. "Every movement of her slender, snaky body in those glittering Oriental robes was a poem. She reminded me of some wonderful orchid—an exotic—a creature from another world. I just couldn't seem to realize that she was flesh and blood at all. . . . I don't believe Mrs. [Potter] Palmer herself comes up to her."

Ned and another boy also "suped" in *Fedora*, and Ned, who played a police officer, actually had a line to speak. The boys had never rehearsed their parts with Madame Bernhardt herself, and they were quite unprepared during the performance for the paralyzing shriek which she gave, just before Ned delivered his line informing Fedora that her lover has been killed. But happily Ned recovered his equilibrium and spoke his part on cue. After the final curtain Bernhardt came up to him, held out her hand and exclaimed, *"Mon brave, vous étiez superbe!"* To which Ned, never at a loss, bowed low over the hand and murmured, *"Et vous aussi, Madame."* The remark evoked a delicious smile from the actress, and years later Sheldon, remembering her response to his undergraduate wit, said, "Ah, she was a very great gentleman!"

A few weeks after Bernhardt's departure from Boston, a sonnet by Sheldon appeared in the *Harvard Advocate* entitled *"Phèdre."* It began:

> *A golden-voiced vision white with passion's fire,*
> *And golden like a daughter of the sun . . .*

And on the same note of rapturous tribute it ended:

> *The white throat quivers as her high voice rings,*
> *.And trails the liquid sweetness of her song*
> *Far to the golden westward—far and long.*

From this moment on Bernhardt's signed photograph (a reward for Ned's services more precious than any mundane lucre) was the most conspicuous ornament of his college room. If up to now he had been merely a stage-struck youth, there is no doubt that from this first contact with the professional theatre and its high priestess he was a completely dedicated soul.

CHAPTER II

". . . Hell's Kitchen Piping Hot"

WITH all the distraction of falling in love, meeting beautiful actresses, and having his first taste of backstage life—not to mention other extracurricular activities—one might have expected Ned's studies to suffer. But what struck everybody now was that the more he had to do, the more his fund of energy increased and the higher the quality of his work mounted. By the end of his sophomore year he had made an "A" average, and this he maintained until graduation.

Ned took his bachelor's degree in June, 1907, *magna cum laude*. He had not only done four years' work in three; he was the first to take the degree with special distinction in literature and history under a plan inaugurated that year. This involved a final oral examination lasting three hours and covering the whole field of English literature. It was a grueling affair. At the end Ned was sure he had not passed and wrote his mother to that effect. But the next day he received a note from Professor Wendell, offering the congratulations of the faculty on his successful showing. A week later Mrs. Sheldon in Chicago received a dog-eared postcard, which had evidently remained for some days in Ned's pocket forgotten, stating laconically, "I have it."

For Ned the degree was simply a milepost he was glad to have behind him so that he could get on with the serious business of living. The matter of a career was very much up in the air. He had come to Harvard to prepare himself for teaching, and upon graduation he had been offered a fellowship in the English Department. But he was not sure now that he wanted to take this. What interested him most was writing, and everything else seemed beside the point.

As he looked back over his three years at Harvard, so crammed with varied activities, he saw that this was where his development had been most consistent. He had had great success with short stories written in Professor Copeland's composition class. Some of these had found their way into college publications, and one he had actually sold to *Smart Set* for eighty dollars. As an editorial writer on the *Advocate* he had become a power in the Yard. One of his *Advocate* pieces had led to the founding of the Harvard Dramatic Association, an enterprise in which he was abetted by young H. V. Kaltenborn. But the real impetus had come from Professor Baker's playwriting course. Into this he had poured his passionate interest in human nature and the fruits of his years of playgoing. His work, as Baker himself cautiously admitted, had a professional quality.

Ned's last assignment for this course had been a full-length play entitled *A Family Affair*. Baker was so impressed by it that he suggested sending it to a play agent in New York. He even supplied the name of an agent, Alice Kauser—without mentioning apparently that one of his own works had been gathering dust in her office for three years. This would not have discouraged Ned had he known it, since in submitting his own play he had no expectations beyond hoping to learn something of the professional ropes. Baker made a few suggestions for changes in *A Family Affair* which Ned carefully followed. Then he bound the manuscript together and shipped it off. That done, he turned to immediate problems.

He was determined not to go off the deep end in choosing a career. Above all he did not want to waste time with false starts. He wanted to be a writer, but he wanted to be practical about it. Systematically he began to canvass the Harvard faculty for informed advice. He received scant encouragement from Professor Bliss Perry, then the editor of the *Atlantic Monthly*. If he wanted to write, Perry advised that he approach the matter obliquely, say through teaching. On the other hand, Dean Briggs, Professor Wendell, and Professor Baker, all consulted in turn, pointed out the fallacy of trying to write and teach at the same time— unless he wanted to write textbooks. All knew from personal experience that nothing so deadens the imagination as constantly handling the dry bones of scholarship.

Ned was in a quandary. He saw clearly enough that teaching was no road to literary success; yet he lacked the confidence simply to set out as a writer, with no further background. Rather disconsolately he decided the thing to do was to return for a year of postgraduate work at Harvard, during which time perhaps the way would open up more clearly.

Meanwhile, he wanted more than anything else to go to Europe. The summer before he had motored through England and France with his family, and this had whetted his appetite. It now seemed to him that Europe with all its romantic glories was an absolute necessity to a full rich life. Besides if he must go back to Harvard next year, he at least deserved a little fling first. There was not much promise of excitement in his family's plans to spend the summer in Denver.

But in the European project, as on the question of his life work, he had reckoned without his grandfather. Since the death of Theodore Sheldon, Sr., "G–pa" regarded himself as the natural arbiter of the Sheldon children's destinies, and he immediately made his views known. He ignored the possibility of a writing career as too preposterous for comment. But he made himself clear on the other issues:

NORTHWOODSIDE,
LAKE GENEVA, WISCONSIN
JUNE 20, 1907

Dear Ned,

I have your letter. I am glad to know through your mother, of your success; I assume you are a Phi Beta Kappa— I have the pin which I shall be glad to give you— I think you should spend this vacation with your mother and sister. The mountain air will be good for you, also the rest from books— there is no comparison in the expense. A Denver round trip from Chicago is $30, and your expenses there would be little. A hundred dollars would cover everything.

Then you may find something better to do than keeping on with college work. You have been receiving and spending and studying eight or ten years. Continuing to receive and spend, continuing your present time of study for four years longer might land you as assistant prof. in a college at $1,500 a year; ten years' more waiting would bring a professorship at $3,000—a beggarly living in a flat. No outlook, or education, or provision for your children if you should marry.

Always affectionately yours,
GRANDPA

I heard Gordon say that you would make a good capable business man. That was two years ago.

On the subject of teaching English the General in a letter to Ned's mother was even more emphatic:

> . . . *There is nothing to English as a profession, a miserable,*
> *discouraging, overcrowded vocation. With ten pins in each*
> *hole, mostly small pins and small holes.*

On reflection, Ned doubtless had to agree with "G–pa" as to the probable rewards of a teaching career. He had been offered an assistantship in English if he returned to Cambridge to work for a master's degree; but the salary of four hundred dollars a year seemed hardly worth the inroads teaching would make on his time. What really disturbed him was that his grandfather should so high-handedly veto his plans for a trip to Europe.

> *Of course I never for a moment doubted [he wrote his*
> *mother] that he would not sanction my going to Europe.*
> *From his letters I should judge that he wanted me to go*
> *into business at Denver and start making my pile. How he*
> *must scorn all the "beggars" who teach and write to give their*
> *best to the world, rather than squeezing it for as much money*
> *as possible. I'm awfully sorry but the thought of Grandpa*
> *and all his millions makes me rather bitter.*

But no matter how Ned felt, there was no sidestepping the patriarch. The financial security of the family was largely in Henry Strong's hands. His simple formula for eliminating any opposition to his views was the brief statement, "I'll cut you out of my will."

The person who had the hardest time in the frictions between Henry Strong and his grandchildren was Ned's mother. Yet she was well qualified to act as buffer. She not only had her father's vigor but a good deal of his temperament. Her sympathy for Ned did not prevent her from seeing the practical advantages of keeping him in her father's good graces. Her tactics in the present crisis were to side with the General on the immediate issue, the proposed trip

to Europe, and to push the matter of Ned's career into the
background. After all, Ned was only twenty-one. Would it
not be better to wait another year, to let plans for the future
jell? And how better could Ned spend the interim than in
postgraduate work at Harvard?

The compromise was accepted by both sides, and in
the end each got about what he wanted. Ned even had his
trip to Europe before the end of the summer, and at no
expense to his grandfather. His uncle and namesake, Edward Sheldon, a wealthy New York bachelor, decided to
take a brief holiday in England and Scotland and offered
to take Ned along for company.

The early part of the summer was spent in visits, first
with Professor Baker, and later with the family of one of
his close friends at Harvard, George Luther Foote. Foote
was the stepson of Basil King, the former Episcopal clergyman who had now in middle age become a successful novelist. Ned had often been at the King house in Cambridge,
and Mr. King, a perceptive judge of men and talent, had
become keenly interested in Ned. Now in the quiet of
the New Hampshire mountains where his friends had a
summer home, the boy went over the whole question of
his future with King. Without hesitation the older man
told him to write—to think only of what *he* had to say and
to pay no attention to anybody else, including the public.
This was the advice Ned really wanted, and then and there
he resolved to be a writer and nothing else.

No one knows what laws of chance operate in such
matters; but at about the time Ned was talking things over
with Basil King, Alice Kauser happened to turn up an un-
opened parcel under a pile of playscripts on her littered
desk. When she saw the postmark "Cambridge" she sighed.

Another inept and labored effort from some Harvard professor! She started to push it away. Then a hunch told her to open it. When she did so, her surmise seemed correct. The very way in which the manuscript was fastened together—so securely that the pages could not be detached for easy reading—revealed that this was no professional job. Yet having gone so far, still urged by the instinct which was her chief stock in trade, she thought she had better read. She did not stop until she had finished the manuscript. Then she called her secretary and dictated a telegram to Cambridge.

In response to the summons Ned, who had just returned from New Hampshire, crammed a few articles in a bag and took the first train to New York. A few hours later he met the woman who was to play a major part in his professional life.

Alice Kauser at this time was the leading play broker in New York. She was born in Hungary of a father who was a naturalized American citizen and a mother well known as a Wagnerian singer. A girlhood spent in the wings of theatres and opera houses and an extensive acquaintance with important literary figures in Europe had eventually led her into play brokerage. She handled the American rights for works of such dramatists as Ibsen, Anatole France, Maeterlinck, Sardou, and also acted as agent for a select number of American writers. It was generally agreed that any author who attracted Alice Kauser's interest was, if not already a success, well on the way to becoming one. This proved to be the case with Edward Sheldon. From that late June morning in 1907 when he first walked into her office until her death, shortly before his own, Miss Kauser was Ned Sheldon's faithful shepherdess, handling not only his business affairs in the theatre, but piloting him with sure hand around the artistic and social pitfalls that await every newcomer to Broadway. The association was one of unbroken pleasure on both sides. Undoubtedly it brought Miss Kauser handsome financial rewards, but there were other considerations too. Like everyone else, this shrewd, matter-of-fact, often callous-seeming woman of the world warmed to the glow of Ned's personality. People referred to her as Sheldon's stage mother, an image more sentimental than accurate, since there was little to suggest the maternal in Alice Kauser's Valkyrie-like physique and temperament. But it is certain that no mother ever watched with more careful eyes the first steps of her offspring than did Alice Kauser as she guided Sheldon to success.

She never forgot the details of their first meeting. Sheldon gave his name to the secretary in the outer office. The girl eyed him in puzzlement and then called Miss Kauser on the office telephone. "It's a boy," she said in a low, astonished voice. Long afterward Alice Kauser would laugh and say, "It was exactly like the announcement of a birth, which it was—of a playwright!" She was as nonplused as the secretary. In fact her first impression, when Sheldon walked into her office, was that the playwright had sent his son to talk with her. "But it's *my* play," Ned protested. Miss Kauser looked into the brown eyes, so brightly innocent, and then she stretched out her hand. The grip made Ned wince, but it stamped the gesture with permanence. He and Alice Kauser entered upon their lifelong compact.

If Ned had come to New York with high hopes for *A Family Affair*, these were promptly dashed. Despite Miss Kauser's own enthusiasm for the play, she advised him strongly against offering it to anybody. Although she knew that it was a completely original work, in both theme and situation it resembled a current Broadway hit. And she refused to have the future of her new playwright imperiled by the faintest suspicion of plagiarism. The thing to do was to go back to Harvard, or wherever, and write another play at once! Ned was floored at this thought, but Miss Kauser left him no time for misgivings. Nor was there cause for them. A few days later Sheldon reported the visit in a note to Van Wyck Brooks:

> . . . She asked me if I had any ideas—I gave her three. She selected one for me to work on, and told me to have my scenario in by Aug. 10, if I could. She said she could get me a contract on my scenario. . . . Naturally, I was surprised, pleased, and encouraged; but I shan't count on anything or talk about it till I have my contract in my pocket. . . .

The idea which appealed to Miss Kauser had been simmering in the back of Ned's mind for some weeks. Once during the previous winter on a walk through a poor section of Boston, he had stopped to watch a Salvation Army meeting on a street corner. The preacher was a pretty girl who in spite of her bonnet and uniform still carried some faint suggestion of a lurid past. But what struck Ned was the thrilling sincerity with which she spoke, and the rapt interest of the bedraggled group gathered about her. Ned wondered by what route she had arrived at her present state. Out of that wonder sprang the idea of *Salvation Nell*, the play which a year later swept like a fresh gust through the stale atmosphere of Broadway, and carried Edward Sheldon to instant fame.

But between the germ of the play and the finished work lay months of discouraging and sometimes bewildering effort. Ned had left Alice Kauser's office after that first interview on a cloud of optimism, but by midsummer he was beginning to feel that he had bitten off more than he could chew.

> . . . *The play isn't going at all well* [*he wrote to Brooks in July*]. *I have a subject quite out of my line, and don't know how to attack it in the least.* . . . *Please don't look forward to sitting in a box at my imminent first night. You may be disappointed in such an idea.* . . .

The truth is Ned knew nothing about the Salvation Army or the atmosphere in which it operated, and, with a natural aversion to squalor and poverty, he was not eager to explore the field. Yet the fact that he was now committed to write the play pushed him on to get some first-hand material, for without it there was no way to develop the story he had in mind.

When he went home to Chicago on vacation, he made visits to Salvation Army headquarters and found out everything he could. He carefully studied the personalities of those who carried on its work. He also attended several meetings, to absorb the emotional flavor and the idiom of street-corner evangelism.

Later in the summer Ned visited Denver and enlisted the aid of his cousin Elsa Denison in gathering more color. The two young people, dressed in their oldest and most inconspicuous clothes, ventured together into the slums to watch a Salvation Army meeting. They entered zealously into the spirit of the occasion and acted the parts of lowly and repentant sinners with fervor. But the evening was not productive in the way they expected. The pretty Bryn Mawr girl soon attracted the eye of a burly reprobate very much the worse for wear, and Ned was obliged to remove her quickly from his aggressive attentions.

Yet if actual experience failed to give Ned more than a few useful facts, these were enough to set his imagination going. Before he left Denver, *Salvation Nell* had "coagulated," as he put it, and by mid-October two acts were completed.

Ned was now back in Cambridge, as he had planned earlier, to take his master's degree. He signed up for courses and attended lectures, but with less verve than in other years. His heart and a good deal of his mind were on Broadway, and to one within touching distance of the glittering world of the theatre, Harvard seemed a dull place. Most of Ned's close friends were now gone. Professor Baker was in Paris lecturing at the Sorbonne, and Van Wyck Brooks was in England, settled down to writing his first book.

Fortunately Jack Wheelock was still in Cambridge. He and Ned again had rooms together in Prescott Hall. For both young men the literary career had become more important than the academic. Although Wheelock was still an undergraduate and would not take his degree until the following June, he was already getting a toe hold as a poet. Manuscripts went out regularly to the magazines, and Ned found his friend's productivity infectious. Wheelock was now editor-in-chief of the *Harvard Monthly*, and Ned had been named president of the *Advocate* board the previous spring. The publications took a great deal of time and added a sense of pressure to the writers' other activities. Though both performed their editorial functions conscientiously, both were looking with somewhat jaundiced eye upon the student effusions which filled the *Monthly* and the *Advocate* mailboxes. Wheelock found himself rejecting contributions to the *Monthly* with rather a high hand and for reasons not always clear to him. One morning, for example, he found in his box a brief unsigned poem. There were only four lines; and, though tossed casually aside at the time, they remained fixed ever afterward in Wheelock's memory:

The Prairie

No boundary to earth's immensity,
  To vast, unfathomable loneliness,
    Forever holding back a dumb caress
And hopeless as the twilight-laden sea.

It was not until long after that Wheelock discovered the poem had been written by his roommate.

Although increasingly absorbed with his play, Ned did not wholly withdraw from Harvard's social life. Under any circumstances, people were as necessary to him as food and drink; and he was happy enough when, along with Wheelock, he was elected to the Hasty Pudding Club. He even wrote the skit which he and Wheelock and another friend performed as part of the initiation, in which Wheelock proved the hit of the evening. He played the role of a lady of tarnished reputation and, at Ned's insistence, was laced into a corset to the point of asphyxiation. Indeed at the climactic moment of the play he fainted dead away, an effect greeted with bellows of delight.

But such shenanigans really belonged to another life now. *Salvation Nell* was completed at Christmas; and early in January, Ned took it to his friend Basil King, then at work on his novel *The Inner Shrine*. Ned read the play aloud to King, and the reaction was all any playwright could wish. "He wept," Ned wrote his mother. "It left him without anything to say. Don't tell anyone."

Caution had now become the order of the day. As Ned moved closer to his goal of a Broadway production he was fearful lest a false step upset everything. Miss Kauser warned him continually of the importance of keeping details of his work to himself. She made it plain to him that the theatre was a world in which no holds were barred and the cutting of throats a matter of routine. Good ideas for plays commanded a price, and literary larceny was commonplace.

Before *Salvation Nell* was finished, Miss Kauser had talked with two or three actresses about the possibility of doing the play, for she knew that the casting of it—particularly the leading part—was of supreme importance. She had shown the manuscript to Margaret Anglin who declined it, to her later regret. Then she had taken it to Carlotta Neilsen, whom Ned himself hoped might do it. But Miss Neilsen was already committed for the coming season. Of course the ideal choice would have been Mrs. Fiske. Unfortunately she was involved with Ibsen, and this would continue through the following autumn. But Miss Kauser, chancing to witness a performance of *Rosmersholm*, thought she detected in Mrs. Fiske a slight weariness with Ibsen, and on one of her famous hunches sent the actress a copy of Ned's play. Mrs. Fiske read the manuscript during intermissions of a matinee performance, and was carried away by the play and its heroine. In *Salvation Nell* she saw a role different from any she had yet played but made to order, as it seemed, for her personality. She had depicted plenty of fallen women in her time, but none of them had risen to preach on street corners. And though she had plucked many hearts in gilded salons, she had never gathered souls from the gutter. Before the afternoon was over—so it was reported—she was trying on Salvation Army bonnets.

The news that Mrs. Fiske had accepted the play sent Ned's spirits to such a pitch that his feet scarcely touched the ground as he went about the Yard. When on January 25, 1908, the New York *Dramatic Mirror* announced that Mrs. Fiske had leased the Belasco Theatre for the coming season, which she would open with "a new and strikingly original play by an American author," his excitement was almost unbearable. But he made every effort to remain calm, still telling himself that anything could happen; that until the curtain actually rose on the opening night nothing was sure.

With all this going on outside, it was difficult to focus on work at the University. Yet somehow Ned managed. He still found his classes with "Copey" stimulating, but Professor Maynadier's course in English Fiction was a trial of endurance. Jane Austen's world seemed so remote from Forty-second Street!

Slowly the semester limped to a close. As soon as he finished his last examination and without waiting to know the result, he was off to New Hampshire to visit the Kings. They were elated over the contract with Mrs. Fiske, and King told him to take every advantage of this opening wedge into a writing career.

Late in June, Ned came back to Cambridge for Commencement, to hear Jack Wheelock read his Class Poem, and to say good-bye. The young poet was sailing for Germany at the end of the summer and would probably be away for two years.

Though the air was bright with his own prospects Ned felt a pang of sadness at the sudden breaking up of the happy life of the last four years. During the next few weeks at his grandfather's on Lake Geneva the realization came to him that he was on his own at last. And though this was the moment for which he had been waiting so long—ever since he had written his mother from Milton Academy that he could not live "a hanging around sort of existence forever" —the thought brought dismay to his heart. His maturity seemed suddenly to desert him. He envied the cool ease with which Van Wyck Brooks in England had plunged into the life of a man of letters. Brooks had just written him about his work and the people he was meeting. Ned suddenly felt uneasy about himself.

> Your letter sounded frightfully grown up. Please don't begin by making me feel very young—I don't know that I could bear it.

At the threshold of his own career he felt lonely for the two friends whose companionship throughout four Harvard years had been an important spur to his work.

> . . . It is awfully convenient to be like Jack [he again wrote Brooks], and be able to move along with the greatest ease without the stimulation and presence of one's friends.

But by the end of August this mood had passed. In reply to a summons from Harrison Grey Fiske, he came on to New York to attend the first rehearsals for *Salvation Nell.* Except for Holbrook Blinn and one or two other principals, the actors were recruited by the company stage manager while Mrs. Fiske was winding up her tour with Ibsen. At the end of the first reading of the play there was a brief whispered consultation between Mrs. Fiske and her manager-husband. Then Mr. Fiske came upon the stage and quietly announced to the cast that its services would not be required.

Ned was dumbfounded at this wholesale dismissal. He had had no inkling of the autocratic powers, or manners, of stars and managers. Every human instinct was revolted by the procedure, especially when he saw the looks of disappointment—in one or two cases, of heartbreak—on the faces of the actors. It was his earliest lesson in the ways of the professional theatre and he never forgot it. From this first reading of his play he understood clearly that the only feelings tolerated on the stage are those manufactured by the actor for the benefit of a paying audience.

It was not until mid-September that a cast satisfactory to Mrs. Fiske was assembled and rehearsals finally began. Ned was on hand every moment. Day after day he sat in the dim theatre watching what went on under the glare of the single worklight over the stage. It was one thing to have written the play, and quite another to see it take on life under the combined efforts of director, actors, and scenic designer.

What struck him as truly wonderful was how much the play contained that he had never been aware of himself, especially when Mrs. Fiske began to work on the character of Nell. It was like some miraculous growth, as day by day the personality born in Ned's mind became merged with that of the actress, flowering in unexpected ways as it did so. There was an unforgettable moment when, just before the opening in Providence, Ned was sitting in the balcony watching the dress rehearsal. Mrs. Fiske had come to the end of the second act where Nell, having made her choice between the life of a Salvationist and one of crime with the tough jailbird whom she still loves, clutches their child to her bosom and cries:

> Come on, Jimmy! We're goin' to pray—we're goin' to pray for your Dad, Jimmy, an' we're goin' to save him! If we only believe—if we're only sure in our hearts—God'll do it!

Then above the fury of the storm raging outside come the opening words of the Lord's Prayer.

The scene gripped Ned as though he had never heard it before, and he was surprised to feel hot tears on the back of his hand. For the first time he saw his heroine as she truly was. To his mother he wrote:

> There stood my Nell revealed to me! . . . Mrs. Fiske made me realize the elemental nature of the woman as I never did before.

The opening in Providence was very festive. A large delegation from Harvard, including Professor Copeland, was on hand, and a number of people had also come up from New York, attracted by rumors of the play's sensational nature. At the final curtain there were loud shouts for the author, but the panic-stricken Ned was nowhere to be seen. Finally Mrs. Fiske had to go in search of him and lead him, blushing to the roots of his thick black hair, before the glaring footlights.

There was no doubt about the audience's approval, but it was hard to tell from the reviews in the Providence papers what the critics thought. All were impressed, but some were also shocked. The realism of the saloon scene particularly, in which streetwalkers, drunks, and touts mingled with rowdy abandon, was something American audiences were not accustomed to. Everybody was obviously fascinated, but it did not seem quite proper to admit it. On this somewhat ambiguous note the play moved into New York.

Ned was full of misgivings. Mrs. Sheldon and his sister Mary had come on from Chicago for the opening. Ned was also expecting his cousin Elsa Denison up from Bryn Mawr, but he warned her, "I strongly doubt the play's success."

In the week's interval before the *première* the tension of waiting was increased by Ned's growing sense of responsibility toward the others involved in the production. Only now did he realize how many hopes besides his own were at stake. The day before the opening he stood on the darkened stage of the Hackett Theatre (at the last moment the Belasco was not available) with Ashton Stevens, critic of the New York *Journal,* and looking out over the empty house he said, "I hope they like the play. If they don't it will be such a disappointment to Mrs. Fiske. I can't tell you what she has done for it, and I don't mean only by acting in it and directing it."

When Ned took his seat before the opening curtain he seemed more like a boy than ever. He beamed with innocent satisfaction at the well-filled house, noting not only the liberal sprinkling of his personal friends but a number of personages whom he knew only by sight. What thrilled him most, a young man hoping to make his mark in the theatre, was a glimpse of the white mane and clerical collar of David Belasco in the shadows of a proscenium box. If his play passed muster under that knowing eye, he would have nothing to worry about.

Perhaps those critics were right who said that without Mrs. Fiske *Salvation Nell* would not have been a smashing success. Sheldon was a complete unknown, and a play dealing with slum life was not calculated to appeal to an audience which had schooled itself not to think about such things (this was in 1908). Mrs. Fiske's special radiance gave something to the figure of the little drudge which Ned had not foreseen, and possibly not intended. But the point must be made—now half a century after Mrs. Fiske's performance —that she had the material to work with.

The story of the barroom slavey, raised by religious fervor above the sordid love affair which has brought heart-

break and degradation, may be trite—as the critic William
Winter was at pains to point out—but it is not so trite as
a good many plots Winter thought refreshingly original.
If there was a certain familiarity in the play's basic situation,
this was completely obscured for the audience by the passionate sincerity of the chief character. In transforming Nell
from a pathetic drudge into a creature of stature and nobility,
Ned kept her faithful throughout to her background and
limitations. The gospel she preaches in front of McGovern's
Saloon is as elemental as her own experience of life.

> It's the old, old story I've told you many times before. Christ
> was a poor man, and He chose poor people to be his friends.
> He knows how hard we have to work ter keep alive. He
> knows how strong and terrible our temptations are. . . .
> But let me tell you that it's you Christ waits for. You've
> sunk to the bottom, you know the bitterness and cruelty
> of life, and it's you Christ wants, to show the beauty and
> the glory and the light. When you and me who have fallen
> rise again, we're greater than our sins, we're bigger men and
> women than if we'd never sinned at all.

These words, spoken in that slightly breathless, silvery
voice—not always articulate but, oh, so moving—were religion made glamorous. And the picture of Nell, her piquant
features turned upward to catch the glow of the street lamp
overhead (bolstered by a few judiciously placed spots) had
the same effect on the audience as on Nell's regenerate lover,
the hulking Jim Platt, and on the motley throng of squalid
humanity which Ned, in happy ignorance of production
costs, had placed in the background. Tears flowed unabash-
edly.

Perhaps the best evidence of the public reaction to *Salvation Nell* was in the well-filled tambourines of the two

Salvation Army lassies who from the opening night through the whole run of the play stood outside the door of the Hackett.

If Ned still had any doubts of his success after the ovation at the final curtain, these vanished when the reviews appeared next day. In the general chorus of acclaim there were only two sour notes. William Winter wrote a column of acidulous comment in the *Tribune* in which he called *Salvation Nell* "a piece of rubbish . . . compact of ingredients of coarse humanity, and low life, and feebly instinct with moral purpose." Shuddering in every fiber of his outraged gentility, he stated: "Those persons who wish to have their minds dragged through the gutter and drenched in the slime of the brothel can gratify their desire at the Hackett."

Louis V. Defoe of *The World* was disturbed, though not indignant. He thought too great emphasis was laid on photographic externals (a criticism time has amply confirmed). But he was mainly distressed that an author so young should be so pessimistic, implying that the world was full of pleasanter subjects than the life of the underprivileged. He compared *Salvation Nell* to Gorky's *Lower Depths:* ". . . both cut from the same strip, both of them gruesomely fascinating and profoundly depressing." However, he felt obliged to add: "A writer of such close observation is certain to be heard from again; and some day he will look back with amazement at the recklessness with which he plunged into his first effort."

These were the only voices of dissent. The general opinion was summed up by Ashton Stevens when he said: "However much tradition may be shocked and polite conversation shattered, the fact must go on record that the boy from Harvard . . . has given New York the most daring play it has ever seen. . . . This play not only dramatizes the Salvation Army, but it serves up Hell's Kitchen piping hot . . . a very remarkable production of a remarkable play."

Perhaps Ned did look back later at his "recklessness," but if he did so it was with amusement rather than amazement—and perhaps with pardonable satisfaction. For the play which stirred New York in 1908 by its sensational realism was really romance in disguise, a morality tale on the Cinderella theme. Yet with all its sentimentality *Salvation Nell* proved a milestone in the history of the American theatre, for it showed an awareness of bigger problems than Broadway had been willing to tackle up to that time. It showed, too, that really vital drama must take its material from everyday life and not depend on the threadbare, overworked stuff of immemorial stage convention.

We know now that the boy who a scant two years before had thrilled to his first taste of backstage life had become a pioneer in a movement which would bring the American drama to the notice of the world. In 1926, seventeen years after *Salvation Nell* appeared, Sheldon—then a prisoner to the four walls of his invalid's room—sent a wire to Eugene O'Neill to congratulate the younger playwright on *The Great God Brown*. In reply O'Neill wrote:

Dear Edward Sheldon:
   I was immensely grateful for your wire about Brown. Your continuous generous appreciation of my work during the past years has meant a great lot to me, has been one of the very few things that have gratified me and satisfied me deep down inside. I say this—and I want you to know I say it!—with the deepest sincerity. Your Salvation Nell, along with the work of the Irish Players on their first trip over here, was what first opened my eyes to the existence of a real theatre as opposed to the unreal—and to me then, hate-

ful—theatre of my father, in whose atmosphere I had been brought up. So, you see, I owed you this additional debt of long standing.

My inner conviction has always been that you are one of the rare ones who really understand and have a right to speak, and to be listened to, whether of praise or blame. And I have always felt that we should be friends—(Not that you haven't proved very much of a friend already as far as my work is concerned!)—if my good fortune should ever be to meet you. And I shall look forward to that good fortune, if I may, on my return from Bermuda in the spring.

With your "every good wish" right back on you a thousand fold!

EUGENE O'NEILL

CHAPTER III

The Golden Hour

WITH *Nell* established as a hit, Sheldon plunged into the life of New York like a schoolboy released from the classroom, which in effect he was. As the author of the season's most important play, he found himself, like Byron, famous overnight. He was suddenly the wonder boy of his generation. Since, in addition to success, he had good looks and a winning manner, he was soon a center of attraction.

He ate up the life of the theatre as a hungry cat laps cream. This was what he had always wanted. Through Mrs. Fiske he met many stage people, and in a matter of weeks he was on first-name terms with half the celebrities of Broadway. He moved in a rarefied atmosphere composed of champagne, glittering nights, adulation, and a sense of ever-widening horizons. It was enough to make one dizzy. Yet if ever a man took success in his stride, it was Edward Sheldon.

His mother always remembered walking up Fifth Avenue with Ned one day and noting a new billboard on top of a building opposite the Library at Forty-second Street. Ned's name was blazoned forth in great letters on an advertisement for *Salvation Nell*. Mrs. Sheldon proudly called his attention to the sign. Ned glanced up and said, "Yes, it's nice. I always wanted to be in New York."

In February, *Salvation Nell* started on tour. Its reception had been well prepared by the publicity and discussion following the New York opening. Wherever the play was performed critics and public treated it as the event of the season. It even excited editorial comment in the papers and one article in the Cleveland *Press*, entitled "We've All Been Scooped by a College Boy" was widely republished throughout the country.

> *Ever since there were newspapers and police courts and policemen [so ran the article] there have been police reporters. . . . It has come to be a tradition of the police reporter to see comedy in rags and humor in whiskey befuddled humanity. . . .*
>
> *Young Mr. Sheldon, fresh from college, has every reason to see the slums through the eyes of tradition, but he did not. Tradition says the people of the slums are tough or they wouldn't live there. Edward Sheldon says the people of the slums are hard because they were born there or have been driven there. . . .*
>
> *And in seeing these things he has scooped the police reporters. For we—police reporters and all—should be able to understand the cry of the submerged, as voiced by Salvation Nell when she says, "For God's sake, Jim, let's be straight and give our kid a chance—we never knowed until it was too late!"*

The tour wound up at Boston where Sheldon was honored with a special "Harvard Night," which gave his Cambridge friends who might have missed the Providence opening an opportunity to salute their recent classmate.

Back in New York, Ned improved the shining hours. He was definitely the social lion of the moment, though he never roared. Despite the maneuvering of hostesses to keep him in the center of their parties, he usually managed to find

a good seat on the sidelines where he might talk quietly
with people who really wanted to talk. He delighted particularly in the group which gathered at the Norman Hapgoods', who had the nearest thing in New York to a French
salon, where people of the theatre and of society mingled
freely and where the conversation was frequently witty and
always gay. It was at the Hapgoods' during this winter that
Ned met two English women, Mrs. Patrick Campbell and
Constance Collier, both of whom were to become friends of
a lifetime. Constance Collier in her autobiography *Harlequinade* remembered the Sheldon of those days as "a rosy-
cheeked, black-haired boy, simple and quiet, taking his
great triumphs with shy gratitude, always thinking of other
people before himself . . . reasonable, just and kind, with
the supreme simplicity of genius and the limitless wisdom of
the ages. Even in those days, young as he was, he gave one
a sense of peace that was quite remarkable."

Certainly Sheldon was a new type on the Broadway
scene. In an atmosphere where self-advertisement and self-
aggrandizement become almost a necessity to survival, Ned
attracted attention by self-effacement. This was not by any
conspicuous belittling of his own achievement. He was delighted when people liked his work and told him about it,
but a few moments in the spotlight were enough. He soon
developed a trick of turning it quickly on somebody else.

His modesty was most apparent at rehearsals. He would
sit quietly in the back of the theatre, seldom speaking unless
asked a direct question. Or if he had a suggestion for some
actor who was straying far from the mark in the interpretation of a character, his criticism would be veiled under a
query: "I wonder what the effect would be if we did that
speech thus and so?" ("thus and so" being the way the

speech ought to be done and the way the author had intended). When the actor read the speech as Ned had suggested, Ned would say, "I really think you have something there—it's great!"—which would give the actor the impression that *he* had been responsible for the improvement, leaving him with the happy sense of his own brilliance.

Ned displayed another quality in the arduous weeks when *Salvation Nell* was in preparation. In the fierce rivalries that sometimes developed between members of the cast he assumed the role of peacemaker. His tact, his gentle courtesy, his ability to make each party to an altercation feel himself the possessor of unique talents which really placed him beyond all danger of competition, were oil on troubled waters. The result was a general feeling of comradeship and harmony throughout the company, never forgotten by those who took part in the play.

With all his modesty, his quiet manner, his consideration for others which won him the title on Broadway of "Sir Galahad," Sheldon was no ascetic. He had luxurious habits that soon found expression in elegant clothes, a handsome apartment on Gramercy Park, and constant entertaining. He liked beautiful things, and one of the gratifications of having plenty of money was that it gave him a chance to indulge his most extravagant tastes. Nothing delighted him more than to walk into a florist's shop and order not a bouquet but a whole windowful of blooms to be sent to the lovely creature on whom his attention was momentarily fixed.

Certainly there was no insufficiency of women in his life. Alice Kauser, who watched with fearful eye for the effect of such distractions on her protégé's work, noted that women fell in love with Sheldon as regularly as waves beating upon the shore. And if they retreated with equal regularity, there were no hurt feelings. One of Sheldon's most graceful talents was his ability to parry the heaviest onslaught of feminine emotion with skill and effectiveness and yet somehow leave the lady in full possession of her self-respect and, incidentally, of her admiration for him.

It was not that women lacked attraction for him. On the contrary, he felt himself drawn all too easily to a pretty face and a softly curved figure. But passion with Ned was inevitably tinged with romanticism, and there was also a good deal of the Puritan in him. From his mother he had acquired the idea that the only definitive relationship between men and women was marriage. Obviously he could not marry all the beautiful women who came his way, and this prevented him from plunging into any affair that could not be ended without undue complications. There were of course plenty of stories about Ned and the various leading ladies with whom he was seen at Delmonico's, or in Central Park, or among the palms of the Plaza. But the same lady seldom figured in any two stories—that is, until Doris Keane appeared on the scene.

Perhaps the real reason for Ned's casualness about the women whose names were sometimes linked with his during the first two years in New York was that his deepest feelings were centered around the piquant, dark-eyed beauty whom he had met during his sophomore year at Harvard. Being in New York brought him very little closer to the object of his adoration than he had been in Cambridge, but the paths of actress and playwright now crossed frequently, and Miss Keane evidently accepted Ned's attentions with a certain show of interest. But that was all—for the moment. The ambitious young actress was still too much wrapped up in her career, as well as in entanglements of a more personal sort, to give Ned much encouragement. In fact she seems to have had the same pleasant regard for him that Sheldon himself had for most women, and nothing more.

But even had he been of that temperament, Ned was in no situation to pine. He was not only immersed in a feverish social life; he was hard at work on another play.

Long before *Salvation Nell* had seen the footlights, Ned had submitted to Alice Kauser a list of ideas which he thought had possibilities for plays. None of the subjects greatly impressed her, and one of them she vetoed energetically. In the form actually jotted down by Ned in his memorandum, this ran as follows:

> *A young Southern statesman, nominated for the governor of his state and engaged to an aristocratic girl in every way, discovers that he has Negro blood in his veins. After a hard struggle he succeeds in suppressing the accusation. Then his conscience awakens and he tells the girl the truth. Although she is horrified at first she cannot let him go. But this decides him; in spite of her pleadings, he resolves to give up his political career and go back to his own race, to work for them as one of them.*

Of all the ideas this was the one Sheldon most favored himself, but Miss Kauser let him know in unequivocal terms that it would never, never do. "The nigger problem is not one that the American people want to see upon the boards," she said sharply. Sheldon's reply to this was a simple question: Why not? He had gotten the idea from an article in the *American Magazine*. If people were willing to read about such things, why couldn't they come to a theatre to see them?

Miss Kauser did her best to dissuade Ned, but the more she opposed the idea, the firmer he became in his conviction that it would make a play. In fact his mentor's disapproval seemed to act as a spur. No sooner had *Salvation Nell* settled down to its run than Ned started to work on the play first called *Philip Morrow*, but later, bluntly, *The Nigger*.

By spring of 1909 the work was nearly finished. The pace of New York, hard labor, and the sense of suddenly becoming stale started Ned to thinking again of Europe. When friends whom he had met abroad in the summer of 1906, a Mrs. Clark and her daughter, proposed that he accompany them on a tour of France and Italy, Ned eagerly accepted the opportunity. He had found the Clark ladies lively and congenial, and the prospect of sharing the delights of Europe with stimulating companions (Ned hated doing anything pleasant alone) was all he needed.

This proved another of those blissful summers filled with new sights, new personalities, and the discovery of hidden beauty in out-of-the-way corners. Although much that he saw was now familiar, he felt the same old surge of joyful excitement that Europe always produced. He drank deep of the magic of Como, more theatrical than any stage designer's dream, and as the party moved on to Rome he wrote, "My feet are dancing! How can *I wait!*"

He was an indefatigable sightseer, never without his Baedeker, which might well have been left behind since he memorized in advance every detail of any spot to be visited. He saw everything that tourists from time immemorial have seen, yet that did not prevent him from admiring the Jungfrau in all her virginal freshness or noting that the Mona Lisa's smile *was* inscrutable. But his acute observation was always turning up something that escaped the orthodox tourist's eye. Years later his friend Ruth Draper wrote to thank him for reminding her, when she visited the Janiculum in Rome, to pause at the gate of the garden belonging to the Knights of Malta and peek through the keyhole, which framed a vista of memorable beauty.

In Switzerland, Ned came upon his old friends the Basil Kings, and a few days later both parties moved on to Paris. Here there was a grand reunion with Jack Wheelock and two other Harvard friends, George Foote and Charles Seeger. These three classmates had been studying in Berlin for the past year, and were taking a vacation trip along the Dalmatian coast when news came that Ned was in Europe. They immediately changed their plans and hastened to Paris. Here the quartet under Ned's expert guidance systematically did the rounds of theatres, cafés, and popular dance halls—as well as the classic points of interest. They saw something of Paris society too when they were entertained by Miss Emily Grigsby, a friend of Ned's from London, who had a charming flat in Paris. Mrs. Norman Hapgood was also living in Paris now, and her salon was much frequented by a cosmopolitan group of writers and artists with, as always, the right admixture of people from good society. Ned's companions were a little awed by his air of easy familiarity in this atmosphere of elegance and sophistication. As Wheelock remembered, "Ned was brilliant among these women of the world, while the rest of us merely trailed along in varying degrees of ineptitude."

Despite the interruptions of travel and constant sight-seeing, Ned worked away feverishly on his new play. *The Nigger* was finished in mid-July and shipped off to Alice Kauser. When he arrived in New York a month later (having cabled Miss Kauser to meet him at the dock with money to see him through the customs, for he was dead broke), he found that the play had been accepted under very favorable conditions and was ready to go into rehearsal.

Throughout the previous winter, Ned had keenly followed the development of the most ambitious theatre project New York had seen for years. This was the construction of the magnificent New Theatre on Central Park West, which, under the management of the intelligent and sensitive Winthrop Ames, was designed to bring new life to the always ailing American stage. Other attempts had been made to revive the "fabulous invalid" but nothing on so grand a scale. The New Theatre building, a gorgeous structure with architectural echoes of the Palazzo San Sovino in Venice, was the last word in comfort and equipment. It was to be operated as a repertory theatre—not the first nor yet the last attempt to realize this fond dream of American drama-lovers—with a permanent company of thirty outstanding players. One third of the productions would be classics, to counteract the inherent Broadway tendency to drift to the lowest level of spectators, and the rest would be important modern drama.

The three-million-dollar project was underwritten by an impressive list of backers which included John Jacob Astor, August Belmont, Otto Kahn, Henry Clay Frick, William Vanderbilt, and a dozen other prominent New Yorkers. At the head of the acting company were to be Julia Marlowe and her husband, E. H. Sothern, who would inaugurate the venture with Shakespeare's *Antony and Cleopatra*. Also scheduled for production during the first season were Galsworthy's *Strife*, Maeterlinck's *The Blue Bird*, a new play by the young playwright Edward Knoblock (also a Harvard man, class of 1896), and Sheldon's *The Nigger*.

Winthrop Ames had seen *Salvation Nell* and was one of

the first to congratulate the author, remarking that he hoped Sheldon would some day do a play for the New Theatre. Miss Kauser, doubtful of interesting more purely commercial producers in Ned's latest work, had sent *The Nigger* to the New Theatre—and Ames's play reader, John Corbin, who was also a distinguished critic, had immediately recommended it. In Corbin's judgment *The Nigger* was an even more promising work than *Salvation Nell*.

Whatever may have been Miss Kauser's misgivings, *The Nigger* proved everything Ned hoped. For the New Theatre it was the bright spot in what turned out to be from beginning to end a chain of disasters. The Sothern-Marlowe production of *Antony and Cleopatra* received a lukewarm reception, largely because the play was swamped by complicated, cumbersome settings. Then the Sotherns, by an almost too fortunate chance, found that they would not be able to play the whole season, since they had not been able to extricate themselves from earlier commitments. This meant the loss of the theatre's two big names, and lesser actors had to be substituted in the star roles. The other plays met with indifferent success. It remained for *The Nigger* really to bring the great establishment to life.

Forty years after the opening of Ned's second play *Cosmopolitan Magazine* published an article entitled "The Ten Dramatic Shocks of the Century." Among the plays on the list were *Sapho* by Alphonse Daudet with Olga Nethersole, which New Yorkers saw in 1900, Bernard Shaw's *Mrs. Warren's Profession* in 1905, and Sheldon's *The Nigger*, the play which (as the article stated) "nearly forty years before Sinclair Lewis's *Kingsblood Royal* treated of Negro blood in a man supposedly white and of his love for a woman of pure Caucasian blood. The theme at that time was theatrically sensational and induced qualms in the audience . . . adding to the general shock was the dialogue presenting the acquiescent Southern attitude toward lynching."

Naturally the play created a storm of discussion—and a good deal of protest. The press took violent issue with the title. Sheldon immediately countered with the statement:

> I surely meant in no way to cast any reflection on the Negro. Quite the contrary. I wanted to get into the title of the play the attitude of the white race to the black. When the play is seen, I am sure that the development of the character will show how ironical the title is meant to be. . . .

Shocked or not, audiences filled the New Theatre, not only on the opening night of the play, but every night thereafter when *The Nigger* appeared in the repertory. And before the season had closed, two road companies set out on tour.

Wherever the play went the query inevitably rose: how could a man so young grasp problems so complicated, and analyze them with such force and vividness? For whatever the shortcomings of *The Nigger* as a play (and there were plenty, of which diffuseness was not the least), the race conflict came across the footlights with a drive that, almost literally, set audiences reeling.

But again, as in the case of *Salvation Nell*, the chief source of the play's power was not facts but the playwright's imagination. Sheldon knew almost nothing about Negroes beyond what he had read, and he had never been in the South. Yet he knew enough of the traditional relationship between whites and blacks to grasp the powerful forces of the antagonism between the races, and by making the

conflict specific, centered in the emotions of a few individuals, he made a gripping play. Yet of real perception
of all the social and economic factors which have weighed
so heavily in this problem, there is little or nothing in *The
Nigger*. Essentially, as in *Salvation Nell*, Sheldon was writing a romantic drama with a realistic setting. The race problem was merely a means to an end—to create greater emotional tension between his hero and heroine.

The Boss, Sheldon's third play, also owed its origin to a
magazine article. In the spring of 1910 Ned and his brother
Ted had both been struck by the publication in *Collier's
Weekly* of a sketch of the career of one William James
Connors, better known as "Fingy" Connors, a Buffalo pol-
itician. Connors was a self-made man who had worked his
way from steamboat roustabout to freight contractor, from
a flourishing asphalt and paving business to the presidency of
the Magnus Brewing Company, and finally to the owner-
ship of the Buffalo *Enquirer* and the Buffalo *Courier*. In
1910 it was reputed that he employed six thousand men, and
his steam yacht, named for his paper the *Enquirer*, was the
badge of his achievement. This was a success story of a type
many times duplicated in the palmy era before World War I
and was the sort of career which for the average man justified
the American Dream. Although the muckraking novelists
like Theodore Dreiser, Frank Norris, and Upton Sinclair
had begun to strip the glamor from such figures of stalwart
individualism, the stage had not yet been given a full-length
portrait of the strong man whose greed carries him to
dazzling heights over the backs of the weak and defenseless.
In *The Boss*, Sheldon started out to create such a portrait,
but, as in his previous plays, the romantic element soon
dominated everything else. Sheldon's hero, Michael Regan,
"The Boss," displays all the bald aggressiveness of his proto-

type, battling his way to power with absolute disregard for any human feelings but his own. In a plot which now seems quite preposterous, he is humbled, not by the awakened proletariat, though this has a part in the story, but by the sacrifice of the woman he loves who finally offers herself to him if he will not foreclose the mortgages on his workers' homes! *The Boss* is a creaky structure at best (which critics of the time were quick to report), but it still shows vitality, not only in the portrait of the leading character, but in the suggestion of social unrest moving toward explosion. The impact on audiences who saw it was undeniable. *The Boss* was not only exciting drama, but an original commentary on historic changes in the American scene, a fact noted by Charles A. Beard in *The Rise of American Civilization:* "In Edward Sheldon's 'The Boss,' offered in 1911, was vividly illumined the raw struggle between capital and labor."

Sheldon was not at the New York opening of the play. He had been out on a party most of the night before, and had risen early that morning to meet his family who, as usual, were coming on from Chicago to see the *première*. By dinnertime Sheldon was exhausted and went to bed in his room at the Hotel Royalton where he was living at the time.

But if the author himself was absent, there were plenty of other notables in the theatre that night, including Mayor Gaynor and other important New York politicians, lured by the rumor that the play portrayed a character well known to them all. Sheldon probably grinned next morning when he read in the *Evening World* that His Honor "betrayed no sign that he had even a bowing acquaintance with such a type as Michael Regan."

More interesting to Sheldon personally were the re-actions of two other spectators that evening. One of these was Henry James, on his last visit to America before returning to England where he would eventually become legally, as he had been so long in fact, a British citizen. James accompanied Mrs. Cadwalader Jones, in whose charming house on Eleventh Street Sheldon had often been a guest, and who was to become one of his closest friends. Immediately after the performance Mrs. Jones sat down and wrote Sheldon a warm letter of praise for *The Boss*. Henry James also wrote the next day, charmingly—but not so warmly. In fact James disliked the play very much, and the audience even more. But he put it all in such gracefully oblique form that Sheldon could not take umbrage. In fact he treasured James's letter to the end of his life.

Although some of the critics had reservations about *The Boss* none denied the play's power. As in the case of Sheldon's two previous works, it gave rise to excited discussion—and this, far more than mere favorable reviews, brought customers to the box office. By the spring of 1911 Sheldon was not only famous, he was also rich.

But there was no resting either on his artistic laurels or his prosperity. It seemed now as though Sheldon were being driven by some invisible whip, to produce faster and faster—to pour his creative energy into plays good, bad, and indifferent—as if in some deep recess of his subconscious mind he feared the golden current might suddenly be cut off.

In rapid succession now followed *Princess Zim-Zim*, an abortive comedy about a Coney Island snake charmer; *Egypt*, a wildly implausible melodrama of gypsy life starring Margaret Anglin, which never saw New York; and then in 1912 *The High Road*—another highly successful domestic drama with Mrs. Fiske.

Despite the failure of Ned's two previous plays, Mrs.

Fiske's confidence in the young playwright was unabated. "I believe in him," she said simply. "He is sincere. He has big ideas. He writes what he wants to express, not what he thinks may be popular . . . I regard him as our most interesting dramatist. . . ."

In *The High Road*, Sheldon returned to the drama of social overtones. Fundamentally the play was a romance, dealing with the perennially appealing theme of the fallen woman and her struggle back to respectability. In this case respectability must be written with a large "R" since it implies nothing less than the White House. Mary Page, the heroine, has had a moral lapse twenty years before the play opens. In the intervening time she has worked in a factory and become a champion of working girls. Then she meets and marries the governor of the state, who is now a candidate for the Presidency. His rival gets wind of Mary's past and threatens to expose her. She counters not only by admitting her youthful misstep, but proposes to make a public acknowledgment of it and thus expose the rival's cowardice in using such means to achieve his own ends. The rival thinks twice about the matter and decides to carry on his campaign by devices less foul.

The High Road was not only sensational as to theme; it was also a very elaborate production. The play required incidental properties in the most fantastic variety, ranging from special Havana cigars to a live horse. These properties —particularly the horse which had to be recruited afresh in each town at which the play appeared on the road—almost proved the undoing of the assistant stage manager. This was young Barrett Clark who later became a critic and stage historian. The production of *The High Road* doubtless contributed to Mr. Clark's decision to leave the practical for the more literary aspects of the drama. It was not only the utter unpredictability of each new piece of horseflesh he had to deal with nightly that proved so harassing. There was also Mrs. Fiske, dedicated to the welfare of all dumb creatures, to reckon with. If Mr. Clark so much as twitched the flank of a recalcitrant beast to get him on or off the stage, Mrs. Fiske would be waiting in the wings with fire in her eye.

But the meat of *The High Road* was in the subject, and the explosion of controversy over this almost drowned out all legitimate criticism. The first shot was fired by an editorial in the *Evening Sun* entitled "Should a Woman with a Past Be Recognized in Society?" The topic was taken up by other papers, and individuals. Anna Nathan Meyer, anti-woman suffragist, proclaimed against the morality of the "new woman" as exemplified by Sheldon's "erring heroine . . . carried through the sacred portals of the White House."

Mrs. Fiske herself, mindful of the publicity value of this sort of thing, wrote a pamphlet defending Sheldon's heroine called "The Moral Status of Mary Page." And Carl Sandburg, a young newspaperman and poet, also championed the lady whom he regarded as a true spokesman for the working class:

> Whatever wrong things, whatever dirty or vicious things there might be down in this working class, she felt this class was cleaner all through and more honest and beautiful altogether than any other class. . . . This play, *The High Road* by Edward B. Sheldon, is one of the most interesting and thoughtful plays of all recently produced.

With the success of *The High Road*, Sheldon more than retrieved whatever ground he may have lost with the failure of *Princess Zim-Zim* and *Egypt*. And even failure had its rewards. Although *Princess Zim-Zim* added little to Ned's reputation and certainly made him no money, it produced returns far more important to him.

To begin with, on the play's opening night in Boston, Ned, sitting in the back of a stage box, was electrified to spy the figure of his grandfather, Henry Strong, sitting in the second row of the orchestra. The old gentleman had made no recent attempts to direct his grandson's life, but he had been cool about Ned's success as a playwright. He happened to be in Stockbridge, Massachusetts, on business when he saw the announcement of *Princess Zim-Zim* in a Boston paper, and decided that this was a good chance to find out for himself what it was all about.

It was a case of instant conversion—of a sort Ned so delighted to present on the stage but which rarely occurs in real life. The erstwhile Holy Terror followed every moment of the play with fierce concentration, and the movements of the lovely Dorothy Donnelly with something less than fierceness. When it was over he applauded vigorously. Then he went immediately to his hotel and sent the following telegram to Ned's mother:

PLAY OPENED LAST NIGHT TO LARGE AND ENTHUSIASTIC
AUDIENCE. NED RECEIVED OVATION.

Princess Zim-Zim was specifically written for the talented and sensitive young Dorothy Donnelly whom Ned had met the winter before. He had been greatly taken not only by her striking gifts as a comedienne but by her winsome, modest personality. Like Doris Keane, she had had but indifferent success up to now, mainly because of poor parts. *Princess Zim-Zim* was Ned's effort to remedy this situation. And indeed the name part, the Oriental snake charmer with an Irish brogue, was ideally suited to her comedy style. Unfortunately the play itself was so poor—floundering as to plot, confused as to tone—that it did little to advance her career. But it certainly brought her closer to Ned. Of all the women whom Sheldon knew in his early Broadway years none was a more serious competitor to Doris Keane. And there is no doubt that the little Irish girl with the lilting voice and luminous smile lost her heart forever to Ned Sheldon.

The other friendship growing out of the short-lived Coney Island fantasy was with John Barrymore, whose part in Sheldon's story forms a chapter by itself. It was during the run of *Princess Zim-Zim* that the two men were first drawn together in what to many people seemed one of the most incongruous friendships in the theatre. Outwardly at least, Barrymore with his volatile, quixotic, and unstable temperament seemed to have little in common with the unassuming, poised young playwright. Even Sheldon's mother never understood the attraction, and when she once asked Ned what he saw in the actor (with a slight edge to her voice—she was no admirer of Barrymore) Sheldon merely said dryly, "I like to be with him."

Actually the two men were admirable foils for each other, and below the surface they had much in common. Both had a passion for beautiful things, and both had an immense gusto for living. It was in no small measure due to Barrymore that Sheldon crammed so much fun into his few remaining years of normal life. And for Barrymore, Sheldon was always a balance wheel, more than once restraining the undisciplined genius from some disastrous move. Although Barrymore at this time was known primarily as a comedian, both off stage and on, Ned saw at once that the mannerisms, the outwardly cynical attitude of the handsome young actor really masked a nature so delicately organized that it needed constant protection; and he readily assumed the role of *fidus Achates*. Furthermore, Sheldon was the first to sense the actor's true potentialities as an artist, and literally pushed him into the course which led to their realization. In the producer Arthur Hopkins' words, "Sheldon put the finger of destiny on John Barrymore" and became "the true director of his rich career."

All this was later. But it was during the brief run of *Princess Zim-Zim* that Sheldon really got to know Barrymore. He would drop into his dressing room after the play, and while Barrymore removed his make-up the two would have long discussions about every subject under the sun. These would continue over pancakes and coffee at an all-night Childs restaurant, and after that over beers in some Forty-second Street or Greenwich Village saloon. And once the pale December sun rose on the two sitting on a park bench, still deep in heated argument. For one thing these two friends had in common that was obvious to everybody. Given the proper circumstances, they could both talk forever.

Sheldon moved now in a golden glow of success and popularity. But the full richness of the harvest of these years lay in the friendships which came to him. At the Norman Hapgoods', at Mrs. Cadwalader Jones's, and at the William Favershams', Sheldon was a celebrity among celebrities and invariably whoever met him felt the magnetism of this young man who seemed so wise to the ways of the world, and at the same time so unspoiled by it.

It was at the Favershams' that Sheldon met that dashing, Gallicized Scottish prima donna Mary Garden. Miss Garden, lately the toast of Paris's Opéra-Comique, was now with

Hammerstein's Manhattan Opera Company for three seasons before becoming the mainstay of the Chicago Opera Company where she would remain for some twenty years. Forty years after meeting Ned, Mary Garden wrote with her characteristic candor: "We admired each other at once and passed most of the evening talking about the new art we were both to bring into the theatre and the opera of the U.S.A."

Another intimate of these first New York years was W. Somerset Maugham, who like Sheldon was then riding the crest of his first success as a playwright. The two had much in common, above all their passion for the theatre and a high regard for each other's craftsmanship. Whenever Maugham was in New York he made his headquarters at Ned's apartment on Gramercy Park. When Maugham married Syrie Bernardo, Sheldon arranged the details of the wedding and served as Maugham's best man.

Ned was also credited with an important part in Maugham's literary career. Though Maugham himself has never divulged the details, friends of both men insist that Sheldon was responsible for Maugham's best-known work, *Of Human Bondage.* As the story is generally told Ned suggested the novel, based on his friend's early days as a medical student, to help Maugham overcome a disturbing sense of inferiority because of a speech defect. It occurred to Ned that he might conquer the defect, or at least change his attitude toward it, if he wrote it out of his system. It was supposedly from this suggestion that Maugham's autobiographical novel grew, the stutter emerging as Philip Carey's clubfoot.

One summer Maugham and Sheldon returned from Europe together. Sheldon had acquired a pair of West Highland terriers, and the dogs were still seasick when the ship landed. An old friend of Sheldon's still recalls their arrival at Gramercy Park with each of the fastidious young men holding a puppy at arm's length outside the taxi window.

The dogs soon became the center of Sheldon's household. Little Weasel was eventually bred, and as her time approached Sheldon set everything aside to attend to her needs. Late one evening she became unusually restless and Ned took her into bed with him. In the middle of the night he was forced to dress hastily and rush Weasel to the nearby veterinarian. He spent most of the next morning on the telephone announcing to all his friends the happy advent of Weasel's litter.

Sheldon was now twenty-six. With the success of *The High Road* he had reached a score of four hits out of six plays written, a record on which many men might have made a career. Yet everyone felt that Sheldon was merely starting. "If he can turn out work like this now, what may we expect from him when he is fifty?" was the continued comment of the critics. As for Ned himself he had no conjectures about the future. The present was rich and full enough, and he had no premonition that life could be otherwise. Even the compulsion to drive himself to ever-greater effort might have come from the stimulus of success, or the general excitement of so much going on around him. Unlike many writers, Sheldon worked best when he was caught up in a whirl of varied activities. New faces, new sights, new books—these had the same effect on his imagination as drink or narcotics are supposed to produce on some artists. The main thing was to live each moment for all it was worth, and the energy he poured into living seemed to return in new abundance to fill the reservoir of his creativeness.

One thing everybody noticed. Success for Ned was

simply a means to an end, and the end was mainly outside himself. Fame was an embarrassment, except that it helped him to do things for his friends. The handsome royalty checks sent by his agent gave him pleasure because they were money that he could spend as he pleased. His principal self-indulgences were the annual trip to Europe and his elegant apartment on Gramercy Park. The summer weeks abroad gave release from the pressures of his New York life, and the chief purpose of the apartment was to provide hospitality for his friends.

Those who knew him even casually in these early years kept in their minds always a picture that was symbolic of his whole life. It was of a young man, shining-eyed and debonair, standing with outstretched hand. Sometimes the hand was passing a ten-dollar bill, or a fifty if he happened to have one in his pocket, to some poor devil. Sometimes it was offering a playscript written to further a promising talent. Sometimes it was reaching out to grasp another hand to give strength and comfort. Already the stock answer to any question of trouble along Broadway was: "Go up and see Ned about it."

CHAPTER IV

Romance

DURING Sheldon's second winter in New York he began
work on the play which was to prove one of the most
spectacular successes in the history of the theatre, and at
the same time the supreme irony of his personal life. He was
never certain himself where the idea for *Romance* came
from. In a sense it had been with him since childhood for
it was as a boy in Chicago that he had first heard the story
of the exotic opera singer Lina Cavalieri. Sheldon's mother
with her strong feeling for all that was romantic and picturesque in life had been captivated by the fabulous career
and sultry beauty of the prima donna, and from some magazine had clipped a photograph of Cavalieri and placed it in
the frame of the mirror over her dressing table. Many times
Ned had gazed upon the exquisitely modeled features, the
smoldering black eyes under high arched brows, the proud
lift of the head, until Cavalieri became the embodiment of
his boyhood ideal of feminine loveliness.

Now in New York, more than ten years later, chance
revived the memories of the singer. After some years abroad
Ned's friend of Lake Geneva days, Henrietta McCrea was
in New York. The little girl who had first fired his interest
by her exotic background and foreign manners had grown
to charming womanhood. She and Ned liked the same

things and they saw each other frequently. Because of their similar tastes and common background of the Chicago Gold Coast, from which they had both successfully emancipated themselves, people began to suspect that they were in love. Yet much as they were attracted to one another, actually each was committed elsewhere. Henrietta was already engaged to the painter Willard Metcalf and was to be married within a few months, while Ned, with whatever slight encouragement, was head over heels in love with Doris Keane. But he was happy to find someone out of his old life who was also completely at home in his new world. In the years since they had last met Henrietta had come to know many stage people both in America and abroad. She regaled Ned with tales of Sarah Bernhardt and Yvette Guilbert. She also had a fund of anecdotes about his boyhood idol Lina Cavalieri whom she had known well in Paris. The details of the singer's life revived memories of his youthful passion and set his thoughts to working.

The new play took shape gradually, but from the start two things were clear in his mind. The heroine would be an opera singer and, to show how vividly he had the picture of Cavalieri before him, she would be called Cavallini. The second point was that the play would make no concessions to the rising interest in social problems. It would be a love story and nothing else, and lest that should slip for a moment from his mind he immediately set down the title: *Romance*.

He had many irons in the fire that winter of 1910. *The Nigger* was an established hit at the New Theatre, and he was tied up with rehearsals of two road companies which would soon start out. A good deal of rewriting was necessary for these, particularly for the company that was to tour the

South. He was also at work on *The Boss*, already so long
in the making that he could not leave it for fear of losing
interest altogether. So *Romance* had to be shelved for the
moment.

The summer of 1910 Ned made his usual trip to Europe.
With a younger Harvard friend Lincoln MacVeagh, the
future publisher and diplomat, he traveled through Devon,
visited Somerset Maugham in London, and then went on to
Italy. In Venice he began to think again about *Romance*.
The prototype of his heroine, the great Cavalieri, had begun
life here. She had been a street urchin, eking out a miserable
existence selling oranges and singing for pennies, until a
traveling Englishman picked her up and launched her on
the road to fame. Ned recalled the details of the story. Sitting
at Florian's in the long twilight hours, under a sky of deepen-
ing blue-green (by now his favorite color), he caught something else. It hung like a gauze curtain obscuring the
wretchedness of the singer's past, softening the gaudy colors
and crude lines of her later career. It was the atmosphere of
Venice itself, of faded splendors, of marble façades and old
frescoes—of a past that could never be wholly recaptured,
yet that never forsook one who had grown up with it. It
was precisely the atmosphere in which he would clothe
his own heroine, the atmosphere of romance.

Ned stored the impression carefully away and returned
to New York. The autumn found him still too busy with
other matters to get very far with the new play. There was
a lot of revision to be done on *The Boss*. Alice Kauser was
frankly irritated with him for having neglected it, and
William Brady, who was to produce it, was anxious to begin
rehearsals.

A far greater preoccupation was Doris Keane. She and

Ned were now seen frequently together, at the homes of friends, at Coney Island, in secluded corners at Sherry's— and rumors began to burgeon. Presently stories appeared in the papers, for the love affair of the handsome and much-discussed young playwright could hardly escape becoming public property. Yet for all the rumors and eventual publicity, few real details of the affair were ever known to anyone except the principals themselves.

Early in May, 1911, just before leaving for Europe, Ned wrote his cousin Elsa Denison to announce jubilantly that he and Doris were to be married. He also informed other friends, including Jack Wheelock and Van Wyck Brooks. But to his immediate family he said nothing about the matter, either then or at any time thereafter.

This is surprising when one considers how closely knit the Sheldons were. However, Ned knew in advance that his mother and grandfather would heartily disapprove his marrying an actress. He wished to hurt neither of them, certainly not his mother whose enthusiasm for the theatre did not extend to the acting profession generally. At the same time Ned knew that whatever protests might come out of Chicago, his decision, as well as his feelings for Doris, would not change. Rather than beat the air with futile preliminary discussions, it seemed that the best course was to keep silent. When the marriage actually took place he would let his family know; by that time discussion would be useless.

Ned refused to let this or any other concern dim his happiness during the spring of 1911. One of his friends still recalls a picture of the two lovers at that time. It was late one April afternoon, and Ned was seeing Doris into a hansom cab at the stage door of the theatre where she was playing.

The warm spring sun had already gone down behind the high buildings, but the theatre alley was filled with golden afterlight which touched the cloud of tulle Doris wore about her dark head so that her face was illumined in a bright aureole. Ned, with one foot on the step of the hansom, was gazing into her eyes as he handed her an enormous bunch of Parma violets. From Ned's gesture, the fixed look of adoration in his eyes, and the smile of his beloved, it was obvious that they were at the moment in a world completely to themselves. They might have been posing for a symbolic picture of young love in the springtime.

But only a few short weeks after this there is a discrepant, if not discordant note. Doris Keane, shortly after Ned's departure for a summer holiday in Italy, embarked for London where she was to do a new play. Just before sailing she saw Alice Putnam (her former understudy and the cousin of Eleanor Whidden), and in response to some inquiry about Ned, she murmured, "Oh dear, he's beginning to talk about getting married—about an apartment and furniture." At that moment there was apparently some difference of understanding as to the exact state of affairs. But by mid-summer the engagement was accepted as a *fait accompli* by the friends of the couple and Doris's own uncertainty seemed to have vanished.

Ned went straight to Tremozzo on Lake Como where in an atmosphere of distracting loveliness he worked in desultory fashion on two plays begun the previous winter. He made little progress, for as he confessed it was "difficult to do any serious work in such a heavenly place as Lake Como," and in June he went on to Venice. Here too there were distractions, but by sheer exercise of will power he managed to finish one play—and then with a feeling of sharp release he rushed to London and Doris Keane.

He found his beloved in a state of characteristic frustration. Her English engagement had turned out to be like so many others, nothing to really advance her career—and she was thoroughly depressed. This was a situation that Ned could not allow to continue. He must have urged her then and there to marry him as soon as possible, that to his mind being the perfect solution for everything. But Doris could not so easily abandon her ambitions; and though she may have consented to becoming engaged, that was not the same thing as setting a date for the wedding. Ned understood how it was. Until Doris had really achieved stardom, the goal toward which she had been struggling for so many years, she would never be happy. So he pushed aside his own impatience and told her not to worry. As Doris herself later related, "He assured me that there was hope still; and just to show his faith in me promised me a play."

Contrary to a widespread notion, Sheldon did not have Doris Keane in mind when he first conceived the character of Madame Cavallini, the heroine of *Romance*, nor even at the time of the meeting in London in 1911. When he promised to help Doris he was thinking of another play, one of the two he had brought with him to Europe that summer. This was the story of a gypsy girl who marries an aristocratic young man but is unable to endure the restraints of ordered society and returns to her wandering tribe—the play later entitled *Egypt*. Ned fancied that the part of the tempestuous and temperamental Romany girl would be a suitable vehicle for the personality of his fiancée. But after Doris had taken a look at one completed act and the scenario for the rest of the play, she tactfully declined the part. In this she showed better judgment than Margaret

Anglin, who produced *Egypt* the following season with most unhappy results.

The play which had been completed that summer was *The High Road*. But this was already promised to Mrs. Fiske while still in outline form. Anyway, as Ned doubtless realized, the part of Mary Page, the ardent reformer who has risen so nobly above her sullied past, was not the sort of thing to appeal to Doris. So the only possibility left was *Romance*, still hardly more than begun. It was not until they were both back in New York the following winter that Ned showed Doris the play, of which by then two acts had been drafted. Rough as it was, she saw at once that this was what she had been looking for. Even with only the main features of the part sketched in, she knew that Cavallini would be the answer to any actress's prayer.

With three plays in progress at once, one might have expected Ned's social activities to be curtailed. But he still managed to see people constantly and to entertain at his Gramercy Park apartment. Here he had surrounded himself with a *décor* suited to his taste, in which the keynote was comfort tinged with theatricality. The walls of the living room were hung with great gun-metal mirrors brought back from London, and the floors were covered with thick-piled black carpet. Everywhere were evidences of his European wanderings—a string of grotesque marionettes, glass from Venice, French furniture, old prints, paintings. At one point, for purely decorative purposes, several brilliantly plumaged live macaws sat on perches about the dining room. The walls of his study were lined with books, and deep, softly upholstered chairs invited lounging rather than labor. The establishment was staffed by a competent Swedish couple.

Ned dropped in often now at the Players Club, to which he had been admitted the previous year. The Club was only a few yards from his own house. This center of congenial fellowship must have offered a considerable temptation to pleasant loitering and talk. Half of Ned's closest men friends were members, and the Club's priceless collection of theatrical mementos and its famous library always had a special fascination for him.

Yet he worked on unflaggingly. One after another the three plays moved to completion. When he was ready to sail again for Europe in June, 1912, *The High Road* and *Egypt* were turned over to their respective producers. Only *Romance* was unfinished. Ned had saved that for the last, so that he might give himself wholly to it in Europe.

The summer of 1913 Ned headed as usual for Italy. At Cadenabbia on Lake Como he joined his friend and fellow-Harvardian Edward Knoblock, who was enjoying the profits of *Kismet*—a current Broadway hit. While Knoblock idled on the lake or explored the countryside, Ned worked on *Romance*. Now the atmosphere of Como was a stimulus rather than a distraction. In the bright sunshine, with a setting of peacock-blue water, of flower-covered marble terraces before him, he caught new inspiration for the character of Cavallini. Had he been able to look into the future his sense of dramatic irony would have been stirred. Not far from this very spot, more than thirty years later, the original of his heroine, Lina Cavalieri, met her end—during an air raid in World War II. This was in 1944, and Cavalieri was living in retirement, an old woman and almost forgotten. But that was after the world was mortgaged to the powers of darkness. In 1912 it still belonged to romance—at least for Ned

Sheldon, as he sat under the unclouded Italian sky, pouring his ardor and lover's dreams into his play.

In July he and Knoblock went to France. At Fontainebleau they joined Arnold Bennett with whom Knoblock was to collaborate on a new play. The three writers settled down in a little inn on the edge of the forest for the remainder of the summer. Knoblock and Bennett completed *Milestones* (which would be a hit the next season in London) while Sheldon put the final touches to *Romance*.

Ned returned to New York to find *Egypt* in rehearsal and casting for *The High Road* under way. He immediately turned *Romance* over to Alice Kauser to place.

Under ordinary circumstances this would have been no problem. Sheldon's was now the biggest name among American playwrights, and producers were competing for his work. But there was a hitch with *Romance*. The play had been written for Doris Keane. It was dedicated to her, and she must play the star part. Despite Sheldon's popularity and the appeal of the play itself, the stipulation was a definite drawback so far as the producers were concerned. Although Doris Keane had some admirers in New York, in general she was regarded as a second-rate or at best merely competent actress—certainly not a performer of star caliber. Besides, Sheldon's last play, *Princess Zim-Zim*, had been a failure, and when in September *Egypt* closed five days after it opened in Chicago, producers did not feel that even the Sheldon name was enough to carry the new play. It definitely needed a well-established star. The more reluctant managers were, the more determined Ned became. Either *Romance* would be produced with Doris Keane in the leading role or it would not be produced at all.

Finally those astute showmen, the Shuberts, decided to take the gamble. At least they went so far as to option the play, and when *The High Road* with Mrs. Fiske was established as a hit in November, thus sending the Sheldon stock up once more, they put *Romance* into rehearsal.

From the first reading with the assembled cast it was clear that Ned had been right. Nothing Doris Keane had previously done had prepared anybody for her handling of Cavallini. She brought to the part of the worldly-wise opera singer a warmth and sparkle, a combination of naturalness and subtlety, that made her seem even to people who knew her well a completely new personality.

Of course by this time it was common knowledge that Sheldon had written the play for her, and it was easy enough to read into the part of Tom Armstrong, the young clergyman who falls in love with the diva, Sheldon's own passion for Doris Keane.

Yet even before *Romance* went into rehearsal the supreme irony had occurred. Exactly when it happened or why is not known. But some time between Ned's return from Europe in late August and the end of the year, his engagement to Doris Keane was broken. It was not until after the play had opened in February, 1913, that the news became public. Gossip was immediately rife—but the facts of the break were a carefully guarded secret between the two people involved, so carefully guarded that even after the deaths of both Ned and Doris the details were still unknown.

In the spring of 1913 Ned wrote to Van Wyck Brooks, now living in California: "You will be sorry to hear that my engagement to Doris was broken last year." This of course meant some time in 1912. Since Ned was still very much in love and full of plans for a future with Doris when he returned from Europe in August of that year, the rupture must have occurred after that time.

One can only guess what really happened. Many years afterward Doris Keane told a friend, who was also a friend of Sheldon's, that it was Ned who had called the marriage off, saying, "I would make a very poor sort of husband for you, Doris." This would imply that Sheldon, at the last moment, was overcome by feelings of inadequacy. However, this does not accord with the general picture of his personality. What seems likely is that something had occurred which to Sheldon's mind created an insuperable obstacle to any real chances for happiness in the marriage, and rather than hurt the woman he loved by telling her the truth, he was willing to put himself at fault.

Doris Keane had had numerous admirers before she ever met Sheldon, and the engagement had not, apparently, put an end to the attentiveness of at least one or two men. For a beautiful actress this is not surprising. But it probably did not occur to Sheldon until he was on the very eve of marriage that this would undoubtedly continue. Despite his proverbial generosity, in matters of love he was as possessive as the next man; and this instinct coupled with his idealistic view of marriage may have made him suddenly see their future together in a different light.

One thing is quite certain. Even while she was engaged to Sheldon, Doris had seen a great deal of a familiar Broadway figure, the millionaire Howard Gould. Not long before the opening of *Romance*, Gould had divorced his first wife, the beautiful Katherine Clemmons, also an actress. Whether this was a preliminary to the serious pursuit of Doris Keane is not clear; but Gould certainly made no effort to disguise his continued interest in her. Sheldon was of course aware

of this, since all Broadway knew about it, and he must have
told Doris that she would have to decide between Gould and
him. The natural supposition is that Doris was unable to
make up her mind in the simple unhesitating fashion Ned
felt the occasion demanded—and on that rock the romance
came to grief.

For the next several months Doris Keane's name was
linked with Gould's in no uncertain fashion, and the Gould-
Keane-Sheldon triangle was a succulent morsel for the Sunday supplements. In the late spring of 1913 one of the papers
carried a full-page story entitled "Ambition or Gratitude—
Which Wins?" in which Miss Keane was depicted on the
horns of a dilemma unable to choose between the two men
who were in love with her—the young playwright to whom
she owed her success and the financier waiting to share his
millions with her. The story was presented luridly and it
did not flatter Miss Keane. It mentioned among other details the fact that *Romance*, now ending its New York run,
had been sold by the Shuberts to Charles Dillingham who
would take the play on the road, and that the financial back-
ing in this deal was provided by Howard Gould.

So when Doris started out on tour with *Romance* in the
summer of 1913, the two men who had competed for her
were both involved, Sheldon as author of the play and Gould
as the angel behind it.

But the story does not end with this rift in the lute.
Whatever happened did not change Ned's real feeling for
Doris. Both during the run of *Romance* and throughout the
later years, they saw each other frequently, and Sheldon's
interest in Doris' career and her personal life never waned.

Romance opened at the Maxine Elliott Theatre in New
York on February 10, 1913. The play was first tried out in
Albany where an event occurred which to the superstitious-

minded was prophetic of disaster. By mistake the stagehands placed palms in the first-act setting which were not called for in the script. Proverbially palms on the stage mean bad luck, and when Lee Shubert saw the baleful omens he had them hastily removed. But it was too late. On Saturday before the Monday opening one of the principals, the actress playing the part of Signora Vanucci, Cavallini's duenna in the play, had a stroke and shortly thereafter died. But both Sheldon and Shubert happened to remember Gilda Varesi who had played an effective bit in *Salvation Nell* and they sent her a wire. As luck would have it Miss Varesi was free at the moment and was able to jump into the part on forty-eight hours' notice. Her performance turned out to be one of the hits of the play.

In New York, *Romance* received a royal welcome. Though one or two critics found Sheldon's story trite and oversentimental, the majority shared the opinion of Acton Davies of the *Evening Sun:*

> Many things of theatrical importance happened at the Maxine last night. Doris Keane, a young actress in the role of a capricious, coquettish Italian diva, took a long leap up the ladder which leads to stardom; William Courtenay, as the courtly old Bishop who renewed—or rather reviewed—his youth for his grandson's sake, scored brilliantly . . . and most important of all, perhaps, the little Benjamin of American dramatists, Edward Sheldon produced one of the most engrossing and fascinating dramas which have been shown here in a long, long time. *Romance* will prosper for this one reason. It is a play which fascinates, and more than that, it tells one of the prettiest and most touching love stories that the stage has unfolded in a long time.

Naturally the production gained interest through the now much-publicized love affair between star and playwright. One critic took pains to point out that Sheldon was obviously "wooing Miss Keane by proxy" throughout the play. There were others who reported a special glow on the dramatist's ruddy cheeks the night of the opening, the unmistakable flush of happiness of the lover who has realized his dream. No one even suspected what had really happened. To everybody the combination of circumstances, the play itself, the beautiful star, the handsome and gallant young author, and true love—gave *Romance* an aura which probably has never been equaled by any other play produced in America.

The fabulous career of *Romance*, from its opening through the decades of its travels around the world, leaves us now a little bewildered. Though just as addicted to sentimentality as our fathers before the first World War, we prefer that commodity with a more brittle coating, or of a chewier texture than that of Sheldon's story of the glamorous opera singer who sweeps a young clergyman off his feet, reduces him to the point of sacrificing his career to his passion, and then in a gesture of renunciation to end all such gestures sends him back to his parishioners (who at that very minute are poignantly caroling in the snow outside). But great popular successes in the arts—as in politics, as in science, as in religion—can only be understood in the full context of the age which produces them. To the generation of 1913, still clinging desperately to the Victorian belief in the ultimate triumph of idealism, there was reassurance in Sheldon's picture of sex ennobled by self-sacrifice.

But *Romance* had something more. Into the character of Margherita Cavallini, Sheldon put every known quality that makes for theatrical effectiveness. As a vehicle for the most striking display of feminine allure the part is a tour de force with few equals in the drama. And Doris Keane made the most of it. For thousands still living, her first appearance in *Romance* is an inviolate peak of theatrical memory.

Not only Cavallini's first entrance as she sweeps up the staircase of the Van Tuyl mansion to confront young Tom Armstrong for the first time, but her personal appearance was carefully planned to draw and hold the most critical eye. She is "a bewitching, brilliant little foreign creature, beautiful in a dark Italian way," according to the author's description. "She is marvelously dressed in voluminous gauze, and her dress is trimmed with tiny roses. Her black hair hangs in curls on either side of her face, and three long, soft curls hang down her low-cut back. On her head is a little wreath of roses. She wears long diamond earrings, a *rivière* of diamonds is about her neck, diamonds gleam on her corsage, her wrists, and her hands. She carries a fan and a bouquet in a silver filigree holder. She speaks in a soft, Italian voice. . . ."

Sheldon lavished attention on the star's costumes and accessories. Everything pointed up the personality of the diva, so as to keep her the focus of the stage picture. For the last act she must wear a gown of black velvet, highly appropriate for the scene of renunciation and infinitely flattering to the wearer. With this went a long string of pearls and a jeweled crucifix—to suggest an awakened religious sense without any abandonment of the worldliness and love of luxury which are a part of the heroine's nature. During the summer of 1912, before *Romance* had even found a producer, Sheldon had spent hours combing antique shops in Paris for just the right crucifix. In Ivanowski's portrait of Doris Keane as Cavallini, which is now in the Museum of the City of New York, one can see it still.

Sheldon was inexhaustible in supplying other touches to

heighten the effectiveness of the star part. One property called for was a pet monkey. Sheldon and Doris spent days visiting New York pet shops to find a suitable animal—one small enough and friendly enough to be manageable. The search was long and discouraging, but Sheldon refused to give up the idea. He knew that the monkey would add a note of exoticism to his heroine—and he knew something else. A beautiful woman ravishingly gowned would attract attention. But a monkey fascinates the dullest imagination. His sure instinct told him that the combination of the two would be irresistible—and of course he was right.

As to the actual merits of Doris Keane's performance, it is impossible to judge. To many people her very name evokes memories of a magic the stage has rarely produced. Although many other stars played the same role in later revivals of the play, and invariably with success, Cavallini and Doris Keane became synonymous.

Doris Keane was certainly not a great actress. The best evidence of this is her record prior to *Romance* and in her later plays. It is true that until *Romance* she never had a really good part, but the test of an actor is his ability to make something significant of a poor part, and there is no indication that Doris Keane ever did this.

Sheldon himself must have had few illusions on this score, for even when he was most in love with her he did not discuss Doris as an actress, though he had a passion for acting as an art, and was an extraordinarily perceptive judge of both natural ability and technique. Yet except for her performance in his own play, which he considered perfect, he had little to say about Doris as an artist. He knew that, given the right role, even modest gifts can be made to dazzle—and Cavallini was that role. Besides he was in love with her, and that was enough.

But the role which made Doris Keane was also her undoing, and this is perhaps the greatest irony of the whole
story of *Romance*. For never afterward could she shed entirely the character that Sheldon had created for her. She
had made Cavallini so much a part of herself that for the rest
of her career she still played the glamorous flame of young
Tom Armstrong, with almost pathetic results.

For several years *Romance* gave Doris Keane everything,
professionally at least, that she had always longed for. After
a successful run in New York and a long tour on the road,
where star and play excited wild enthusiasm, in 1915 the
play was taken to London. As a *bon voyage* gift, Sheldon
assigned all future rights in *Romance* to Miss Keane for her
lifetime.

Londoners gave the play at first only a lukewarm reception, and for some weeks it operated at a loss. Then public
interest quickened. The stimulus of a command performance
before Queen Mary proved all it needed to settle down as a
hit, and when it finally closed in 1918 *Romance* had rolled
up one of the longest runs in the history of the English stage,
with the total of 1,049 performances. During those years
Doris Keane was the toast of London and the idol of thousands of war-weary men. At the front reproductions of
Ivanowski's dramatic portrait were widely distributed. The
figure in the black velvet gown, with pearls and crucifix,
the pale uplifted face, slightly imperious yet so inviting, hung
on many a dugout wall and beside countless hospital beds in
France. In fact Doris Keane was the last "pin-up girl" of
the legitimate stage.

In London performances were frequently halted by
Zeppelin raids that sent audiences rushing for the cellar, and
for part of the run the play was presented with six matinees
and two evening performances a week—reversing the nor-

mal theatrical schedule. But week in and week out, raids notwithstanding, it was *the* play of London, and seemingly indestructible. When it finally closed in 1918 the playgoers crowded to the footlights at the final curtain for an informal reception to the star and her leading man, Basil Sydney—who in the meantime had also become her husband. Afterward, according to the correspondent of the New York *Times*, Doris had to fight her way to the waiting limousine through "thousands of souvenir hunters."

While the play was still running in London, other companies all over Europe began to produce it. In 1916 it was given in Moscow in two theatres simultaneously. In Petrograd it had a longer run than any play in years, and the Russian star, Madame Andreeva Gorky, wife of the novelist, Maxim Gorky, achieved an enormous success in the title role. Some critics, European as well as Russian, maintained that she was the greatest Cavallini of all. This heresy becomes almost credible in view of the fact that Madame Gorky (who was indeed a very fine actress) performed the play throughout Russia for over five years! A later Cavallini, Madame Eugenie Leontovitch, who appeared with Philip Huston in 1934 in one of the many American revivals of *Romance*, was first inspired as a young girl at the Russian Imperial Drama School when she and her class were taken to see Madame Gorky's performance.

In 1921 *Romance* was seen again in New York and then in Chicago, with Doris Keane more triumphant than ever. Before the revival ended, the French Academy took the unprecedented step of inviting Miss Keane to bring the play to Paris. Robert de Flers, a member of the Academy, had seen it in London, and although he understood hardly any English he came away deeply impressed. "I felt the piece without understanding it," he said. "It is pure enchantment." Doris Keane declined the invitation to come to Paris, but two years later a French translation of *Romance* with Madame Madeleine Soria as Cavallini opened at the Théâtre de l'Athénée. Paris was swept off its feet, although there was some bewilderment at the situation of a clergyman proposing marriage! (Despite their great Protestant tradition, the French always think of clergymen as Catholic priests.)

In the autumn of 1926 *Romance* came back to London, where Doris Keane received a tremendous ovation. Since the play had had an initial run of three years followed by some six years of continuous performance on the road throughout England and Scotland, this revival was hardly more than a continuation of the original run, yet the reception given the star was as to a long-lost favorite daughter.

Remembering the lukewarm reviews which the play had originally drawn, Doris cabled Ned exultantly:

> THEY SAY ROMANCE PROCLAIMED BY ALL CRITICS A GREAT PLAY STOP ST. JOHN IRVINE AND CRITIC AGATE OF SUNDAY TIMES WROTE WONDERFUL REVIEW SUNDAY AND AGATE BROADCAST TELLING EVERYONE TO SEE IT THAT IT IS WONDERFUL STOP SO TEN YEARS LATER THEY REVERSE THEMSELVES AND ACKNOWLEDGE THE PUBLIC RIGHT BLESS YOU I KNOW THIS WILL MAKE YOU LAUGH STOP HAVE SPENT ALL DAY IN THEATRE FOR FLASHLIGHTS SURELY THE LAST STOP RONDA WILL BE WITH ME FOR WEEKEND UNLESS MUMPS AT SCHOOL PREVENT STOP PLEASE REPEAT STARK YOUNG AND GLADYS UNGER LOVE DORIS.

Ronda, referred to in the cable, was Doris Keane's little daughter, born in England some years before. Inevitably she too became one of those for whom Ned felt special affection.

After several months in London, the play was again taken on a tour of England and Scotland. And there was another revival in Paris, in 1928, again with Madame Soria.

But *Romance* traveled still farther. It was seen in Norway and Sweden, in Spain, Egypt, India, and throughout the Orient—in Australia and New Zealand and even in Africa. Few plays of modern times, those of Ibsen and Shaw not excepted, have found so varied and yet so uniformly enthusiastic audiences. Its extraordinary popularity led Professor Arthur Hobson Quinn, a foremost authority of the American drama, to observe: "the creator of *Romance* had illustrated again the fact that the shots of the American minute men have not been the only American products that have been 'heard round the world.' "

It was not only in terms of distance covered that *Romance* proved its vitality. The play was soon translated to the screen. In 1920 Doris Keane appeared in a film version, and ten years later Garbo essayed her second speaking role as Cavallini in a performance so honest and poignant that the story took on fresh life.

For another decade, through World War II, *Romance* continued to hold its own. It was seen all over the country with Eugenie Leontovich, with Jane Cowl, with Cornelia Otis Skinner, and other stars.

In each case the actress playing the leading role went over the part carefully with Sheldon beforehand. It was with special delight that Otis Skinner—an old friend of Ned's— saw his daughter, Cornelia Otis Skinner, as Cavallini. During the original New York run of the play in 1913, Skinner had been appearing in Knoblock's *Kismet* and had had no opportunity to see it. Not until 1938 did he have this pleasure. Then Skinner, though tired and ill at the time, journeyed to Ogunquit, Maine, to see his daughter's performance. In a letter to Sheldon, professional criticism and fatherly pride were mingled:

That it was your play and that Cornelia was acting in it were two things that lifted me quite out of myself and made life worthwhile. . . . Plays have a way of hiding their glory under the passing years, but yours holds up its head as youthfully as though it were written yesterday.

The echoes of *Romance* did not die away on Broadway until 1948. That year the Messrs. Shubert gave the play in a musical version called *My Romance,* with a score by Sigmund Romberg and lyrics by Rowland Leigh. Anne Jeffreys was a charming Cavallini, and Charles Fredericks played Armstrong, the young rector. Though loving care went into the production, its run was brief. Whatever nostalgic delight it may have afforded an older generation its pace was too slow, the edges of its sentiment too soft for postwar New York.

In *Romance,* Sheldon reached the peak of his success as a playwright. None of his later works, even hits, achieved the same quality of magic, exercised the same spell over audiences. It was not that he had exhausted his capacities as a writer in this play. It was simply that life does not twice present a combination of circumstances like that which had enabled him to capture in *Romance* the very essence of his youthful idealism, and to give it back to the world in a form that was universally appealing.

But *Romance* did more than add to Sheldon's fame and fortune. The part written for the woman he loved became in his mind forever associated with Doris Keane, and Doris Keane, by the same token, never lost for Sheldon certain overtones of the personality of Cavallini. Though the years were not kind to her, in Sheldon's eyes and to his inward vision when sight was gone, Doris Keane remained forever young and lovely as he had re-created her in the heroine of *Romance.*

CHAPTER V

The Gods Serve Notice

THERE was no outward sign to show the state of Ned's feelings over the break with Doris Keane. But a month after the opening of *Romance* he quietly slipped away to Europe. He had no plans, except to get as far from New York as possible.

He spent a month in Berlin, which he had never seen before, hearing music and steeping himself in the German drama. In early spring he set out for Italy, pausing for a few weeks en route in Switzerland. When May came he drifted to Como where he succumbed as usual to the enchanted air, untouched apparently by bittersweet memories of the summer before.

June found him in Venice, where he realized an ambition of years by renting for a month a magnificent old *palazzo*, full of dim gilding and Tintorettos, complete with gondola, gondolier, and an assortment of servants. The very day he moved in he ran into an acquaintance, a young British playwright, and promptly invited him to dinner. During the meal his guest was taken violently ill and had to be rushed to a hospital outside of Venice. Ned was so concerned about the young man that he not only accompanied him to the hospital but stayed with him until he had recovered from his illness. By that time the lease on the *palazzo* was almost up. In all

Ned spent exactly three nights in it. Furthermore, on his return he found that the Italian staff, as evidence of their appreciation of American tailoring, had removed all but one pair of the *signor's* trousers.

In midsummer Ned was in Paris where he met Dorothy Donnelly and a friend, Miss Daisy Blaisdell, whom he had known years before in Chicago. In the few crowded days the trio passed together, Ned seemed completely himself. He was full of projects and his gaiety was inexhaustible. One night the three friends dined at the Crillon and later went to a small boulevard theatre famous for political satires and amusing singing and dancing. In the course of the performance Ned reached for his handkerchief and pulled out of his pocket instead one of the immense Crillon napkins. For an instant he regarded the monogram with dismay, then a look of delight came over his face. He had recognized friends in a box across the theatre and began waving the large square of linen to attract their attention. Since the curtain was just descending for the intermission the great flapping napkin was taken as a gesture of enthusiasm for the actors, quite in the *opéra bouffe* spirit of the evening, and the whole house burst into laughter. But before he slept that night, Ned did up the napkin in a neat package and mailed it back to the hotel with apologies.

From Paris, Ned went to London where he was cordially welcomed by his now numerous friends of the British stage. The Favershams were settled now in England, and Ned spent several weekends at their charming old Tudor house at Chiddingfold in Surrey. Constance Collier was also a frequent guest, and at the Favershams' he met for the first time Julie Le Gallienne and her daughter Eva. There, too, began his long friendship with May Whitty, her hus-

band Ben Webster, and their daughter Margaret who always remembered "the enormous distance one had (at the
age of five) to look upwards in order to see him!"

The winter of 1913–14 Ned worked steadily on an
ambitious task, the dramatization of Hans Christian Andersen's *The Little Mermaid*, which he turned over to the
producer George C. Tyler before leaving again for Europe
the following spring.

The summer of 1914, which was to mark the end of
European touring for everybody for some years, was Ned's
last among the sights and sounds of the Old World in which
his passionately romantic nature took such delight. In Venice
he was joined by his friend John Barrymore, who, unlike
Ned the year before, made no effort to conceal the de-
pression occasioned by his own affairs. Barrymore's marriage to Katherine Harris (his first) had gone on the rocks,
and this combined with a feeling of hopelessness over his
professional career had sent him to Europe in a frank gesture
of escape. But the encounter with Sheldon, the first of several
in similar crises, gave Barrymore what he needed. Having
poured his troubles into Ned's sympathetic ear, and having
received sound advice from the younger man, he soon put
the past behind him. Ned made him feel that nothing was
irretrievably lost, and that the best of his life was yet before
him. Soon Barrymore began to warm to his friend's unquenchable excitement over Venice, and the two men, so
unlike fundamentally yet so congenial in their capacity for
enjoyment, were soon exploring *palazzi* and galleries as
though nothing in life mattered more than to soak up the
color and splendor on all sides. Together they went on to
Rome where Ned introduced Barrymore to all his favorite
haunts. They walked along the Appian Way and browsed

in the Vatican Library. They stood silently beside Keats's grave in the English cemetery. At night they haunted a little café where a young girl, a fiery beauty with a voice to rival the very nightingales of the Pincio, was an unforgettable attraction.

They traveled to Florence and plunged again into the thick air of the Renaissance, looking at Botticelli's pictures, exploring the Bargello, climbing the road to San Miniato, storing unconsciously a thousand details to be revived years later in that gorgeous venture, *The Jest*.

Their last night in Florence neither of them could sleep. The tumult of impressions filling their minds, and perhaps the sense that something fateful hung in the air, kept them talking almost till dawn. Finally, as they looked from their hotel window at the city whose life seemed to smolder under the shadows like a banked fire, Barrymore suggested that they climb up to a cupola on the roof of the hotel and watch the sunrise. In pajamas the two friends cautiously inched along the tiles until they reached the little tower jutting out over the river. There, leaning against the railing, with the Arno bending below, they talked until the first crimson flashed against the windows across the river.

The two parted next day. Barrymore, fired with new ambition, returned to America, and Sheldon went on to London. He was there when the assassination at Sarajevo brought Europe to the realization that she had reached the brink of war. In London, however, the effects of this event on the public were almost equaled by the shock of the divorce of Lady Randolph Churchill and her husband, George Cornwallis-West, and the latter's immediate remarriage to Beatrice Stella Campbell, known throughout her professional life as Mrs. Patrick Campbell. Sheldon's acquaintance with the ravishing and tempestuous "Mrs. Pat" had begun two years before in New York. On his arrival in London he was immediately welcomed to her house, and during the next weeks the two saw each other often. This summer marked the beginning of one of the rarest of all Ned's remarkable friendships with older women in the theatre. From 1914 on, Mrs. Pat Campbell began to depend on Sheldon for advice and to look to him for comfort as the vicissitudes of life bore down on her.

Through Mrs. Pat Campbell, Sheldon met more people in London. It was at her house that he first knew young Denis Mackail, grandson of the painter Sir Edward Burne-Jones, son of the great Oxford scholar John William Mackail, and brother of a then unknown but aspiring young writer with the pseudonym of Angela Thirkell. Mackail had designed stage settings for Barrie and Shaw, and Sheldon immediately discussed his own forthcoming production of *The Garden of Paradise* (as the dramatization of Andersen's *Little Mermaid* was called). Mackail even made some colored sketches for the play, although the producers, the Liebler Company, eventually employed Joseph Urban to do the settings.

Throughout July the feeling of panic in Europe increased. Americans were rushing for homebound steamers, and when chance presented Ned with an opportunity to secure passage he took it. In August he read the words of Viscount Grey of Falloden, "The lamps are going out all over Europe; we shall not see them lit again in our lifetime," and he felt the prophetic significance of the statement as it applied to the world of his youth. What he did not realize then, as he did later, was its application to his personal life.

Meanwhile, he was busy as usual. In November, *The*

Garden of Paradise opened and in ten days closed. Despite much admiration for the production, in particular for the settings of Joseph Urban, recently arrived from Vienna and struggling to establish himself, the fragile tale of the mermaid who gambled on winning the love of a mortal and lost was far too delicate for the hearty Broadway appetite. The production cost the Liebler Company fifty thousand dollars and sent it into bankruptcy. As usual Sheldon was nonchalant about his own loss, a year's work gone for nothing. His concern was for the producers and particularly for the gifted Joseph Urban. Fortunately the production had caught the eye of Florenz Ziegfeld, who not only had Urban revamp some of the sets for his *Midnight Follies* at the New Amsterdam, but later engaged the young Viennese to design the handsome Ziegfeld Theatre on Sixth Avenue.

That fall Ned also undertook another dramatization, *The Song of Songs*, based on the novel *Das Hohe Lied* by Hermann Sudermann. The play was immediately bought by the Shuberts, who before it reached production sold it to Al Woods. This producer, whose genius for mismanaging the English language rivaled that of Samuel Goldwyn, was greatly taken by Sheldon from the first. This was another of many friendships between the playwright and people of totally different tastes and background. Woods summed up their relation accurately when he said, "Ned for class—me for mass!" What Sheldon really liked about the producer, aside from the loyalty which was part of Woods's nature, was his occasional willingness to trust intuition as against common sense. "He knew I would always take a chance on an unknown," said Woods, adding, with a deft manipulation of grammar, "if they smelled just right." And Woods put implicit faith in Ned's judgment of actors. "I

always had power of attorney to send young hopefuls up
to Ned, who knew more about picking actors than anyone
else in the world."

The two worked happily together on *The Song of Songs,*
which opened on December 21, 1914, and despite mixed
notices ran into the following spring. Neither Woods nor
Sheldon regarded it as a complete success. Woods was content to get back his original investment, and with another
real hit on his hands (this was *Kick In* with John Barrymore)
he refused to take a ten-thousand-dollar share of the author's royalties to which Ned felt Woods had a right since
he had greatly assisted in pulling the script into shape. This
did not suit Ned who went to Tiffany's and purchased a
magnificent black pearl which he sent to his co-author. The
pearl became one of Woods's greatest treasures.

Life was considerably brightened during this winter by
Mrs. Pat Campbell who had come to America with Shaw's
Pygmalion, and was in and out of New York. It was during
this time that "Mrs. Pat" inaugurated the habit, which lasted
the rest of her life, of talking for an hour every morning on
the telephone with Ned when he was within calling distance.

Denis Mackail, the young designer and future biographer
of Sir James Barrie, was also in America that year and when
he was in New York he stayed with Sheldon on Gramercy
Park. Once the friends trekked over to Brooklyn to see
Maude Adams in *Quality Street.* Though Sheldon had lived
now for several years in New York he had never been to
Brooklyn, and as a precaution on this expedition he took
along a Baedeker, explaining to Mackail that so far as he was
concerned Brooklyn was a foreign city.

When spring came Ned yearned as usual for Europe,
and despite wartime conditions he thought he might go at

least as far as England. His friend the producer Charles Frohman had passage on the *Lusitania* and urged Ned to come along with him. Ned had about made up his mind to accompany Frohman when a call from his friend and classmate George Foote caused him to change his plans. Foote was to be married within a week and insisted on Sheldon's being his best man.

Five days after seeing Frohman off, just as Sheldon was leaving New York for Keene, New Hampshire, where the wedding was to take place, news came of the horrible tragedy off the Irish coast. The torpedoing of the *Lusitania*, which cost the life of Frohman among hundreds of others, brought the war home to Sheldon along with the rest of the country. He went on up to New England with the sense of horror heavy over him, despite the fresh beauty of the spring countryside and the wedding festivities.

Up till now Ned's life had been like a long bright summer day. He had only tasted tragedy in the death of his father, when he was a student at Harvard, and in the disappointment of lost love. In the nature of things neither was an extraordinary occurrence, and both were softened by youth and a world of consuming interests.

Now, in the late days of August, 1915, came the first intimation of something which no man of twenty-nine can expect or easily accept as part of the inevitable design of life. Ned spent July and August of that year on the North Shore of Massachusetts with his mother, who had taken the house of Robert Haven Schauffler, the poet and music biographer. It was a delightful spot and Ned worked happily, varying his routine with a daily swim and an occasional set of tennis. Toward the end of their stay he noticed an unaccountable stiffness in his knees, particularly after playing tennis. He thought little of it but he was annoyed and complained to his mother. Mrs. Sheldon was alarmed for there was a history of rheumatic tendencies on both sides of the family. She insisted that Ned go to Boston and have X-rays made. These revealed nothing unusual in Sheldon's knee joints; yet some days later when he arrived in Chicago for a long-promised visit with his family, he was a very sick man. An examination showed that his tonsils were seriously infected. These were promptly removed; but when still no relief came, Dr. Lillian Taylor, a friend of the Sheldon family, suggested that Ned consult another woman physician, also highly regarded by the Sheldons, Dr. Clara Ferguson.

Dr. Ferguson watched Ned closely for several weeks, observing that normal activities during this time were becoming increasingly difficult for him. A marked ankylosis of shoulders and hips had set in, and certain movements caused excruciating pain. There was no mistaking the symptoms. Ned had fallen victim to a crippling, progressive arthritis.

Though suffering acutely, the patient assumed that his illness was a passing affair which medical treatment would soon clear up. This was of course before the days of cortisone, and before the study of arthritis in its relation to the general nervous system. The disease was assumed to result from the operation of low-virulence bacilli springing from some infection. The main thing was to locate the source of infection, which Ned was confident would be done.

Regarding his own troubles as temporary, his chief concern at the moment was for his friend Jack Barrymore. The actor's recent run of parts had done little to display the genius Sheldon was determined must have its chance. While in Chicago, Ned had read a new play, *Justice*, by John

Galsworthy. There was a part in it that Ned considered ideal for Barrymore, and as soon as he could travel, in the early autumn of 1915, he took the train for New York. There he talked with his friend John Williams, a newcomer to the producing field and a Harvard man, and persuaded him to do the Galsworthy play, with John Barrymore in the leading role. The part was totally unlike anything Barrymore had attempted before, but Williams was willing to take the gamble. The result was the revelation of a completely new Barrymore. As Falder, the sensitive, weak-willed hero of *Justice*, Barrymore gave a heartbreaking performance. The play became a hit, and Barrymore was established as a serious actor of the first rank.

That winter Ned took life somewhat easier. He worked in desultory fashion on two or three ideas for plays, but mainly he was content to see old friends, especially Barrymore whose success touched him as deeply as any achievement of his own. When *Justice* closed, early in the summer of 1916, the friends spent several weeks together in California. Here in the mild but stimulating air of Santa Barbara, surrounded by new faces, caught up in the fast pace of the Barrymore social life, Ned's condition seemed to improve. But it was clear to everybody that movement of any sort was difficult for him.

The fall of 1917 Ned was back in New York again, trying in the face of everything to carry on his usual full life. He started to work seriously on a new play, but this was pushed aside in order to lend a helping hand to another friend.

During the winter the British actress Constance Collier arrived in America after two years of wartime England and a run of bad luck. Ever since they had first met at the

Favershams' eight years before, she and Ned had kept in close touch. Ned considered her one of the finest actresses of the time, and his esteem for her as a human being was even greater. When she arrived in New York her prospects were uncertain, and she needed a job. So Ned placed his services at her disposal.

Miss Collier had brought from England the manuscript of a play, a dramatization of Du Maurier's *Peter Ibbetson*, which she hoped to do. She was fascinated with the story, and the part of the Duchess of Towers, the heroine, seemed to offer special opportunities for her. Unfortunately the script, written by a newspaperman, John Raphael, had such serious weaknesses that no producer was willing to consider it. Sheldon, a great Du Maurier addict as well as a friend of Miss Collier's, determined that the play would be done and he undertook to put the script in order. Throughout most of the winter he worked on it, changing certain scenes, tightening others, cutting, rewriting the dialogue—making it, in short, really stage-worthy. He then showed the play to John and Lionel Barrymore. He had no trouble in convincing John that the part of Peter Ibbetson was right for him. But Lionel was more reluctant to do the overbearing Colonel Ibbetson, Peter's father. But in the end he yielded, as people usually did to Ned, and was grateful ever afterward. With the three principals lined up, Sheldon offered the play to the Shuberts who took it at once.

Peter Ibbetson opened on April 17, 1917, ten days after the United States declared war on Germany. The tense state of affairs did not promise well for a romantic dream fantasy, but perhaps because it offered a complete escape from the unpleasant truth that war had at last come to America, people flocked to it. For two years it delighted Broadway audiences, providing a strong impetus in the careers of Ned's three friends and bringing handsome profits to the original playwright, Raphael, and to the Shuberts. For his part in rewriting the play and making its production possible, Sheldon took nothing, neither a share of the author's royalties nor any public credit. He would not even allow his name to appear on the program.

Ned's happiness over the outcome of *Peter Ibbetson* had the same effect as his reaction to John Barrymore's success the previous year. For the next months he was convinced that his physical condition was nearly normal. The country was now deep in preparations for war, and Ned was determined to go into the Army. But any illusions he may have had about his condition were crushed at the recruiting station where he tried to volunteer. At the preliminary physical examination the officer in charge merely looked at him and said, "What are you doing here? You ought to be home in bed!"

Ned did not take this advice, but the Army's rejection was a serious setback. He doggedly tried to go about his affairs as usual, but by late spring his friends noted that he could no longer cross his knees and that he walked with a stiff, halting gait. About this time his friend Henrietta McCrea, now Mrs. Willard Metcalf, arrived back in New York with her husband and a very young baby. Ned happened to be at the Metcalfs' apartment one day when the baby was being bathed and asked to watch the performance. Mrs. Metcalf had not seen Sheldon for some months and was astonished at his unsuccessful effort to bend down over the baby's tub. She asked what was wrong, and Ned answered with a wry grin, "I guess it's just old age," and let it go at that.

He spent the summer of 1917 in California, at Montecito, where he took a house and engaged a Japanese manservant to look after him. During the summer his Chicago physician, Dr. Clara Ferguson, visited him. Dr. Ferguson saw at once that his health had seriously deteriorated, and she secretly despaired that anything could be done for him. But what struck her as more significant than his physical condition was a change in Sheldon's spirit. He seemed to have become both quieter and stronger. He had lost none of his old good humor, but there was a deeper current of seriousness in him. His sympathies for others, always alert, were even quicker now, and in the long talks between physician and patient he showed a grasp of human problems which Dr. Ferguson would have thought impossible in so young a man. Most remarkable of all, as she later stated, was the extraordinary feeling of peace and healing which, in the very midst of his suffering, seemed to emanate from him.

Though every movement now meant agony, Ned could not stop working. The fall of 1917 he quickly revamped Dumas' *Dame aux Camélias* for Ethel Barrymore, and in December he traveled East for the opening, a disappointing affair. Despite all his efforts, the piece showed its ancient mechanism, and Miss Barrymore was not quite the fragile type demanded by the story and tradition. To her admirers she was ravishing in a blond wig and sumptuous costumes, but neither Ned's cunning nor the star's charm were sufficient to keep the creaking apparatus going. Ned refused to allow his name to appear on the program, but the critics had no difficulty in recognizing certain Sheldon touches. He had always had a predilection for using music wherever possible to heighten an emotional effect, and he had tried to cover some of the weaknesses of the old play by this means.

But the results were none too happy. One reviewer commented pointedly on "Mr. Sheldon's inordinate affection for piccolos, fife and drum corps, love birds, harps, choirs, music boxes, military bands, street organs, and victrolas in the wings," remarking that, " 'Music off' is to the Sheldon faith what 'clothes off' is to Ziegfeld. . . ."

Sheldon was as devoted to Ethel Barrymore as to her brothers, and he shared her despair at the failure of *Camille*. Her heart had been set on the play (with all odds against them, leading ladies still persisted in thinking they must at some time in their careers play Dumas' heroine), and he had done what he could to help. What this cost him, even Ned did not realize. When he returned to Chicago in January to visit his family and to rest, his condition had greatly worsened.

He stayed very quietly at home with his family throughout the spring and summer, thinking that by foregoing all activity there might be improvement. But by October he was bedridden. At this time Gordon Strong, his mother's brother, saw him and made the following note in his diary:

> To Bellevue Place for dinner. . . . Afterwards to the third floor where Ned lies, propped up in bed, looking very badly. Trained nurse in Ted's old room, with a wagon-load of medicines and apparatus. While Ned is probably not dangerously ill, his confinement and appearance are distressing. His mind is clear enough—he thinks straighter, I believe, than anyone in the family—perhaps than anyone I know—particularly in [regard to] human beings.

Dr. Ferguson now decided that Ned could not survive the bitter Chicago winter, and recommended the dry climate of Arizona. So before Christmas, Ned was painfully lifted

aboard a train and started for the Southwest accompanied by
his mother and a trained nurse. There was irony in the fact
that while the miles were increasing between the playwright
and Broadway an article appeared in the *American Magazine*,
stating that "among playwrights Edward Sheldon must be
considered the best we have in this country. He has the
education, the experience, and what is more, the fires of
youth burning within him. In a few years he will be writing
plays which will make him as well known in the tradition
as Ibsen, Shaw or Thomas."

But for Sheldon the handwriting on the wall was becoming clearer with each passing week. In Chandler, Arizona,
where the eye met vast distances in every direction, he felt
acutely the slow contraction of his own horizon. The fact
that nothing in his previous life had prepared him for the
fate which was overtaking him only made the situation more
difficult. He could not guess the full extent of what lay
ahead, but he sensed that he would never again know complete freedom of movement, and that knowledge cast a black
pall over the whole picture of the future.

He had taken with him to Chandler a trunkful of personal letters, memoranda, notes for plays, papers pertaining
to past and projected work. One day Mrs. Sheldon came
upon him, destroying the contents of the trunk, wincing with
the effort to tear and burn envelopes and manuscripts, but
working frenziedly while strength remained to wipe out
all reminders of his past life. For it seemed to him now that
whatever lay before him would make a mockery of his
brilliant youth, and he could only face the future by wholly
forgetting the past.

Soon it was evident that he required more expert medical
care than was obtainable in Chandler, and he was moved to
Los Angeles. Here an operation was finally decided upon,

to break up the calcification in his knee joints in the hope of re-establishing articulation. The operation was followed by long and complex treatment, involving daily stretching of the legs. This was so painful that the sweat poured from Ned during the process, but no one heard him cry out, and when he was able to write he made no mention of the agony he was undergoing.

Only once was there something like a protest, in the early days of 1919 when it was evident that the operation had not succeeded, that it had not even halted the progress of the disease. It was then that the full realization of what was in store came over him, and he cried out to his mother in despair, "If I only knew what I have ever done to bring all this upon me!"

Yet he had no sooner faced the future squarely, seen it with all its implications of pain and bleakness, than his mind turned away from himself. Though flat on his back in a hospital bed, he determined to carry through a project already begun for Jack Barrymore. This was the adaptation of the Italian Sem Benelli's play *La Cena delle Beffe*, which he had begun the summer before, and which he had carefully preserved from the destruction of his other papers, simply because—though the work was his own—it was destined for somebody else.

Barrymore had become interested in this play a couple of years before. It was a violent but gorgeously colorful melodrama laid in the period of the Medici which Barrymore and Sheldon had studied with such zeal during their stay together in Florence in 1914. The story deals with the dastardly attempt of two powerful nobles, the Chiaramantese brothers, to steal the betrothed of a sensitive young artist, Gianetto Malespina, and to eliminate Malespina by having him drowned. Malespina escapes and turns the tables on the brothers by a trick more diabolical than their own machinations against him. The part of the young artist, combining aesthetic sensitivity, charm, and a Machiavellian brilliance, was to Sheldon's mind a perfect role for John Barrymore, while that of the domineering elder Chiaramantese brother lent itself admirably to the brand of stage villainy which Lionel Barrymore had by now made so peculiarly his own.

The play had attracted much attention abroad. Duse presented it originally, and Bernhardt had later given it in Paris under the title *La Beffa*. In Sheldon's version, called *The Jest*, nothing was lost of the original drama, and much was added in the beauty of the dialogue. Without resorting to archaic language Sheldon wrote the play in a flowing, musical, richly colored free verse which excited as much comment from critics and public as anything else in the production. He had never attempted verse drama before, and *The Jest* revealed another talent little suspected even by those most familiar with his work.

Added to the exciting story and brilliant acting of the two Barrymores were the masterful settings by Robert Edmond Jones. Seldom has so much talent been combined in such perfect harmony as in *The Jest*. The play was a tremendous success. It opened at the end of the 1919 season (on June 4), and John Corbin, writing in the New York *Times*, said: "*The Jest* has fallen across the sky of the declining season like a burst of sunset color."

The good news of *The Jest* brought some comfort to the invalid isolated in his Los Angeles hospital room. At the same time the feeling that he was so far from everything that most interested him, and cut off from those whose friendship was so necessary to him, added to his forlornness. Ned had now struck the darkest period of his ordeal. Added to the constant physical pain was the anguish of loneliness.

It is true that his mother was close by, but he missed acutely the companionship of his contemporaries, the easy talk, the gaiety, the intellectual stimulus of New York. These had been the very breath of life to him, and he suffered now from a kind of spiritual strangulation.

He had not seen his old Harvard classmate Van Wyck Brooks for two years. When he learned that Brooks, now an instructor at Stanford University, was spending some months at Carmel, he wrote to him eagerly:

> . . . I wish I could see you. I have been more or less ill for the last couple of years and am now here in this place unable to move my legs or I should take tonight's train for Carmel and burst in on you. I wonder if you have changed. I don't suppose so really. I know when I think of you I don't think I have. Do you ever come down here? . . .

Later when his doctor suggested a long voyage, if his condition improved, Ned impulsively wrote again begging Brooks to go with him. It never occurred to him that Brooks, now married and with a family, might find such a project impracticable. To the invalid, clinging desperately to a last frail hope of at least partial recovery, there was tonic in the very thought of moving again amid new and stimulating scenes in the company of his old friend.

This notion had to be abandoned before it even reached the stage of definite planning. In April, 1919, Ned wrote Brooks that he had walked eight steps ("It took five minutes and two nurses, but I am as proud as if I had had twins"). But a few days later there was a relapse and he was again bedridden. Then in a mood very close to hopelessness he wrote:

> I will come to Carmel just as soon as I can. I would come now, if I could manage the trains, etc., but I know they wouldn't let me. . . .

*I am trying to read Science and Health but I can't. I
cnvy Christian Scientists so. All these people have something I want—they see something I can't and I am just
greedy enough to feel angry about it. I never felt the need
of a definite religion until recently. I used to think I could
stand up to anything that came along but I don't any more.
Of course now that I want it I can't see why I don't get it.
Perhaps wanting and getting haven't the sweet simple connection that people think. . . .*

Ned had now reached the bottom of the abyss. In late
April final tests were made and the hospital laboratory report
showed the presence of *streptococcus viridans* in his blood
stream. Against this deadly bacillus there was then no known
antibiotic. In Sheldon's own mind this meant the end of any
real hope. There was no way of telling how long the disease
would take to complete its work, but he knew that it would
not stop until it had reached every joint in his body and he
lay stretched in immobility forever.

Except for the announcement to his mother of the laboratory findings, he made no comment on the news. In the following weeks there was no sign of rebellion against the
sentence that had been passed on him. Only in the letters
to Brooks was there any hint of despair. What thoughts
passed through his mind during the long wakeful nights in
the hospital may be surmised. But there was no unguarded
moment in which he let down the barrier of reticence about
his inmost self.

Yet during the next weeks he came to grips with destiny,
and from some hidden reservoir of the spirit drew the
strength to go on. He not only found the courage to endure,
under a blight from which death might have seemed a welcome release, but he formed the sure belief that affliction
could not destroy the purpose of his life. There was nothing
—at least in the outward circumstances of his previous

history—to prepare him for the blow that had fallen. He had no prop of formal religion or orthodox creed. Still, in the moment of crisis he found a faith which would not only sustain him in the thirty remaining years of his life, but which would also reach out in powerful and mysterious ways into the lives of countless other people.

While he was still under the shadow of the first days after the laboratory report had come in, Ned received an anguished letter from Mrs. Patrick Campbell in England. Since the death of her only son, killed in the war two years before, Mrs. Pat had turned to Ned as her unfailing source of courage and solace. Now domestic troubles had brought her fresh sorrow and she naturally poured out her heart to Ned, having of course no idea of the seriousness of his condition. Ned responded as he always had. With fingers almost too stiff to move he grasped a pencil and wrote out a cable:

> STELLA DEAR: I LOVE AND BELIEVE IN YOU. WISH I WERE THERE. SURE THIS CANNOT CONQUER YOU. TENDEREST THOUGHTS AND AFFECTION. NED.

A few days later he managed a brief note to her:

> *I wish courage and wisdom could keep you from suffering. I know they can't but they will carry you through it, anyway. . . . I know you hate to walk in darkness, but you won't for long.*

Whatever else may have been taken from him, the impulse to give was intact. Perhaps this was what Ned learned in the long dark hours of questioning in the hospital. No matter what happened to him, short of death itself, he could always give something to others, if it were nothing more than a few words. So long as he could do this, his life still had a meaning.

CHAPTER VI

"A Real Live Human Being at Last"

SHORTLY before Christmas, 1919, Sheldon left the Good Samaritan Hospital in Los Angeles and moved to Hollywood. He was able to stand for a few moments at a time and take two or three halting steps. But all the therapy, operations, and patent exercising devices (such as an overhead trolley arrangement) had failed to help him walk. Though he bore his disability cheerfully, he was beginning to chafe at the lack of human contact his sociable nature craved. Through his theatre connections he had met some of the film people, and in Hollywood he could at least catch echoes of his beloved Broadway.

Though already the center of the motion picture industry, the Hollywood of 1919 gave little hint of the fabulous things to come. Sagebrush and wild pepper trees still grew in vacant lots on Sunset Boulevard, and social life centered around the Los Angeles Athletic Club. "Pickfair" would not be built for another two years, and the private swimming pool as the mark of social acceptability had not yet been thought of. Most of the actors who did not live in Los Angeles were content with simple bungalows like the one Ned rented. The word *glamor* had scarcely emerged from its native habitat in the murky glens of Scotland, but there was already a certain glitter in the air. With warm

118

sunshine, easy money, and the adulation of audiences vaster
than actors had ever known before, temperament blossomed
luxuriantly. Hollywood was already developing its special
brand of personality, and the popping of champagne corks
mingled with the explosions from colliding egos provided
continuous fireworks.

To Edward Sheldon emerging from the depths, this
scene offered a momentary lift. He was pleased to welcome
Charlie Chaplin and Douglas Fairbanks to his house, and
there was a happy meeting with John and Lionel Barrymore
who, like other Broadway friends, were beginning to look
to Hollywood as a bulwark against lean days in the theatre.
But it was a small world and Ned soon found its limitations
irksome. He began to yearn for New York and the theatre
of flesh and blood, where the values were closer to real life
and where illusion was at least three-dimensional. Besides
it was now evident that the slight gain from his stay in the
hospital was only temporary. In Hollywood he had succumbed to one of those universal nostrums in which, even
then, the film capital specialized—with discouraging results.
This was a new kind of electrical treatment whose purpose,
as Sheldon described it, was to make one "jump and grow
strong!—on the same principle as making a corpse dance."
Instead of halting the progress of arthritis it produced the
opposite effect. By the summer of 1920 he was completely
bedridden once more.

This turn for the worse made Ned all the more eager to
get back East. Perhaps the overbright sunshine, the atmosphere of specious youth and vitality which infused the
Hollywood dream world were added irritants to his condition. At whatever cost, he was determined to reach New
York before it was too late.

Already travel presented serious difficulties. In Los Angeles his physicians warned that if Ned undertook the trip he might not live six months. But this was a risk he was willing to run. However, he decided not to make the journey without a break. At his mother's urging he agreed to see another doctor in Chicago, and possibly later to go on to the Mayo Clinic in Rochester, Minnesota.

Once the decision was made, the actual problem of transportation had to be met. Since Sheldon was now flat on his back, unable even to sit up, the chief difficulty was in getting him aboard the train. It was his brother Theodore in Chicago who finally arranged the matter. Thanks to a friend, then president of the Pullman Company, and to officials of the Santa Fe Railroad (whose interest was aroused when they learned that Sheldon was the grandson of an early president of the road), the details were worked out. The windows and a steel mullion were removed from a drawing room on the Chicago train, and Ned, immobile on his stretcher, was passed through the opening. A special crew of workmen then put back the windows with temporary fastenings so that they could be readily removed at the other end.

Two days later Sheldon was in Chicago. He was taken at once to the Presbyterian Hospital, whence, after a few days under the observation of Dr. Frank Billings, he was moved to Rochester. Here the verdict of the California doctors was confirmed. Even the Mayo Brothers could offer no help in halting the arthritis which was steadily moving into all parts of Sheldon's body.

Yet in the midst of this final extinction of his hopes, Ned's thoughts could not remain wholly on himself. While in Rochester, he received news of a terrible tragedy that had struck the family of his old friend Henrietta Metcalf, "the little girl next door" of Lake Geneva days. Ned sent her a wire (she was then in Chicago), urging her to come to Rochester and stay near him during the time of a harrowing inquest. Henrietta came thankfully and found comfort and peace at Ned's bedside.

Late in the fall he was back at the Presbyterian Hospital in Chicago for further tests and treatments. For the sake of his family, who still refused to give up hope, Ned submitted stoically, though with the full knowledge now that there was no real help for his case.

One ray of sunshine brightened these dreary weeks. Another patient in the hospital was Ruth Gordon, a gifted young actress whom he had first seen with Maude Adams in *Peter Pan,* and later in Booth Tarkington's *Seventeen.* Hearing of Sheldon's presence in the hospital, Miss Gordon immediately sent him a note. Messages flew back and forth, and when Sheldon could be placed in a wheel chair he paid her frequent visits. At Christmas, Miss Gordon's room was livened by a huge laurel wreath and gaily decorated little Christmas tree, sent by Sheldon. In long talks with the young actress about the theatre and mutual friends, Ned's longing for New York rose afresh. The treatments in Chicago had brought no relief, and when his mother proposed further consultations Ned cried out, "I don't think I can stand any more. Will you take me back to New York?"

The matter was settled then and there. His last thought at the hospital was of Ruth Gordon, and he asked to be taken to her room. She noticed, as the litter was wheeled away, that when Ned said good-bye he could no longer turn his head.

It was again Theodore who arranged the details of the

train journey with the Pullman Company and the New York Central Railroad, and rented an apartment for his brother in New York. Sheldon now set forth for the last time over the way made familiar by countless trips since his boyhood when he had first gone East to school. As he lay in his berth he watched the wintry landscape flash past the window. Trees and fences were etched black against the snow, which lay in heavy drifts along furrows and railway embankments. Except for a brief glimpse of the ice-packed Hudson and the Palisades next morning, this was Ned's final view of the world beyond the rooftops of New York, which henceforth would bound his visible horizon, until they too vanished in darkness.

Waiting on the platform at Grand Central Station as the Twentieth Century rolled into New York was a young physician, then working at the Rockefeller Institute, who was to play an important and continuing part throughout the remainder of Sheldon's life. Carl Binger and Sheldon did not then know each other, but Mrs. Sheldon had met the young man on a transatlantic crossing and had been impressed by his perceptive and deeply humane nature. She had kept in touch with him since. When the move to New York was decided on, Mrs. Sheldon, fully understanding how much her son would depend not only on expert medical care but on a grasp of personality problems beyond the range of many physicians, sent word to Binger and persuaded Ned to put himself in the young doctor's hands. From that winter morning on, for twenty-five years Binger was the anchor to windward of the Sheldon household, ready with care and advice in every major crisis. Mrs. Sheldon came to regard him as another son, and for Ned he became a second brother. The circle of friendship was

soon enlarged when Binger married the charming Chloe
Garrison, granddaughter of William Lloyd Garrison, and in
time Binger children were included on the same terms of
affection.

Since Binger at this time was about to leave general
medical practice for psychiatry, he called in Dr. Kenneth
Taylor, who from the early twenties until Ned's death had
the chief responsibility for the invalid's physical care. But
Binger was always close at hand for consultation, acting as
general adviser to Ned and Mrs. Sheldon in personal as well
as strictly professional matters.

Sheldon's physical condition was naturally a matter of
constant anxiety to his family and friends. In the early years
of his illness scarcely a day passed without the suggestion of
some new treatment or medicine from well-meaning friends.
Remedies proposed and tried included sulphur baths, trans-
fusions, compressed air treatments, high-frequency sound
waves sent through water, serums, vitamins without end—
and other aids less orthodox. It became one of the functions
of Carl Binger to evaluate these, discarding the obviously
useless ones, deciding how far those of possible benefit could
be adapted to the patient's condition.

Although the study of psychosomatic medicine was in
its infancy when Sheldon was first stricken—the word
"psychosomatic" had not even been coined in the early
twenties—there were those who felt from the beginning
that his illness had an emotional origin, or at least a psycho-
logical bearing. This was based on the simple observation
that his condition tended to worsen under stress, and to improve when something happened to give him an emotional
lift. One of the physicians who frequently saw Sheldon at
this time was Dr. George F. Draper (inventor of the term

"psysomatic," later altered to the more euphonious "psycho-somatic"). Draper, noting Sheldon's reaction to certain shocks, characterized almost every time inevitably by increased ankylosis in still partially articulate joints, felt this to indicate if not a subconscious retreat from life, at least "a sort of self-immolation—of not moving forward into life." To a certain extent this view was also shared by Binger, who at the time he welcomed his new patient was already beginning the research in psychosomatic medicine in which he would win distinction. Yet never once did this physician, who was most closely and most continuously in contact with Sheldon for more than twenty-five years, exploit the friendship to probe the depths of a personality which could not fail to excite his scientific curiosity.

What amazed Dr. Binger from the first was the extraordinary adjustment Sheldon had already made to illness. Even now, however, from the vantage point of after-years and with all the added knowledge of a long career as a psychiatrist, Binger cannot say what part emotional disturbance played in Sheldon's case. What was important was the way in which Ned met the conditions of his life and what he made of them.

But if Binger himself was reserved on the subject, other friends were less so. In 1923 Emile Coué was in New York, and Sheldon was persuaded to see him. The little Frenchman, whose famous "day by day in every way" was practically a household phrase to the post-World-War-I generation, produced some remarkable results with auto-suggestion, particularly among shell-shocked veterans of the war. Sheldon, more perhaps because of his interest in a colorful personality than through any conviction of Coué's ability to help him, approached the interview, according to a witness, as one "curiously and critically observing. Not that he was anything but the most appreciative person and generous to the extreme. The picture of the dramatic, and, in one sense, rather pathetic little man, standing, in his worn frock coat beside the bed repeating his well-known phrase to the prostrate figure, lying practically immovable—and the effect of these two personalities, one seeking to give and the other to receive—was naturally a moving experience, particularly to one who realized the incongruity of the whole affair."

Despite an occasional experiment of this sort, Sheldon's health was primarily the concern of men of the regular medical profession, and the number of these who were called in at one time or another for special treatment or consultation was very large. As a patient Sheldon naturally excited special interest and challenged the highest skill— and it would be folly to underrate the contribution of these doctors to his physical survival.

Nevertheless, the fact remains that almost without exception each of these men in his association with Sheldon had a sharper sense of benefits received than of services rendered. One of the first specialists called in by Binger was the otolaryngologist, Dr. John B. Kernan. Long after his professional visits ceased Dr. Kernan continued to visit Sheldon regularly. When radio came into Sheldon's life, Kernan was a favorite companion for Saturday afternoon football broadcasts. Sheldon's personality fascinated him, and he was quick to see one source of his former patient's hold over people. "Sheldon had it in him to give himself uniquely to each person who knew him, so that when I was with him, I felt for the time being that he was all mine."

So it was with the oculist Dr. William Brown Doherty, to whom, furthermore, Sheldon's vitality and the seemingly endless range of his interests were a constant marvel. Even in the hard months when Sheldon's sight was fading, the patient's intellectual activity was a challenge which this doctor-friend was hard put to it to meet. In fact Doherty admits that when he was fatigued himself he simply could not face Sheldon, whose mental gymnastics could be quite overpowering. Their discussions covered plays, plots, crime, medicine, and science, and, once, "the most hideous words in the English language." These, they concluded after careful search, were "intelligentsia," "funeral parlor," "housewife," and "galluses."

There were numerous instances when the doctor-patient role was reversed, when Ned brought healing and comfort to a weary and discouraged physician. Once Carl Binger wrote to Sheldon's mother:

> *Last evening I spent with Ned. He is so very splendid. . . .*
> *I was in a blue funk when I went there, but his transcen-*
> *dental—I know no other word for it—quality lifted me out of*
> *it and gave me more faith in myself, which is as much as*
> *one man can do for another.*

This was also the experience of Dr. Henry A. Murray, another close physician-friend, whom Sheldon met in 1924 through Binger. There had been an instant flash of recognition when these two first came together, but the friendship remained in suspension for two years while Murray was studying in England. When he returned to New York in 1926, they took up where they had left off. After their reunion Murray received the following telegram from Sheldon:

> YOU GAVE ME A VERY DELIGHTFUL EVENING. THANK YOU
> AGAIN. WILL YOU PLEASE LET ME KNOW WHEN THE NEXT
> CHINK IN YOUR TIME OCCURS SO THAT I CAN SUGGEST AN-
> OTHER PARTY? IT IS A LUCKY THING FOR YOU THAT I HAVE

ARTHRITIS BECAUSE OTHERWISE I MIGHT COME AROUND ONE
OF THESE EVENINGS DEDICATED TO SCIENCE AND TAKE YOU OFF
TO AN ARMENIAN RESTAURANT OR CONEY ISLAND OR SOME
OTHER BACKGROUND FOR CONVERSATION.

This message arrived at the very moment that Murray
was writing to Sheldon. Murray's letter not only expresses
his own feeling about Sheldon, but summarizes the attitude
of all those who knew Sheldon well:

> . . . I take it you want no sympathy, old man, but I hope
> you will not object if I say that you are the most heroic of
> men. When I am with you I speak with a divinity, and life
> seems a glowing thing. In all these two and a half years I
> have had your presence, the image of you, continuously on
> the fringes and periodically in the focus of my conscious-
> ness. The concrete fact of your transcendence over bodily
> affliction fills me with awe and humility. I did more than
> enjoy myself last night. I felt as if the incumbency of body
> and matter were somehow removed and that our ideas could
> glow into another level and meet in another medium. . . .
> It is a highly thrilling experience, your intuitive grasp—
> short cuts to direct apprehension. What others have lost
> mucking around the world, you have gained, my dear fel-
> low, in your incomparable fashion—through reflection and
> inner revelation. . . .

Murray was one of those rare people with whom Sheldon
could dwell continuously on the plane where he was happiest.
The physician and psychologist shared Ned's thrilled wonder at the eternal mystery of life. When they were together
both men were conscious of an extraordinary spiritual release. "It raises the tide of my mind to speak with you!"
Murray once wrote. Ned's attitude toward Murray is
summed up in a telegram sent shortly after his friend's return from England:

DEAR DOCTOR: IF YOU HAD BEEN A ROMAN ABOUT TWO THOU-
SAND YEARS AGO A ROMAN WHO HAD WON CUPS IN CHARIOT
RACES AND IF YOU HAD HAPPENED TO BE WALKING HOME TO
YOUR VILLA ONE EVENING ALONG THE SHORE OF THE SEA OF
GALILEE AND HAD MET THAT STRANGE LITTLE GROUP COMING
IN THE OTHER DIRECTION I THINK YOU WOULD HAVE BEEN
STOPPED AND A FEW WORDS SAID AND WHEN THEY WENT ON
YOU WOULD HAVE GONE WITH THEM AND STAYED WITH THEM
FOREVER. I WISH I COULD HELP YOU ALTHOUGH I DON'T BE-
LIEVE ANYBODY CAN HURRY OR DELAY WHAT LIES IN STORE
FOR YOU BUT YOU CAN HELP ME. YOU DON'T AT ALL REALIZE
THE POWER AND THE GLORY THAT COMES POURING THROUGH
YOU BUT THE PEOPLE AROUND YOU MUST FEEL IT IN THEIR
DIFFERENT WAYS. I AT ANY RATE HAVE FOUND SOME ONE WHO
CAN TURN MY WATER INTO WINE.

Without exception these men who knew so well the weakness, the despair, and the humiliation to which pain can reduce the human spirit were affected by the simple fact of Sheldon's heroism. In 1924, another physician entered his life, Dr. Russell Hibbs, an orthopedist, whose skill coupled with a generous measure of Virginia charm earned him a special niche in Sheldon's regard. A few hours after their first interview Dr. Hibbs called in his "good right hand," Miss Emma Schrampf, head of the physical therapy department at the New York Orthopedic Hospital. She found the surgeon deeply moved. "I want you to do something for me," he said. "I have just seen the rarest person. . . . I went home and *wept*." He explained about Sheldon and described his condition. The patient was not paralyzed and could use most of his muscles, but not his joints where extensive calcification had already taken place and where the inflammatory processes were increasingly active. He must have daily massage and muscular exercise. Would Miss Schrampf herself take on this unusual and difficult case? Miss

Schrampf would and did—and continued her services until
the week before Sheldon's death more than twenty years
later. For ten or twelve years she worked daily with him
for an hour and a half. In the later years her work was supple-
mented by that of Miss Anna Kantor, another highly skilled
therapist.

These, among many others, were the people in whose
hands Sheldon's life rested after his return to New York in
1921. In their professional capacities they were able to appreciate, as the layman could not, by what frayed threads
his physical mechanism was held together. Other than to
bring some ease to the pain-wracked body their efforts
were limited. The unending marvel to them all was how little
the patient's life seemed to depend either on his body or
their ministrations. What they all observed as the years
rolled on was the constant growth of another organism,
sturdier, healthier, more reliable—and more alive than mere
flesh and bones.

On this final return to New York the Sheldon household
was first installed in an apartment on the corner of Thirty-
fourth Street and Madison Avenue. Here as soon as word of
the invalid's arrival got around Ned's friends began to
gather. If they were at first shocked at the condition of the
young man who had moved with such vigor and gaiety
among them, this reaction was promptly replaced by admiration at his stoic acceptance of his situation, and his
determination not to let his illness separate him from the
life and the people he loved. Soon they ceased to think of
his apartment as the home of an invalid, but rather as a
haven of repose in the hectic life of Broadway. It was soon
discovered also that the bright, gaily decorated living room
in which Ned spent his days was a clearing house of news

and information about everything that was going on in the theatre. Friends, anxious to make Ned feel a part of the Broadway world, carefully collected every item that might interest or amuse the invalid when they came to see him. Because of his gift for intimacy and his reputation for never having betrayed a confidence, Ned became also a repository of details concerning the personal lives of the ever-expanding circle of his friends and acquaintances. This was one of the sources of his great influence in the theatre. His effectiveness in helping those who came to him with their problems was due not only to his deep sympathy and understanding of human nature, but to the mass of facts in his possession.

Among the very first people to see Ned when he returned to New York were Doris Keane and her husband Basil Sydney. After its second triumphant run all through England, *Romance* was coming home. The simultaneous arrival of *Romance* and its star, along with the author, made the first night of the New York revival more dazzling than the *première* in 1913 had been. It simply went to show, as the New York *Times* pointed out, that the original run had nowhere near exhausted interest in the play. At the end of the performance there was thunderous and long-continued applause. Then the audience swarmed upon the stage for an informal reception of the star. It was the sort of scene, all too rare in the modern theatre, which made one think, as one reporter said, "of the favorites of the English stage in the seventeenth century." The same evening Doris Keane, asked by newsmen if she had not wearied of the role she had played for so many years, cried out, "I think I shall tire of everything before I tire of Cavallini. I shall weary of life first!"

If nothing else had given Ned the feeling again of being

really a part of the theatre, the presence of his greatest success and of the woman he loved would have sufficed. Doris came often to the Thirty-fourth Street apartment, and kept Sheldon advised of all the details of the run. Usually she brought with her the current edition of "Adelina Patti," the little monkey—still a vital property in the play. Sheldon was always delighted with the antics of the tiny creature, which would frisk about the room or crawl up on his wheel chair to stare curiously into his face. Once it bounded upon the brick parapet of the roof outside Sheldon's living room, and then leaped into the void. Doris was panic-stricken, not only at the thought of losing a pet but because the monkey required long training for its role and she could not contemplate the evening's performance without this valuable supporting member of the cast. On the streets below passers-by gasped to see the small form come hurtling through the air, strike the canvas awning of the luggage shop below, bounce two or three times into the air, and then come lightly to the sidewalk, startled but unscathed. Adelina was immediately captured and restored to Miss Keane's firm grasp.

It was not only Ned's theatre friends who welcomed him on his return to New York. John Hall Wheelock and Van Wyck Brooks were both in the city to close again the tight circle of that special intimacy. The Basil Kings were also near at hand. Through the Kings he had constant news of his other classmate George Foote, and of their daughter Penelope King, now Mrs. Reginald Orcutt, both with growing families in whom Ned took a lively interest. King's *Conquest of Fear* was now in preparation for publication, and Ned went over the manuscript carefully. Every syllable of the book seemed to strike a responsive chord in him; indeed one statement might have been taken from the very

creed on which Ned had based his existence. He found himself reverting constantly in the next months to King's chal-
lenging assertion that "Life is more or less dynamic according to the measure in which the individual seizes it." Years
ago he had told Eleanor Whidden, "Why do people ask if
life is worth living, when it all depends on the way one lives
it!"

Another old friend who came at once to see Ned was
Mrs. Cadwalader Jones. She never forgot the glow his
presence had cast over the gatherings that had made her
Eleventh Street drawing room one of the most stimulating
spots in New York. Now that Ned could no longer join the
circle of bright spirits Mrs. Jones drew about her, she made
a point of bringing her world to his bedside. Until her death
in 1935 there was a tacit understanding in Sheldon's household that Thursday evenings belonged to Mrs. Jones. Ned
looked forward eagerly to these visits, for Mrs. Jones was
one of the last of that dying race of great conversationalists.
There was both grace and point in everything she said, and
her talk ranged over the theatre, art, literature, politics (of
a very genteel sort!), and of course people.

Through Mrs. Jones, in the early years of his illness, Ned
met her sister-in-law Edith Wharton. He had a special
sympathy for both these women. He well understood the
conditions that made their approach to life so conventional,
since he had a somewhat similar background himself. At
the same time he admired them for their perspective on the
world in which they grew up. Once Sheldon wrote to his
cousin Elsa Denison (by then Mrs. Jameson):

> My old friend Mrs. Jones, who lived for sixty years on East
> Eleventh Street but never forgot she was born on Ritten-
> house Square, once said, "We Philadelphians think of all
> Southerners as Corsicans, and all Bostonians as bigots, and

of all New Yorkers as vulgarians." I asked, "And what do you think of Chicagoans?" To which she replied very firmly, "We don't think of them at all."

In Mrs. Wharton's case the struggle for emancipation had been long, and Ned respected her for her perseverance. Mrs. Jones once told him that her sister-in-law "had overcome the worst environment in which an artist could be born. Something far worse than poverty, ignorance, intolerance, etc. In short, pudginess." She described Mrs. Wharton as "a self-educated, self-made woman, who had pulled herself up entirely by her bootstraps." Commenting on this description in a letter to Ruth Gordon, Sheldon remarked, "I think this is a fair statement, but of course she was born with another great gift—that great serpent of her imagination which lay coiled and sleeping for so many years in the back of her mind. You remember how strikingly she refers to it in *A Backward Glance*."

When Mrs. Wharton returned to Europe she wrote Sheldon of "the instant sympathy between us" which she had recognized "on that very first afternoon when I sat down beside you in your blue aquarium room, and said to myself, 'Why, this is a live human being at last!' "

On Edith Wharton's rare visits to New York she spent long evenings with Sheldon. When she was back in France where she made her home, there was a lively and steady correspondence between them. The first letters from this shy woman, so rigidly correct in her outward manner, began "Dear Edward Sheldon," but in a very short time the salutation became "Dearest Ned" and the signature, "Your devoted Edith." Mrs. Jones once reminded Sheldon that "Edith is a lonely woman who has many friends, but none of them close to her, so she holds to you and me."

From her villa on the Riviera, Mrs. Wharton sent exquisite descriptions of the Mediterranean and of the gardens below her terrace, bringing all the artistry of her great gifts as a writer to bear on the task of making him see and touch and thus share the world in which they both felt so at home.

One interest shared with Mrs. Wharton—and a choice inner circle of his friends, including Alexander Woollcott and Mrs. Belloc Lowndes—was the literature of crime and the macabre. Neither cared greatly for detective stories which concentrated principally on the intellectual unraveling of a mystery, but stories of passion and gore, intermixed with diabolical horrors, exercised an endless fascination for the two friends.

Both collected such tales with the exacting taste of the connoisseur, and books which each had enjoyed were constantly exchanged. When Mrs. Wharton returned to Europe after a visit to America in 1925 she wrote Sheldon:

> When I got back from England the other day I found a rich new book on murder awaiting me. After a first all-night gulp, I am now preparing to sip Lizzie Borden . . . like a liqueur. Bless you for sending me such choice vintages.

At Christmas time, in reply to a cable from Ned, she wrote:

> I like to think that the little lamp of friendship we lit three years ago burns on so steadily, with a leap up for holidays and anniversaries—and a big bonfire for our next meeting, one of these days, I hope. There are so many things I want to talk to you about. I hope that 1926 will bring us a great deal more fiction and biography—and some really good crime.

Sheldon had the highest regard for Mrs. Wharton's taste in this esoteric realm, and once years later in commenting to

Woollcott on the works of Montagu James, he remembered that "Mrs. Wharton always said they had terror, but not horror. She was, however, hard to satisfy."

Sheldon's friendship with Woollcott (another of those close intimacies with a fundamentally dissimilar personality) dated also from the period of his return to New York as an invalid. Woollcott was just beginning his career as a drama critic but he had already won a special group of admirers, not only for his acute observations on the theatre, but for his critical manner in which malice and sentimentality were neatly blended.

As a master of repartee, somewhat studied but often amusing, Woollcott brought a note of individualism into the group about Sheldon which was particularly appreciated. Sheldon enjoyed Woollcott's company from the beginning, although apparently without really warming to the critic's personality. Yet Woollcott from the first was open in his admiration and liking for Sheldon, and went out of his way to please him. He brought the rarest of his stories and retailed the latest gossip with all the mastery of detail and innuendo for which he was noted. Yet it was some time before he discovered that some of his most amusing stories were missing the mark, since they were at the expense of people who had no way of defending themselves. Matters came to a climax when one of the Woollcott barbs struck a particularly sensitive spot in Ned's own feelings.

In 1925 Doris Keane opened in an unfortunate piece called *Starlight*, by Gladys Unger, in which she played the part of an actress of casual morals. In such a role inevitably comparisons with her performance as Cavallini were made to the detriment of both actress and play. Woollcott, in the course of his general denunciation, could not resist a par-

ticularly scathing and needlessly cruel comment on Doris
Keane. When he saw the notice in cold print he thought of
Sheldon and realized that his remarks might be taken amiss.
He at once wrote Sheldon a letter which presumably attempted to excuse the review on the ground of critical im-
partiality. Sheldon, no longer able to write, dictated the following reply:

> *Dear Woollcott:*
>
> *I have your message and I think I had better tell you
> straight out what I feel. I did not like the notice you gave
> Doris Keane in Starlight. I understand perfectly your right
> to like or dislike any performance that happens to come
> along, but this particular notice seemed to me to go beyond
> the bounds of dramatic criticism. I am distressed about this
> because I always looked forward to your visits and enjoyed
> them like anything. I like you a lot but I like Miss Keane
> even more and suppose that is about the size of it. . . . I
> want to send you all sorts of good wishes and to thank you
> again for being so kind to me during these last years.*
>
> Yours sincerely,
EDWARD SHELDON

There was no mistaking the implications in this letter.
In a way calculated to give as little pain as possible, Sheldon
was telling Woollcott plainly that he did not want to see
him again. The letter must have caught Woollcott off balance. He had hurt plenty of people before, and their reactions had been largely a matter of indifference to him. But
with Sheldon it was otherwise. In the months that he had
come to know him better Woollcott like everybody else
had grown to esteem Sheldon's friendship as a special treas-
ure beside which his own reputation as a wit and literary
enfant terrible (a reputation which he cultivated assidu-
ously) was of secondary importance.

One can only guess what burden of guilt and regret Woollcott carried with him during the next weeks. The break with Sheldon must have borne heavily on him until he finally wrote to ask forgiveness. Sheldon destroyed this letter, for he would have been the last man to wish possible disclosure of a fellow being's humiliation. But it must have contained more than apology, must indeed have been a frank unburdening of a nature fully aware of its short-comings and capable of expressing them with humility. This is intimated in the wire Sheldon sent Woollcott in reply:

YOU ARE A GENEROUS MAN AND YOUR LETTER HAS MORE THAN MADE EVERYTHING ALL RIGHT. I HOPE YOU WILL FEEL LIKE DINING WITH ME TOMORROW OR THURSDAY AND TELLING ME ALL ABOUT YOUR EUROPEAN PLANS. THANK YOU DEAR WOOLL-COTT.

It is revealing that Woollcott kept both Sheldon's letter of reproach and his telegram of forgiveness.

From this time on the friendship was one of undiluted pleasure for both men. When he was in New York, Woollcott came weekly and sometimes oftener to see Sheldon. When he was away, at his summer home in Vermont, or traveling, letters flowed in an unbroken stream. When Woollcott entered Peter Bent Brigham Hospital in Boston, at the beginning of his final illness, he could no longer communicate himself, but the messages from Sheldon came daily.

In the autumn of 1922 the Sheldon household moved into a new building at 35 East 84th Street. Henceforth the spacious penthouse fourteen stories above the northeast corner of Madison Avenue would be the background for Sheldon's life, the setting forever associated with him in the minds of his friends.

The apartment had been selected while the building was still under construction. The arrangement of rooms, closets, windows had been to some extent optional with the tenant, who had planned all details with a view to the varied interests of his life and his physical needs. In addition to an enormous living room with windows on both the south and west, there was a large roof garden from which one could see the treetops of Central Park. The apartment included a bedroom and bath for Sheldon, and accommodations for the members of his staff who lived in the house.

Supervision of the arrangement and decoration of the apartment was the responsibility of Ned's mother, who was at hand to keep a close eye on her son's health and to see that his needs were taken care of. Even while the new building was under construction this indomitable woman, then nearing seventy, made certain that Sheldon's wishes were carried out to the letter. One morning while the building was hardly more than a steel skeleton she rode up to the penthouse on the open platform elevator used to hoist workmen and materials, in order to check the location of partitions and communicating doors.

There have been a good many conjectures as to Sheldon's relationship with his mother. Some of the playwright's friends believed that Mrs. Sheldon, who was so close to her son in temperament and understanding, exerted undue pressure on him throughout his life. But the existing evidence points in exactly the opposite direction. From Ned's boyhood on, Mrs. Sheldon strove to make him independent. If she brought any pressure to bear, it was to prevent interference in the decisions which she knew Ned must make for himself, both in the matter of his career and in his intimate personal relations. There was much in his life that she did not approve of. She was fascinated by the theatre, but she had a profound mistrust of the people connected with it. She was enormously proud of her son's achievement as a playwright, although she could never quite reconcile herself to Ned's predilection for actors—and actresses. If she sometimes let her disapproval be known, she did not let it wear on Ned.

When illness struck Sheldon it was wholly natural that his mother, who by that time had no other pressing family duties, should have devoted herself to him. When he was most helpless she stayed close by. But she always discreetly withdrew when his condition improved or when she knew he was in capable and devoted hands.

She came with Ned when he returned to New York in 1921, and took an apartment in the same building where he was first installed. Here she remained for several years after Sheldon moved to Eighty-fourth Street. However, in time it became increasingly difficult for her to supervise Ned's household at this distance, and she decided to take an apartment beneath her son's on Eighty-fourth Street. She did this only after considerable hesitation, feeling that Ned might consider her presence in the same building an intrusion. She discussed the matter at some length with Carl Binger, and asked him to sound Ned out on the matter. Binger did so, and Sheldon's reply was, "Why shouldn't she move uptown if she likes it better?"

Although Mrs. Sheldon engaged Ned's servants and organized the details of his housekeeping, once everything was running smoothly she returned to her own affairs. As Ned's life became ever more crowded with the constant procession of people who came to him, Mrs. Sheldon was distressed that he might overtax himself. But she soon realized it was the very number of demands made upon Ned that kept him going, and she retreated even farther into the background. She seldom met Ned's friends, unless they were old and close ones of her own also, and was scrupulous to avoid intruding on any visit unless she had been asked in advance. She never came to see Ned under any circumstances (although she lived only four floors beneath him) without first telephoning like everybody else.

While Ned himself lived almost entirely in a world of his own making, remote from that in which he had grown up and from that of his mother's New York friends, he remained always a deeply loyal and devoted son. Though his world was filled with gifted and brilliant people, he could still prize the extraordinary qualities of his mother's mind and her vitality which he had inherited in such generous measure.

Sheldon also never lost his childhood feeling of closeness to his brother and sister, although both lived in Chicago and were raising families of their own. Mary Sheldon was married to Alfred MacArthur, brother of the playwright Charles MacArthur who later married Helen Hayes. Theodore Sheldon had married Margaret Lewis, whose people were old Chicago friends of the Sheldons, so that she made a new link with Ned's happy childhood. Although Ned never discussed his family with his friends except in a casual way, everyone knew how devoted he was to his brother and sister and their children, and understood that when they were in New York his time belonged to them. Even friends of long standing could expect appointments to be summarily canceled if there was an unexpected arrival from Chicago. A note, such as this one to Grace George, was usual under the circumstances:

I am sorry I did not see you before you went away. My family was in town all that time, and as I do not often have them with me, I just dropped everything and saw as much of them as I could.

Surrounded by friends and anxiously watched by physicians, Ned began to create a unique existence. By the end of 1925 he was permanently bedridden. At the same time he had completely reversed the customary invalid's role. In steadily increasing numbers people of the theatre, writers, scientists, and others with the simple but sufficient distinction of having somehow gotten to know Sheldon, were beating a path to his door. They came not to sympathize with, or to comfort someone who had lost the promise of a brilliant future and was doomed to a prison more confining than walls or bars could ever make. They came drawn by the spell of a man so dynamic, so sensitive to every vibration of life, yet so perfectly at peace with destiny, that simply to be with him gave a sense of beginning all over again. If there was a mystery at the bottom of his personality, no one attempted to pluck out its heart. It was enough to realize, in Edith Wharton's words, that "here was a live human being at last."

CHAPTER VII

The Way Back

To FRIENDS who had not seen Sheldon in the intervening
years since he had moved, as one of them said "like a young
lord in an atmosphere of champagne and flowers and the
best restaurants," the sight of him now came invariably as
a shock. When his college classmate Hermann Hagedorn
saw him for the first time after he had become completely
immobilized, he found Ned "rosy of face as ever, lying like
a living corpse on his catafalque. He had all the old warmth
and friendliness, but I have never gotten over the horror of
seeing him so dreadfully manhandled by destiny."

Sheldon was well aware of the picture he presented and
he did everything his ingenuity could suggest to divert attention from his invalidism. For his own sake as well as
that of his friends, he sought to create an atmosphere of
normalcy about him. He knew that continued pity weakens
its object and that self-pity destroys; so it became funda-
mental to his whole scheme to make people think of him
not as a sick man, but simply as a man in unusual circumstances.

Happily his face was not marked by pain. The strong,
finely cut features were bronzed from the sunbaths which
were part of his daily routine. His voice, always so compelling, lost nothing of its full resonance until the very end. If

anything could dissipate the feelings of compassion his condition sometimes aroused, it was his deep ringing laughter, which completely filled the big living room.

His very clothing belied illness. Luncheon guests would find him sometimes in a white turtleneck sweater, or a gaily patterned pullover complete with shirt and tie. Dinner was always a more formal meal, for which he usually donned a dinner jacket and all the accoutrements, including a boutonniere. Obviously it was impossible for him to wear regular clothing, especially in the later years when it was difficult for him to be moved in any way. But Sheldon's knowledge of stage tricks enabled him to get around this problem. His jackets and shirts, so flawless in every visible detail, were in reality bib-like arrangements, open in back, which could be slipped over his chest. He was scrupulous always about his grooming, and in this as in other respects no one ever caught him unawares. And to an almost uncanny degree he achieved the effect he sought. If some friends like Hermann Hagedorn who had known him from early youth were taken aback when they first saw him as an invalid, others found it difficult to imagine the true nature of his condition. Even to an old friend like Louise Closser Hale, he seemed "like a young man just lying down for a moment."

His success in putting others at ease was due to the fact that Sheldon himself, despite all his suffering, had retained so much of his capacity for enjoyment. Though his real life was increasingly of the spirit, he made the most of the physical means still left to him. However much his being had freed itself from his body, this was the link which kept him in touch with the world, and whatever pleasures of the senses were still accessible he enjoyed heartily. He was as concerned as anyone else that the physical machine, however limited its function, should continue to operate as efficiently as possible.

The chief care of Sheldon's medical advisers was to keep the organs working and the muscles responsive, no easy matter since the patient himself was completely paralyzed and therefore incapable of exercising. This was where the work of Miss Schrampf and Miss Kantor was so important, perhaps decisive in the prolongation of Sheldon's life. Under their skilled manipulation and guidance he learned to use every muscle of his body until the joint condition interfered. By self-discipline he gained an extraordinary control over the whole muscular system. This plus expert and unceasing massage kept his digestive and pulmonary apparatus efficient. Carl Binger remembered only one serious digestive upset during all the years of his acquaintance with Sheldon. Ned had always been something of a gourmet and never lost his interest in good food, even though for many years he had to be fed with a spoon and liquids could only be taken by tube. It was certainly no small blessing for a man who enjoyed the pleasures of the table that his condition did not prevent him from eating almost everything he liked.

There were other ways in which he showed to the end that illness did not mean asceticism. Indeed, in his combination of rare moral qualities and love of luxury Sheldon reminded one of those great Romans of the early empire. He had, as Wheelock put it, *virtus* in the classical sense of the word, valor and goodness which were demonstrated in such high degree. At the same time he loved beautiful and sensuously appealing things, and in some of his tastes there was even a touch of grossness. He enjoyed curdling the blood of tender-minded friends with tales of cannibalism and other horrors, in all the savory details.

In his sun-flooded apartment, surrounded by pictures and *objets d'art*, with a staff of expert attendants, Sheldon's invalidism was shorn of much of its ugliness. Everything that could be done to mitigate the bleakness of his situation was done, and this undoubtedly affected the climate of his spiritual development. One has only to recall the almost unbearable desolation of a charity ward for total arthritics in some great hospital to realize that, for all the tragedy of his life, Ned was spared the ultimate misery of poverty added to sickness.

To Sheldon's friends it did not matter that he was wealthy, not only in his own right, but with a substantial family fortune in the background. The qualities that raised him so obviously above the ordinary run of men were untouchable by outward circumstance. Since wealth had not corrupted nor success spoiled him, why should it be supposed that poverty would have warped or soured him?

The question of what Sheldon's life might have been without money is not really pertinent. If money eased the rigors of his position, that position did not prevent him from making more money. For years his talents continued to command a high premium, and if what he earned was largely diverted into the pockets of others, it was by his own wish and forms another part of the story.

In 1920 he completed the last play of which he was sole author. *The Lonely Heart* was begun some time during the months in California when he was struggling with the dark vision of his future. He was spurred on to finish the play in order to provide a good part for Basil Sydney, Doris Keane's husband, a newcomer to the American stage. *The Lonely Heart* never reached Broadway, by Sheldon's own decision. After the Baltimore tryout, the producers Lee and

J. J. Shubert were convinced that Sydney was not right for the leading role and insisted on a change. Having promised the part to Sydney, Sheldon refused to make a substitution, and the play closed.

The Lonely Heart is not a good play, but it is of interest as a reflection of Sheldon's own personality at the time. It deals almost wholly with the inner life of an individual, as contrasted with earlier plays in which action and character are shaped largely by external forces. The play presents four crises in a man's life, emotional and moral crises in each of which the hero is confronted by the vision of the mother who died in giving him birth and for whose love he has always hungered. Disregarding any Freudian implications in the mother-son motif, one can see clearly in *The Lonely Heart* how inner, spiritual values now dominated everything else in Sheldon's thinking.

The fiasco of *The Lonely Heart* brought disappointment to another member of the cast beside Basil Sydney. Sheldon had assigned the part of the young mother to a charming and ambitious actress, Margaret Mowrer, who looked forward to the role as her first great chance in the theatre. She was heartbroken to have her hopes shattered, and Sheldon did everything possible to comfort her. He insisted that she keep the gray tulle gown she wore in the play, telling her to "wear it whenever you come to dine with me." And he gave her good advice too. "Don't let the theatre ever hurt you. People may, but the theatre mustn't."

Before the end of *The Lonely Heart*, which he had hoped would carry Basil Sydney on his way, Sheldon was hard at work on a vehicle for Sydney's wife. The end of the revival of *Romance* had left Doris Keane very much at loose ends. None of the run-of-the-mill parts offered her seemed worth doing after her career as Madame Cavallini, and in desperation she turned again to Ned. The result was Sheldon's adaptation of Melchior Lengyel's comedy-drama *The Czarina*, a flamboyant costume piece based on the life of Catherine the Great. The star part had that mixture of comedy and pathos in which Doris excelled, and the play had good notices, though with a run of 136 performances it could scarcely be considered a hit.

Increasingly as time went on Sheldon's services to the theatre were those of collaborator with other dramatists, play doctor, and adviser on technical problems. In the summer of 1924 he worked on a play with Ruth Draper, whose unique art as a monologist was one of his great admirations. Sheldon devised the scenario for the play, a fantasy on the personal life of the Three Fates, and Miss Draper did the dialogue. *The Three Fates* was never produced, but it attracted notice. Years later when Miss Draper was performing to great acclaim in London, Sir James Barrie read the play and was greatly taken with it. "I am sure that Barrie's estimate of the sustained, tremendous dramatic quality will please you," Miss Draper wrote Sheldon. "That is all yours and I am proud to think I kept it alive with you. What fun we had anyway, working on it that summer!"

Another friendship which led to joint dramatic effort was with Sidney Howard. The year before Howard won the Pulitzer prize for *They Knew What They Wanted*, he was greatly depressed with personal problems and wrote Sheldon to ask if he might come to see him. The upshot of the visit was the decision to do a play together. This was Howard's first attempt to work with another writer, and in an interview later he said:

> I cannot imagine myself collaborating with anyone but Mr. Sheldon. He has a great love of acting and a great instinct for the theatre as entertainment. When collaborating,

> *Sheldon was the boss, though we both contributed an equal amount of work and ideas. He started the story and wrote the scenario; then we got together on the dialogue. . . . Working with Sheldon put me in touch with a man with a directing mind. With him I got theatre as theatre.*

Sheldon, as usual, was reluctant to take such credit. When Professor Arthur Hobson Quinn asked him about the collaboration all he could get was the brief comment, "That's Howard's play."

Bewitched opened at the National Theatre in New York, October 1, 1924. The night of the opening Howard mentioned to reporters that Sheldon's *Romance* was then being presented in no less than five South American theatres and in Vienna. *Bewitched*, however, was no second *Romance*. The story of a World War I airman who parachutes into a French forest and finds himself in a dream world full of sorcery, sex symbols, and incidental music was described by Gilbert Gabriel as "Parsiful plus. Likewise a Yankee at King Jurgen's court." Other critics were even less kind, and on that note the play quietly folded.

Before *Bewitched* had come and gone Sheldon had another "pot simmering on the back of the stove." Edith Wharton had written from her Riviera retreat in the spring of 1924:

> . . . . *I am pegging away at my new novel, The Mother's Recompense, but the heat has somewhat cooled my ardor. It's great fun, though, to carry about a creative thought inside oneself, isn't it?? How about your Bewitched?*

Sheldon's answer told less about *Bewitched* than about the dramatic possibilities of Mrs. Wharton's *Age of Innocence*, which he had just read. In August, Mrs. Wharton wrote again:

*I need not tell you how interested I am in all your sug-
gestions. I never see a play in any of my tales. . . . The most
exciting thing in your letter is your admirable scenario of
The Age of Innocence. It is most interesting to me to see
how your stage technique remodels mine of the novel, con-
tracting there and pulling out here. Thank you for having
taken the trouble to give me that lesson in your art. How I
wish you felt like dramatizing the book yourself—or I should
wish it if I could ever conceive of a real dramatist wanting to
drag a reluctant play out of a novel. . . .*

If Mrs. Wharton's interest had been keener or her need
more pressing, Sheldon would probably have set about dramatizing the novel at once. But since the author already had
both fame and a comfortable fortune, there seemed no
urgent reason for doing anything about it at the time. But
a year later, from a completely unexpected source, the
stimulus developed.

Meanwhile, Sheldon was deep in another collaboration.
As early as August, 1925, New York papers were quoting
David Belasco's modest statement that on his schedule of
productions for the following season "was just about the
greatest play ever written by an American, *Lulu Belle* by
Edward Sheldon and Charles MacArthur." Belasco's hyper-
bole may be questioned, but the box-office record stands to
confirm the play's success. It opened at the Belasco Theatre
on February 9, 1926, and ran until the early autumn of
1927.

This four-act play, "a colored Carmen," as the critics
called it, concerned a mulatto cabaret dancer who lives and
loves indiscriminately until her past catches up with her—
a long, long way from her native Harlem. In Paris where
she has been taken by a French nobleman and where her
café au lait beauty creates a furore, an abandoned lover finds
and murders her.

Although the plot was threadbare before Mérimée used it, Sheldon and MacArthur revitalized it with local color, a swift pace, a liberal measure of sex, an enormous cast of some sixty people—and above all a star with sure-fire appeal, that sultry human tornado Lenore Ulric. All this combined with Belasco's opulent staging made the piece a long-remembered sensation.

Both during the long New York run and on the road *Lulu Belle* was a handsome money-maker. The box office was helped everywhere by the constant threat of censorship as one group after another protested against the play's uninhibited display of sex. To many people close to Sheldon it was difficult to believe that he had a hand in it, for *Lulu Belle* has no trace of his characteristic idealism and delicate sentiment. But there were others who perfectly understood that under Sheldon's gentle manner and cool, seemingly detached outlook on life there was a well of primitive emotion. Denied normal outlets, this was sublimated in various ways. It is not surprising that a good deal of it went into *Lulu Belle,* and other plays that followed.

Early in the spring of 1926 a friend of Sheldon's childhood came back into his life. Nothing gave him greater pleasure than to pick up the threads of associations that had been seemingly lost in the shuffle of time. In this case the renewal of old friendship had dramatic and, for the friend, decisive results.

Sheldon had never forgotten sitting on the bank of Lake Geneva the summer of his fourteenth year and reading aloud Rostand's *L'Aiglon* with a lively, keen-minded little girl named Margaret Ayer. And he remembered Christmas holidays during his Hill School and Harvard years when Margaret Ayer was a much-sought-after partner for cotillions and dinner dances. He had not seen her in years though he knew that she had married a Chicago attorney, Cecil Barnes, and was now the mother of three strapping sons. Early in March, 1926, he learned that she was in New York for a serious spinal operation, following a motor accident in France some months before. After unsuccessful treatment, first abroad, then in Chicago, she had come to New York to be operated on by Sheldon's own surgeon, Dr. Russell Hibbs.

As soon as word reached him that she was in the New York Orthopedic Hospital, Ned proceeded to surround her by that "imaginative goodness" which so touched him in other people. He knew all too well the dreary boredom of hospital days, the inflexible routine, the long wakeful nights, the efforts to walk again "on legs like boiled macaroni," as he described them. He showered her with reading matter of the most diverting variety—ghost stories, novels by Henry James, plays by Ibsen and Pinero, copies of the *Daily News*, the *Police Gazette*, *True Story*, and the *Ladies' Home Journal*. Recalling the painful monotony of hospital food, he sent containers of special broth and fruit juices, jars of exotic jams and jellies, and once a rare cherry cordial complete with two graceful crystal liqueur glasses, as relief from the ponderous white teacups of hospital crockery. His inventiveness for beguiling the tedium of an invalid strapped rigidly to a spine board was endless. One day an enormous cluster of colored balloons arrived to brighten the ceiling overhead. There was a constant flow of messages, telegrams, letters, telephone conversations as the two embarked on the rediscovery of their old friendship.

Sheldon found that the clever schoolgirl had matured into a perceptive, witty, and highly articulate woman. One morning he sent her a list of old Chicago friends, people whom he had long ago lost track of, and asked her to write a brief paragraph about what had happened to each. The request was partly to satisfy his own curiosity, but mainly to give his friend something to do. Mrs. Barnes obligingly performed the stint with "the unforeseen result," as she later reported, "that it read like a prose *Spoon River Anthology*." Sheldon was so impressed by the way in which she handled the bare details of the several lives that in their next telephone conversation he asked, "Why don't you write a story?" From this casual and quite unpremeditated beginning blossomed one of the country's distinguished literary careers. Probably at that time no one would have been more incredulous than Margaret Ayer Barnes at the suggestion that in five years she would win the Pulitzer prize for her novel *Years of Grace.*

While in the final stages of recuperation from her stay in the hospital, Mrs. Barnes came often to see Sheldon. The evening of her first visit he suggested that she try her hand at dramatizing Mrs. Wharton's *Age of Innocence.* The still unbudded author thought Sheldon was proposing some kind of game. As she later said with complete candor, "I don't know just how seriously he himself took the venture at first. He persuaded me to try to write the play, and then we talked over the construction in detail. Then I went back to Chicago."

Sheldon had no intention of letting the matter drop. But when he sent on the novel for her to study she wrote back that she regarded the project "with a poignant sense of inadequacy. How *could* I write a play. *Really* in all seriousness—a play! Well, I'll read the book with the most solemn consideration. Of course, Ned, I'd love to do it. It would be the lark of the ages. Wouldn't we have fun?"

Under Ned's prodding, by telegram and long-distance telephone, she wrote the first act and sent it to New York. Then she waited for Ned's reply. "When I read it," she informs us, "you could have knocked me over with the proverbial feather." Ned's telegram said:

HAVE CABLED MRS. WHARTON FOR DRAMATIC RIGHTS. WRITE THE SECOND ACT.

From then on, the work proceeded without halt. As each act was drafted it was mailed to Sheldon, always with a sense of panic, for it seemed to the burgeoning playwright that she had plunged into very deep water and might at any moment go over her head. But she soon realized what a firm hand was holding her up. In New York, Sheldon went over each scene with scrupulous care, giving the full benefit of his genius for stagecraft to every entrance and exit, to characterization and to dialogue. For every criticism or alteration he made, there were also words of encouragement and praise for the new writer's own accomplishment. He knew how difficult it was for a sensitive nature to display its first creative efforts, and he had just the right word always to allay the beginner's qualms. "How you have cheered me!" Margaret Ayer Barnes wrote. "I must have been more afraid than I knew of showing you that dialogue! You yourself once said that one never got over being shy."

Before the play was completed it was submitted to Katharine Cornell, the young actress who had made such a hit in Michael Arlen's *The Green Hat* and for whom Sheldon predicted a brilliant future. Miss Cornell felt at once the appeal of Ellen Olenska, the American-born countess and heroine of Edith Wharton's tale of New York high life in the early seventies. The news that she would do the part, and that the play would be staged by her husband, Guthrie McClintic, was promptly relayed to Mrs. Wharton who, though somewhat vague about Miss Cornell's identity, expressed approval.

However, Mrs. Wharton's pleasure in the dramatization began to wane as she learned of the changes to which her novel was being subjected in preparing it for the stage. The chief difficulty centered around the hero, Newland Archer, the man-about-town with whom Ellen falls in love after she abandons her dissolute Polish aristocrat and returns to New York. Both Mrs. Barnes and Sheldon felt that in order to gain sympathy from a modern audience Archer's character must be changed from that of a merely eligible young man with vague cultural interests to a more dynamic personality. With the career of the young Theodore Roosevelt in mind they decided to make him a political reformer with a taste for adventure. Both Mrs. Wharton and her sister-in-law Mrs. Cadwalader Jones were shocked at the idea. Mrs. Barnes, who had discussed the changes with Mrs. Jones, acting as proxy for the remote Mrs. Wharton, wrote to Sheldon:

> Mrs. Jones and Mrs. Wharton feel absolutely with the van der Luydens [characters in the play] that a genteel young man could not dabble in politics. She [Mrs. Jones] said, "Edith thought he would not have been so vulgar," meaning so vulgar as to have fought Tweed. And they also thought it would have been a bit common to join up with Custer to fight Indians. They feel a U. S. Senator is "very distinguished" so the political career can be left in—just the mud and sweat toned down a bit. Mrs. Jones asked very sweetly, "Why would Archer have gone to a fireman's ball? It makes him seem very provincial, my dear, to be a crusader. One of the points of the book was that he was very conventional." Mrs. Jones said it nearly killed Mrs. Wharton to have us say that

*Archer had never been abroad—but they will compromise
on a grand tour of Europe before the opening of the play.
She didn't comment on Ellen's fall from virtue. The chas-
tity of the heroine sinks to complete unimportance compared with the gentility of the hero! It is apparently imma-
terial whether or no Archer spends the night with Ellen so
long as he doesn't go to the fireman's ball. Our Archer appears a monstrous changeling in the cradle of Mrs. Wharton's
hero!*

Gradually these difficulties were ironed out, and when
news of the play's success finally reached Mrs. Wharton, in
her refuge at Hyères, all misgivings were forgotten.

> *. . . The miracle seems to have been accomplished, and you
> and Mrs. Barnes and the actors all have a share in it, while
> I have sat here shivering in my tower, remembering the sad
> disaster of The House of Mirth so many years ago. I see now
> that that disaster was entirely due to bad acting, and a vulgar
> interpretation of the play which Clyde Fitch and I had
> written together. . . . Besides as Mr. Howells remarked to
> me one evening when he went with me: "The American
> public always want their tragedies to have a happy ending."
> . . . As for you, I can only tell you again how deeply touched
> I am for all the trouble you have taken about the play, and
> how much I appreciate your friendship. I hope some day to
> say it to you again instead of writing it. Meanwhile this
> brings you all my best wishes for Christmas and the New
> Year. I know that in one respect it will be a happy season
> for you because you have put so much of your heart into
> the success of The Age of Innocence, and you will enjoy the
> success as much as I do.*
>
> *Always your affectionate friend,*
> EDITH WHARTON

And Sheldon did enjoy the success of *The Age of Innocence*, but not for any direct share he may have had in
it. His satisfaction came from the knowledge that he had

recognized another's gift and forced it to realization. In that completely imperious fashion which he could assume, especially in the interest of others, he overrode the vigorous protests of Mrs. Barnes and refused to have his name stand with hers as author of the play. But his protégée never ceased to proclaim her debt, declaring emphatically, "I simply couldn't have done it without him."

Although the critics were quick to acknowledge the new dramatist's ability, there were those who also detected the Sheldon touch, particularly in the love scenes of the play. When one Baltimore reviewer voiced his suspicion, Mrs. Barnes wrote Alice Kauser:

> *That bright boy is wasted in dramatic criticism—he ought to buy himself a pair of rubber shoes and sign up with a Pinkerton agency.*

Sheldon showed his own esteem for his pupil's achievement by proposing that they do another play together at once, and this time his collaboration would be official. The result was *Jenny*, a frothy sentimental comedy about an actress and a middle-aged business man, whose chief merit was that it served as an admirable vehicle for Jane Cowl and her leading man Sir Guy Standing. *Jenny* was produced by Dwight Deere Wiman and William A. Brady, Jr. (whose father had produced *The Boss* eighteen years before). Though only moderately successful in New York, it proved very profitable on tour. More important for the two playwrights, however, were the indirect results of this second joint effort.

Before *Jenny* was finished, the Sheldon-Barnes combination had already begun to play with an idea of a very different sort. Sheldon had become increasingly interested in stories of crime and the atmosphere of the macabre. This taste was stimulated by his association with Edith Wharton and Alexander Woollcott, both of whom reveled in literary gore. The notion of doing a play involving passion and murder may have been prompted by a desire for relief from the airy inconsequences of *Jenny*. At any rate long before *Jenny* had been put into rehearsal the partners were busy perusing Roughead's *Notable English Trials* in search of a situation sufficiently meaty for their purposes. Finally they found what they wanted in the account of the trial of Madeleine Smith, a well-born Glasgow girl who in 1857 murdered her French lover in order to prevent him from betraying her to the respectable young man to whom she had become engaged. It was a grisly tale in which horror and sex were most promisingly blended. When *Dishonored Lady* was unveiled to the public, a program note stated, "The authors gratefully acknowledge their indebtedness to Miss Madeleine Smith of Glasgow, whose public and private life suggested to them this play!"

Using only the basic situation of the original source, Sheldon and Mrs. Barnes set their story in contemporary New York, made the heroine a wealthy society girl, her lover a Latin-American night-club dancer, and juxtaposed the murder on a love scene of torrid intensity.

From the beginning Sheldon had pictured Ethel Barrymore in the title role. But Miss Barrymore, after holding the script for some three months, discovered that she was already committed elsewhere and regretfully declined the part. One suspects that, fascinated though she must have been by the role, she doubted whether even an actress of her standing could survive the portrayal of a personality as unpleasant as that of Madeleine Smith.

Eventually the assignment went to Katharine Cornell. She too may have had doubts, but they faded before the pos-

sibilities of a role such as she had never played before. Her
subsequent triumph fully justified her expectations. Curiously
enough, Sheldon himself never felt that Miss Cornell was
right in the part or that her interpretation corresponded to
the authors' own conception of the passion-torn Madeleine.

Dishonored Lady opened on February 4, 1930 (Sheldon's
forty-fourth birthday), at the Empire Theatre in New York,
and became one of the season's hits. Though melodrama, it
was not, as Robert Benchley pointed out, "hokum melodrama," and Richard Watts of the *Herald-Tribune* praised
its "thoroughly gripping quality, not often found in the
local drama." The murder scene had a quality of terror which
kept even blasé New York theatre-goers stiff in their seats.

The play brought up some of Ned's friends with a start.
Despite memories of *Lulu Belle*, no one was prepared for the
uninhibited display of physical passion, the rampant sexuality
of one or two scenes. To those who knew Sheldon as the
helpless invalid, whose heroic transcendence of the world and
its evils had created about him an atmosphere of saintliness,
the knowledge that he was even partly responsible for this
probing into the most elemental passions came as a shock.

The person most affected in this sense was Sheldon's
mother. Anticipating her reaction, Ned had sent her the
manuscript of *Dishonored Lady* to read before the play was
produced. From her country place in West Redding, Connecticut, Mrs. Sheldon wrote:

> *Ned dearest:—*
>   *It is three o'clock in the morning. I have finished the*
> *Dishonored Lady and have done it up to catch the next mail*
> *(1st class registered). Thank you for letting me read it. I*
> *know my opinion means little or nothing to you because to*
> *you I seem ignorant and perhaps Victorian, but I can't let*

it go back without a word. I recognize the brilliancy of its character drawing, the accuracy of its technique, its solidarity—its splendid march. And I realize how tempted Miss Barrymore would be to do it—for you fairly hear the tones of her voice as you read it. But oh Ned dear must it continue to be the kind of play which makes it questionable it could escape the censor, that draws that awful kind of an audience that associates your name with just daring and daring themes and situations, that makes people of the better sort leave the theatre dreading to think of the mire of a mind like that shut away from so many things in life. Can't it ever be a play written with that same sure vivid touch, that accurate sense of the theatre yet not in the least theatrical but showing some traces of your real self with some faint manifestation of these years of growth of an always rare and exceptional spirit—

Why do you put between yourself and the world (the needful world) these strange barriers. They are in no sense revelations, because never are they you. . . .

I do care so tremendously for you and I am so jealous for your reputation before a waiting public and above all I am so desperately eager before I die to have you write and put on a play that will at least be by Edward Sheldon, the real and potential Edward Sheldon. . . . There were glimpses in Salvation Nell, more in The Nigger, halting but yet clear evidences in The High Road, much more of the real you in Romance but now—

Those of us who think we know you, the real you the best, and certainly love you the most disinterestedly, feel and know that there are plays within you of a sincerity and loftiness you have hitherto only touched upon, because your soul is great. If you would only let it sing, plays like the Dishonored Lady would be with all its cleverness as a gargoyle to a cathedral!

Please, please,

I love you so—
MOTHER

Sheldon fully understood his mother's point of view, and he would not have wantonly pained her. What Mrs. Sheldon could not realize was that *Dishonored Lady* was as much a part of the *real* Ned as *Salvation Nell* or *Romance*. At least his share in the play had come straight from his own imagination, and his integrity as an artist demanded that he express himself freely, even though it hurt.

This last of the Sheldon-Barnes collaborations belongs properly to a later chapter in Sheldon's story because of its spectacular sequel—the plagiarism suit which won the authors one of the handsomest settlements ever made for a copyright infringement. For Sheldon the immediate satisfaction of the partnership with Margaret Ayer Barnes lay in watching the growth of the talent whose germs he had first detected, and in demonstrating that illness had not deadened his own creative powers.

Even while urging Mrs. Barnes along the first steps of her career as a writer, Sheldon was involved in the struggles of another friend. In 1927 Dorothy Donnelly, who had earlier given up acting for writing, was doing the lyrics for a musical comedy for which Sigmund Romberg had composed the score. This team had already made musical comedy history with *The Student Prince* and *Blossom Time* and Ned was very proud of Dorothy's part in those two phenomenal successes. The new show was called *My Princess* and was based on an old, unproduced play by Sheldon—whose name appeared as co-author of the libretto. It was a very tenuous affair about a socially ambitious oil heiress trying to crash New York society with the aid of an Italian organ grinder posing as a foreign prince (and turning out, in the inevitable way of such things, to be a real prince). Jerry-built though it was, the play seemed to offer possibilities for a musical, and all through the spring of 1927 while long-distance operations were pushing *The Age of Innocence* on its course, Sheldon worked with Dorothy Donnelly on *My Princess*. After a successful opening in New Haven and a brief run in Boston, the musical was presented in New York on October 7. *My Princess* was lavishly mounted, and the star part was performed by Miss Hope Hampton who made a long-heralded emergence from the still silent motion pictures to display not only a pleasingly solid figure but (in the phraseology of Alexander Woollcott) "tresses of assertive gold" and a surprisingly good voice. There was also a vigorous band of Albertina Rasch girls and of course the familiar Romberg music—perhaps a little too familiar in this case. With all these adornments *My Princess* failed emphatically.

Sheldon felt this disaster with real poignancy, for it marked the final chapter in one of his oldest and deepest friendships in the theatre. Even as *My Princess* closed, Dorothy Donnelly, the witty, warm-hearted Irish girl who had been Ned's Princess Zim-Zim, had also played in *The Song of Songs*, and had shared so much of the fun of his early success, lay mortally ill. No one had done more to keep Sheldon close to the world of the theatre than Dorothy Donnelly, and when she could no longer visit him they still talked together daily by telephone. In the hospital when her strength was almost gone she begged that Ned might be brought to her so that she could see him once more. Sheldon himself was by now completely rigid on his back, and the visit would have involved so many hazards that his physicians refused to take the responsibility for arranging it. Sheldon's grief at the loss of this old friend was heightened by his despair that he was not able to help her in her final hour.

Dorothy Donnelly's death followed by one day the even more tragic end of another woman to whom Sheldon was greatly attached. Emily Stevens, who had been the leading woman in *The Boss* and was a cousin of Mrs. Fiske's, had also come to lean heavily on Sheldon for advice and help in late years. When she became afflicted with a conspicuous facial tic and her career as an actress was doomed, she turned to Ned in anguish. He exerted all his power to help her find a solution for her difficulty and, failing this, he tried to give her courage to face life on different terms. But perhaps because he was himself struggling against the sense of heavy loss, as Dorothy Donnelly's life flickered out, his strength for another was somehow diluted. At Christmas time, 1927, Emily Stevens came to him in bitter desolation. In her handbag she carried a bottle of poison, enough to insure extinction for both of them. She begged Sheldon to make an end of it with her then and there. Neither of them had anything to live for, she asserted, nothing but an increasingly barren stretch of years ahead.

It was not the first time Sheldon was confronted by the alternative to the destiny which had overtaken him. If he had not debated the matter secretly to himself, he knew it had sometimes been in the minds of people who loved him. More than once when his suffering was most acute he had read in the pitying glances of those who came to him the question: "How can you go on?" And he knew that more than one of the friends he had so generously helped would willingly have served him in providing a way out of his prison.

Yet since those crucial weeks in the Los Angeles hospital when he saw the full extent of what lay ahead, the matter had never really come to the point of decision. It was not that Sheldon felt either moral or religious strictures against suicide. It was simply that the principle of life was stronger than anything else in him.

This was confirmed again and again. Once when told of a terrible motor accident in which a friend had had such shattering injuries that he longed for death, Sheldon cried out almost angrily, "But my God, the man is *alive*, isn't he? That's all that matters!" This was the essential in Sheldon's credo. Life on any terms was better than no life. And so long as intelligence and imagination were left him, a man was still, in a measure, master of his fate.

Thus he reasoned with the despairing Emily Stevens, insisting that there could be no ultimate answer in her solution. She must throw the bottle away at once, and come back to dine with him the following Saturday. But before that time, she had made her choice. While he was waiting tensely for the final news of Dorothy Donnelly, word came that Emily Stevens had killed herself.

Sheldon began the year 1928 with a heavy heart, but with no lessening of his grip on life. In June of that year, on the occasion of the Twentieth Anniversary of the Class of 1908 at Harvard, his brief report on himself gave evidence of a man who had made his peace with circumstances.

> For the past five years I have been living rather quietly in New York City, writing on various plays, talking to various friends, and thinking a good deal. I find at the age of forty-two that there is a good deal to think about, all of it interesting, and some of it beautiful.

CHAPTER VIII

The Dark Curtain

By 1930 Sheldon's body was fixed in the rigidly supine position, with the head slightly raised on his pillow, in which he would remain for the rest of his life. Although friends continued to believe that somehow, perhaps miraculously, his condition might improve, Sheldon himself had no illusion. He not only accepted the situation as final; he planned his life, organized his household, and serenely contemplated the future as a man who would never move again.

But he had scarcely adjusted to this state when the disease which had taken possession of his skeletal frame passed into a second phase. For some time he had been aware of dimming vision and a gradual contraction of the optical field, but in his struggle with the more immediate effects of arthritis and the routine of his busy life, he had not considered what this might ultimately mean. However, toward the end of 1930 his opthalmologist and faithful friend Dr. William Brown Doherty found it necessary to prepare him for what lay ahead. This was a delicate matter. Doherty did not wish to risk the shock of a blunt announcement, but he knew that some warning might ease the blow when it came, and that furthermore it would give Sheldon precious time for adjustment. Without telling him that he faced total blindness, the doctor hinted that there would probably be a further considerable loss of vision. Sheldon, with his long experience of doctors, knew at once what Doherty really meant though he made no comment when the news was broken. However, later that evening he telephoned his mother. When she answered the call he asked abruptly, "Mother, did you know I was to be blind?"

Mrs. Sheldon, stunned not only by the verdict but by Ned's awareness of it, could not speak for a few seconds. Then, controlling her voice as well as she could, she said, "I had feared it as a possibility." There was another brief pause, then with a change of tone the voice came from the other end of the line. Sheldon spoke slowly, as though steadying himself. "Oh, it's quite all right—only, it took me a little by surprise. Goodnight."

Even his mother could do nothing to lighten the despair of the next weeks as the dark curtain descended. What went on during this time neither Mrs. Sheldon nor the members of Ned's household had any way of knowing. The only indication of suffering was his insistence that he be left entirely to himself. As in that other desolate period at the Good Samaritan Hospital in Los Angeles following the laboratory verdict on his disease, Ned turned away from the world in order to find strength for the ordeal from which the world could not save him.

Pain, to which he thought himself inured, came now in a new form. As the inflammation reached its climax, first one eye and then the other was subjected to searing attacks of iritis. More than once, beside himself with agony, Sheldon pleaded with his physician, "Please, Bill, take out my eyes." But to no one else was there any outcry. Only once did an attendant catch any sound of protest. In the first hours of a

December dawn, as a night nurse watched outside his closed door, the silence was shattered by a sudden, heart-wrenching "Oh, my God!"

To bodily torture was added a bitter torment of the mind. The spiritual discipline that had come from his first experience of catastrophe certainly helped Ned to face this new disaster. Yet the fact that he had endured and finally accepted the loss of bodily movement did not soften this second blow. However greatly he had suffered in no longer being able to stride the world at his own sweet will, blindness meant something else. So long as he could look out of his windows and see the treetops at the edge of Central Park, or watch the changing pattern of clouds above his penthouse terrace, or study the faces of those who sat by his bedside, Sheldon could still feel himself a part of the world of other men. But to be cut off from all these things, no longer even to know the line between light and shadow, must have meant something like extinction.

But he did not give way, either to the temptation to make an end of everything (with means which he might easily have obtained) or to exhaustion. If there had been iron in Ned's soul before, it became steel during this journey into darkness. Somehow in the black hours of despair and pain, the high sharp moments of panic, he found the courage to go on. More than that—in the very midst of his suffering he forged a new framework for his existence.

In one of the rare moments of retrospection which Sheldon permitted himself he referred to the early months of his blindness as "my submerged period, when I came up for air." By the beginning of 1931 his sight was completely gone. There followed a few weeks when no one saw him, and then he faced the world again. At first only his oldest and closest friends came to the penthouse. One of those who came back into his life at this critical moment was Dr. Florence Sabin, the brilliant woman who had first opened Ned's eyes to the hidden marvels of nature back in his boyhood on Lake Geneva. Now a member of the Rockefeller Institute and an anatomist of international reputation, Dr. Sabin's wisdom guided Ned to a deeper understanding of what had happened to him, helping him to accept this too as the work of nature and not simply of a malign fate.

The friends who came to him were prepared to give whatever strength they possessed to push back the desolation which now must surely engulf him. But when they were at last admitted to see him they found Ned serene, cheerful, and as acutely interested in everything going on about him as before.

Indeed, to Sheldon's closest friends it seemed that the new affliction had, paradoxically, brought him new strength. "It would have been an impertinence to pity him," said Florence Reed when she saw him again after he had become blind. Charles MacArthur spoke of him as "that iron man in bed," not in reference to any grim will to survive, but because he now seemed clothed in invincible armor which no further blow of fate could dent.

The final secret of Ned's triumph was his own. Since he never talked of himself or his illness except in the most casual way, no one knew the stages of the battle he had fought, and one could only guess the weapons he had used. The one thing certain was that he had done it all by himself.

Heritage had of course played its part. Ned had all the tough instinct for survival that had kept his pioneering ancestors, both Sheldons and Strongs, pushing steadily westward for two hundred years. And the same faith that had brought his Puritan forebears to the New England wilderness in the seventeenth century had come down to him intact, despite the abandonment of formal religion and the exposure to wealth.

Childhood training also counted. Perseverance was a prime tenet in the Sheldon creed. In his earliest boyhood Ned had learned that no job seriously undertaken could be left until he had given it the best that was in him. Mrs. Sheldon had taught her children to admire valor also, and if she clothed this virtue in rather poetic garb, borrowed from the heroes of Arthurian legend and the drama, it was still a perfectly human quality. Moreover, Ned had seen it demonstrated, in the last months of his father's life. The elder Sheldon was stricken with angina and suffered repeated attacks of excruciating pain. But he gave no sign of his agony, and the memory of this stayed with Ned always.

But Ned's own life was more than an example of heroic endurance. His steady growth after blindness struck him was due to qualities peculiarly his own. Every step of his young life had reflected a superior intelligence; and it was this that prevented him from slipping now into a void of stunned resignation. He had taken with him into his ordeal the absolute certainty that nothing happens without a reason. Throughout the long months of pain and bewilderment this idea hung in his thoughts, a faint but steadily glowing spark in the blackness. He had an unshakable belief that there must be some kind of design back of what had happened to him. The need to learn something of the design, if only a small part, strengthened his resolve to go on. He once said to Ernst Steuben, his orderly, "I live merely out of curiosity."

Ned had another powerful aid in the great gift of his imagination. The same creative drive that had led him as a playwright to build some fragmentary episode or impression into vivid drama now challenged him to take the wreckage of his life and make it into a new structure, finer, more solid, more purposeful than the old one had been. For all his brilliant success as a writer for the stage, it was not until he began to work on his own life that the true artist in Edward Sheldon emerged.

Finally and immeasurably more potent than anything else, because it was a part of the instinct for living—perhaps *the* instinct—was the need to give. This was the point to which everything came back, and from which everything started over again. If there was any defiance in Ned's attitude under affliction, it was in the steady reassertion of this need. It was as though with every fresh loss he cried, "Take what you will! I still have more to give!"

During the next months Sheldon quietly and systematically arranged his life so as to make the most of the faculties left him. The sense of touch was of course denied him. His fingers, stretched in frozen rigidity, could not grasp anything or move along a surface. He still had hearing and speech, and through these the way to the outside world was kept open.

Reading had become more important than ever, and for this he was totally dependent on others. In the early months of his blindness when the pain of iritis was greatest, his nights were like waking nightmares. In brief intervals of sleep the faces of friends and loved ones would be restored. But on awakening there would be darkness again, and pain to sharpen the sense of what he had lost. Only by being read to constantly during these hours was he able to endure the endless nights. The habit thus established persisted for the rest of his life. He always slept fitfully, a few hours at a time.

As soon as he awoke the reading would begin again. This meant that his night nurse, in addition to her strictly professional qualifications, must also be an expert reader, a combination not easily come by.

Sheldon was fortunate during the last twelve years of his life in having as his night attendant Mrs. Katherine Grey, a practical nurse who had grown up in a family whose favorite pastime was reading aloud. Mrs. Grey not only read well but she also had a sturdy critical sense. There would sometimes be heated discussions—at two, or three, or four o'clock in the morning—of Hemingway and Faulkner, of *Gone With the Wind, The Tragic Sense of Life, Tristram Shandy*, or anything else that fell within the seemingly limitless range of Sheldon's tastes. Mrs. Grey had another asset that endeared her to her employer. She was the widow of an actor and knew backstage life. Sometimes their talk would drift to old days on Broadway, and Sheldon would speak of his own past, as he rarely did with other people.

Reading was also a regular duty of his orderly, Ernst Steuben, the member of the household closest to its master. Steuben came to Eighty-fourth Street in the first months of Sheldon's blindness. He was then a very young man, a German, university-educated, who had emigrated to the United States to make his career. He began to work in a hospital as a stopgap while completing his education, and because of his skill and intelligence had been strongly recommended to Sheldon. In time Steuben became a close friend as well as attendant, and without him Sheldon would have been lost. He not only took care of his employer's intimate physical needs, he served as eyes and hands as well. He came to act almost by reflex in anticipating Sheldon's wants. During the war years there was occasional friction between them, for Steuben never forgot that he was a German, but this had little effect on the relationship. The most dismal time of the year for Sheldon was the month when "Mr. Ernst," as he was known to the rest of the household, took his vacation, and the orderly's return was properly celebrated. The career Steuben had originally planned was abandoned. Sheldon was his career.

Steuben spoke English with a slight accent, but Sheldon enjoyed his reading. The orderly was one of the few people he trusted completely in the matter of "skipping." During the mornings, after he had given Sheldon his bath, while Miss Schrampf worked, or later when they went out on the terrace to get the sun, Steuben would read. Magazines and newspapers had an important place in keeping Sheldon posted on the everyday world and on political happenings. Two daily papers were read almost from cover to cover, including certain advertisements and stock market summaries. If he kept an astonishingly accurate picture of the life around him, it was largely due to the newspaper. For instance, he carefully followed all the changes in automobile design from the rectangular, explosive vehicle of his own experience to the sleek silent affair of later times, which he never saw. Though once in a while he made a slip in the matter of women's apparel, as when in the mid-forties he inquired if women still wore "the sheer black silk hose that used to be so attractive," even in this department he kept amazingly well informed.

Everybody in the household, from cook-housekeeper to secretary, was required at some time to double as reader for Sheldon, so that there was no unfilled gap in the day. Friends performed the same service if they were properly qualified, though with these Sheldon preferred usually to talk.

He had his own standards for reading aloud. Because of

his searching imagination and acute sense of word values, he preferred to be read to in an expressionless monotone, letting his own inner ear supply the inflections and emphases, as though he were receiving the words directly from the printed page. He taught his staff to read this way; but tact prevented him from instructing his friends, and there were few who understood the value of this kind of reading to him.

One of those most expert in what Sheldon called "sewing machine" reading was Mrs. Winthrop Ames, wife of the producer of *The Nigger*. Long practice in reading play scripts to her husband, who would listen with closed eyes while visualizing the work on the stage, had given Mrs. Ames the "sewing machine" technique. For years she was Ned's most devoted reader, and at times she performed valiant service. John Marquand sent Sheldon the manuscript of *So Little Time* (first entitled *In That Year*) three days before a dinner appointment. In a series of meetings Mrs. Ames went through the entire manuscript with Sheldon in time for him to discuss it when the author came to the apartment. Sheldon described the book as "brilliant reading" even though the chief ingredient was "pure nitric acid."

In the case of poetry Sheldon did not insist on the "sewing machine" style, in which of course the music of the lines would have been lost. Though his friends included most of the great artists of the stage, he had distinct preferences when it came to poetry reading. Julia Marlowe, a boyhood idol, became a close friend in Ned's later life. Long after she was an old woman living in seclusion at the Plaza, she came regularly to Eighty-fourth Street to read Shelley and Keats. Her intonations, her flawless sense of the nuances of rhythm, were always thrilling. After one of her visits Sheldon wrote Alexander Woollcott that she had read a new poem by Joseph Auslander with "a voice like golden trumpets at dawn."

But his favorite was his old comrade John Hall Wheelock. The poet's reading had not only the appeal of long association, of so many great experiences of poetry shared in youth; he himself had, as Ned said, "the voice for it." Years ago, for his twenty-first birthday, Wheelock had given Ned a little black leather-bound copy of *The Oxford Book of English Verse*, and this lay always on the table by his bed. When Wheelock came he would read from its well-worn pages Shakespeare's sonnets, Milton's "L'Allegro" and bits of "Comus" (Ned never asked for *Paradise Lost*), and the early, as well as the later, poems of Keats. And there was always a call for Byron, especially the Greek lyrics which had the same charm for him now as in his undergraduate days.

Sheldon's tastes in poetry were narrower than in prose, a clear case of one kind of development, at any rate, which had been arrested by invalidism and his remoteness from the ordinary struggles of life. The pessimism of most of the modern poets, or their attempt to idealize our mechanical civilization, left him cold. Though he admired T. S. Eliot's technical virtuosity, *The Waste Land* was distasteful to him. His delight in some of Yeats's lyrics was offset by his revulsion at an occasional idea. Once Wheelock read "Sailing to Byzantium," and when he came to the lines

> *Consume my heart away; sick with desire*
> *And fastened to a dying animal*
> *It knows not what it is . . .*

Ned cried out passionately, "No, no, no—not that! Not an animal!"

There was more than aesthetic pleasure in these poetry sessions with his old friend. The mood created by the reading, and the presence of one whose comprehension he could perfectly trust, aroused a need to communicate things which otherwise he kept scrupulously to himself. Through certain poems he could say what he had never been able to put in his own words. He often asked for Landor's "Rose Aylmer." It took courage to read this to him, for the last stanza of the poem told with poignant directness the whole story of his lost love:

> Rose Aylmer, whom these wakeful eyes
>   May weep, but never see,
> A night of memories and sighs
>   I consecrate to thee.

There was another request that came almost like a ritual at the end of Wheelock's visits. When the poet rose to leave, with his hand on Ned's shoulder in his usual gesture of farewell, Ned would say, "Good night, Jack—but before you go, please say the 'moonlight' lines for me."

The "moonlight" lines formed the closing stanza of an early poem of Wheelock's entitled "Departure." The poet always felt a slight embarrassment at this somewhat formalized exhibition of his own work, all the more so because these lines, even more pointedly than the stanza of "Rose Aylmer," spoke on the subject that in their most intimate talks had never been mentioned:

> Where my youth has sorrowed, now lies only moonlight,
>   Moonlight on the bed, moonlight on the floor—
> And across the pillow where your head lay dreaming,
>   O my lost belovèd, moonlight evermore.

Sheldon's general reading covered enormous territory. He not only kept abreast of the best contemporary work (many manuscripts, like John Buchan's autobiography which Wheelock read to him, were sent to Sheldon even before publishers saw them), but he reread familiar things unceasingly. On the long table of his living room, piled high with a welter of books, play manuscripts, magazines, and pamphlets, were always to be found two volumes which he read at least once a year. One of these was *The Count of Monte Cristo*, which had been his father's favorite novel, and the other was Henry Adams' *Chapters on Erie and Other Essays*, a book to which his uncle and namesake, Edward Sheldon, had been devoted. His fondness for these works was perhaps sentimental in part, but it went deeper than that. To read them was to find himself again in the company of two men whom he had loved and admired. He had discovered long ago that people survive not only through the books they have written, but also through those they have read with deepest enjoyment.

He never lost his taste for adventure stories. When he was despondent with the knowledge of Doris Keane's last illness, he wrote Charles Auchincloss:

> Last night I started to read *Treasure Island*, and the instant Bill Bones appeared at the Admiral Benbow Inn, the old spell began to work again, and R.L.S. had me firmly by the scruff of the neck. . . .

Ned's undying allegiance to the romantic and picaresque caused him to rank John Buchan's *Greenmantle* among the imperishable examples of this genre. Admiration for this book led eventually to acquaintance and warm friendship

with Lord Tweedsmuir himself when the novelist-statesman
was Governor-General of Canada.

For all his joy in literature of the sort that had first
kindled his imagination, he found increasing pleasure in
the ancient classics. In the summer of 1941 he wrote Alice
Buchan Fairfax-Lucy, Lord Tweedsmuir's daughter:

> *I have been reading Aeschylus, Sophocles, and Euripides
> An American woman named Hamilton has translated Eu-
> ripides better than Murray. Sharper, rougher, craggier (if
> there is such a word). But then in all the translations—even
> those by country clergymen and maiden ladies of the early
> nineteenth century the overwhelming dramatic power of the
> original crashes through triumphantly. . . . I have found in
> these dramas a good war-time diet.*

His insatiable curiosity took him into strange byways
There were always books of criminology about. His interest
in education and young people made him an avid reader of
college catalogues and annuals. Once a friend was astonished
to find a treatise on forestry on the book-laden table that
stretched along one wall of his living room. Another time
there was a handbook on glass-making, and one on steel
alloys. His lifelong passion for history had led him to an
intensive study of the Civil War. One of his great heroes was
Robert E. Lee, whose silver-framed photograph hung near
his bed, and among the volumes regularly drawn from the
Society Library there were always one or two dealing with
the Confederacy.

Through others Sheldon continued to gratify far more
than his appetite for reading. Friends also provided second
eyes to keep his spirit roaming about the world, as he once
so eagerly had voyaged in the flesh. People made a special
point when traveling to supply him with detailed verbal

pictures of what they saw and did. And there was some expert reporting at his service.

With Thornton Wilder, whom he had met in the early thirties, he shared many summers abroad. In 1937 Wilder traveled from Paris to the French countryside where he visited Gertrude Stein, then on to Salzburg and the music festival. Everything was reported faithfully to Ned, along with remarks on the progress of *Our Town* which Wilder was then writing. There was another trip recorded by his friend that reawakened tender memories of Ned's happy childhood. Wilder was visiting on the shore of Lake Geneva, Wisconsin, not far from Henry Strong's house. Once he took an early morning walk along the path Sheldon had known so well as a boy.

> It was beautiful, of course, with early mist and horizontal sunlight and dew on the cobwebs, but I wondered why it was poignantly beautiful; and then suddenly I knew. It was the lake's smell and the particular seaweed moss on the stones at the water's edge and the crayfish holes beside the piers; that was my boyhood, too. Until the age of nine I lived in Madison, Wisconsin, and spent my summers at Maple Bluffs on Lake Mendota, less than a hundred miles away. And though since then I have known lakes in England and China and Ohio—Carnegie Pond in Princeton and Lake Whitney and Lake Sunapee (very treasured, that one) and Lake Como and the Austrian lakes, none of them have that particular bundle of smells, nor those effects of light and air. My joy was an atavistic rediscovery.
>
> And now to it has been added the news that you and I have the same standards for lakes; there we first heard waves lapping on shores with a sound that other lakes never quite repeat.
>
> So call us cousins.
> We're related through the lakes. . . .

There was a constant flow of foreign-stamped letters to the penthouse on Eighty-fourth Street, as one or the other of Ned's friends and often several at a time reported from distant corners of the earth. With the brothers Charles and Alfred MacArthur he saw the Alhambra and sun-baked Spanish plains. He shared the life of Henrietta Metcalf and her children during several years in France. And Mrs. Wharton, with all the magic of her power with words, re-created her glittering Mediterranean world.

He stood with Dr. Kernan in a storm on a hilltop above the Killarney Lakes. With Margaret Ayer Barnes and her family he saw again old haunts in England, and breathed the sharp clear air of Norwegian fjords. Robert Sherwood took him to the summit of the Parthenon to look out through the great dusky yellow columns at the violet mountains and the "wine-dark" sea, while thunder rolled and lightning flashed— "Zeus," wrote Sherwood, "still furious!" With Mrs. Cadwalader Jones, in an elegantly chauffeured Hispano-Suiza, he motored to Delphi, and from the top of the wild gorge gazed out across the Gulf of Corinth.

One of the most faithful and talented of these foreign correspondents was Ruth Draper, whose friendship dated from Ned's youth. She appreciated as no one else his intense feeling for color, and her letters brought not only the forms and sounds of remote places, but every tint that crossed her consciousness from the "peach-colored velvet jacket" which she happened to be wearing when she once wrote, to the "mauve jacarandas" on the shores of the Indian Ocean. She knew well the spots that he had loved as a young man; she made him see again the fresh green of London parks, the snow on the Cotswolds, and Florence with its

*. . . blue sky, that row of tiny yellow houses that lies along
the Arno beside the Ponte Vecchio; the green shutters,
brown-tiled roofs, broken stained walls. . . .*

From Australia, as she was winding up a long tour, Miss
Draper wrote:

*I shall have so much to tell you—so many things, places
and people. My thoughts leap to my chair beside you—and
the silence and intimacy of your room, and I hear you laugh
and see you smile and know that you will understand and
feel everything as if you had been with me everywhere. . . .
I'll book my first evening with you when I land.*

Another friend, Daisy Blaisdell, after a trip around the
world, spent a series of evenings with Ned, devoting each
visit to an exciting discussion of a particular country. Miss
Blaisdell was amazed at "the extensive study he had made of
those far-distant lands that he could only see through the
eyes of those who loved him. He astonished me by his
searching questions. . . ." And when they talked of the Taj
Mahal he quoted softly, "It is the proud passion of an
Emperor's love wrought into living stone."

A large collection of Baedekers provided Sheldon with
some of his happiest reading. Ernst Steuben remembers a hot
summer afternoon on the penthouse terrace when Sheldon
with the help of a Baedeker mapped out a tour of the Welsh
Coast, the Scottish Highlands, and the French Riviera. He
visited or revisited many countries in this fashion. Then
there was a day during the second World War when the
row of little red volumes disappeared from the bookshelves.
Miss Blaisdell, who happened to call at the time, saw that
they were gone and asked what had become of them.

Oh," said Sheldon, "didn't you know that the government wanted them to teach geography to our boys in the

service? I miss them, of course, for I was always looking up something or other in them; but I'm thankful that they're in the fight."

In his blindness another interest acquired special importance. He had always been a great music-lover. With the loss of sight his hearing took on the compensating acuteness usual with the blind so that his musical appreciation gained in depth and subtlety. Radio, which was reaching its great development at the onset of his blindness, was an incalculable blessing. When the Metropolitan Opera commenced its broadcasts he was as excited as a boy anticipating his first circus. Even the football season was curtailed to make way for the Saturday afternoon broadcasts of the opera. This was a sacred time which he did his best to keep free, though he might tolerate the presence of another properly educated opera fan. His knowledge of opera was encyclopedic, and his information on any current season was complete. When somebody asked how he could possibly memorize the opera schedule for the whole year, with dates, conductors, and guest artists, he burst out, "But I have to remember! There just isn't time enough in life to be told things twice over!"

Radio and the phonograph, with an enormous collection of records, were only part of his musical life. In the galaxy of Eighty-fourth Street habitués were some of the most resplendent names of the concert stage and the opera.

He had met Geraldine Farrar when he first came to New York. With her beauty and her turbulent background, she became something of a successor to the fabulous Cavalieri. When she was in New York she never failed to see Ned. She was always on the wing, and would dash up to his apartment in a breathless whirl that gave him the feeling of being on the edge of great adventure, as a visit from Farrar usually proved to be.

Edward Sheldon
circa 1910

Mrs.
Theodore
Sheldon
Senior
mother
of
Edward
Sheldon
circa 1930

FROM THE
PORTRAIT
by
Frank
Salisbury

Minnie Maddern Fiske
1906

Mrs. Patrick Campbell
circa 1905

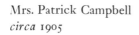

John Barrymore

Edith Wharton
1923

Somerset Maugham

PHOTOGRAPH BY *NBC*

Margaret Ayer Barnes
1933

PHOTO FROM *Wide World*

*Photograph
on opposite page*

Doris Keane as La Cavallini
in *Romance*

PHOTOGRAPH FROM THE MUSEUM
OF THE CITY OF NEW YORK

Florence Reed as the fortune-teller, George Abbott and Helen Hayes as Mr. and Mrs. Antrobus, Mary Martin as Sabena, in Thornton Wilder's *Skin of Our Teeth*

Thornton Wilder
1947

Katharine Cornell

PHOTOGRAPH BY *Vandamm*

John Hall Wheelock
1948

Van Wyck Brooks
circa 1945

She would drop exhausted into a chair, relate some harrowing problem with which she was beset, then pass on to comment about a personality they both knew. Presently the talk would veer to music, and there would be sharp discussion about the phrasing or interpretation of some passage. To settle the argument she would fling herself at the huge grand piano that filled one corner of the room, and dramatically demonstrate the point in question. Without waiting for this to take effect she would plunge into a Schubert *Lied*, or the score of *Butterfly*. Then for an hour the penthouse would be flooded with golden sound.

Sheldon not only delighted in Farrar's music. As a personality of unpredictable movements and reactions, in whom temperament was no pose but the expression of immense vitality, she was one of those rare people who had known and been able to make the most of freedom. And there was variety in her life for all tastes. Ned never failed to chuckle when he remembered the famous story of the backstage row at the Metropolitan when Farrar bit Caruso's ear.

Geraldine Farrar was only one of those whose music gave happy release to the prisoner in the penthouse. Frances Alda, Emma Eames, Lucrezia Bori, Lotte Lehmann, Florence Mills, Edward Johnson, Deems Taylor, Walter Damrosch, and many more came to sing, or play, or simply talk with Sheldon. Once there was a puckish note in the celestial harmonies when Mildred Dilling brought her harp —and Harpo Marx.

Jascha Heifetz's first visit was one to remember. The violinist had not thought of playing. He had simply looked forward to meeting the almost legendary figure that so many of his friends talked about. The two men had an exhilarating visit, in the course of which some perceptive remark of Sheldon's revealed how much music meant to him.

Impulsively, Heifetz asked, "Would you like me to play for you? If you would, I'll send for my accompanist."

A telephone call promptly located the accompanist and sent him on his way to Sheldon's apartment. Then for more than two hours Heifetz played. During this time the intent expression on the invalid's face never changed. And Heifetz himself sensed what was indeed true, that Sheldon had utterly escaped from the limitations of physical existence into a world of pure beauty such as the artist himself had rarely known.

When it was over and the final note had died into absolute stillness Ned made no sign to break the spell. It was Heifetz himself who finally said quietly, "Of course I shall never play in Carnegie Hall as I have played for you today."

But it was not merely that his old enjoyment of music had been sharpened to more acute appreciation. He now took a new interest in the musician as a special human type; he delighted in musical history; and with his alert story sense he developed a special relish for anecdotes of the musical great.

In 1943 during a visit from an English friend, Lady Kenneth Lee, he was vastly intrigued to learn that she was the niece by marriage of Adelina Patti. Lady Lee had much amusing family lore to relate about the diva, a specimen of which Sheldon promptly passed on to his cousin Elsa Jameson:

> It seems that there was another Patti daughter, about twenty years older than Adelina. This daughter was a singer, too, as indeed they all were. She was practicing the extraordinarily difficult Casta Diva from Bellini's Norma one day when Adelina—small, dirty-faced, aged seven—piped up with "I can sing that much better than you can." So with the

idea of fixing her, her brother-in-law lifted her by the shoulders on to the piano and said grimly, "All right, Miss Impudence, sing it." And the miraculous child sang it flawlessly from beginning to end. . . .

The elder sister burst into tears, gave up her career, and Adelina triumphantly took over all her concert engagements and started right on being the one and only Patti.

Did you ever hear any of her records? They were made when she was in her sixties, but the voice has all the effortless ease and something of the tone of a wood thrush. The same type of voice was Galli-Curci's, but far more beautiful in timbre. "O Lyric Love, half angel and half bird"—as Browning wrote of his wife's poetry.

As music acquired greater meaning in his life, Sheldon's sympathies for the problems of the musician also increased. His old friend of Lake Geneva days, Henrietta Metcalf, once described a soirée where most of the guests were celebrities, gathered by a charming hostess to provide an audience for an adored younger brother, a singer with more ambition than voice. Mrs. Metcalf related the details of the party (knowing well how such accounts brought the world alive to Sheldon), describing the guests as they fidgeted in their chairs for an interminable hour of uninspired *Lieder*, and their *sotto voce* comments on the singer and his pretensions. Mrs. Metcalf was a gifted *raconteuse*, and her anecdotes usually evoked a hearty response from Sheldon. But this time the end of the story was followed by a long silence, the kind of silence that always gave Sheldon's friends food for thought. When he finally spoke his brow was furrowed and he was unsmiling.

"I was thinking, Henrietta, what a dreadful thing it must be to be born with a desire to do something above all else and for which one is totally unsuited, especially like singing, for one cannot sing alone—one must sing to someone. An artist can paint and a writer can write, regardless. But a singer must have an actual public."

His voice was gentle, compassionate. Mrs. Metcalf had the feeling that "his words were in no sense intended as a rebuke to my callous interpretation of the evening, but rather just what he had seen in the hopeless plight of the would-be artist, doomed through no fault of his own to dismal failure."

Through reading, music, the reports of friends from all over the world, Sheldon was able to penetrate the second wall that fate had tried to set up around him. Instead of cutting him off from people, blindness actually brought him closer to them. Those who had known him through the years noticed how much his perceptions of human impulses and motives were sharpened with the loss of sight. The men and women who brought their problems to Sheldon (and most of the people he knew did bring him their problems now) were sometimes awed by what seemed an almost clairvoyant penetration of their inmost selves. It was as though in seeing the world only through the eyes of others, he possessed himself of others' minds and hearts as well.

One thing was apparent to everybody and tended to check any feeling of pity his new affliction might have aroused. The loss of his sight, instead of closing him in a world of private tragedy, had opened new channels to life. Blindness, which at first had seemed to drop like a pall over the bright landscape of his youth, was in reality a curtain lowered for a change of scene. There was a moment of darkness, then the stage was visible once more and the view disclosed was one of limitless horizons.

The ancient Japanese servant of one of Sheldon's friends

had followed the growing legend with intense curiosity. It was not until late that he learned Sheldon had long been blind. Then he understood everything. "Mr. Sheldon *blind? That* why he is wise. When man's eye close his mind open. His mind work, instead only his eyes. Man who see use only part brain. Man who cannot see he use all brain, all heart. He see important things now, not just things. He teach all people because he have full spirit now."

CHAPTER IX

Life in the Blue Room

BLINDNESS had little effect on the routine of Sheldon's life. His days, and sometimes his nights, were crowded with appointments, and though there was no tension in the air of the penthouse, there was always a feeling of controlled activity.

There were a few changes in his surroundings that one could not fail to notice. One of these was the disappearance of the small stage that had always stood at the foot of his bed directly in the line of vision. This had furnished him much entertainment, and it had also had a considerable usefulness. When he was no longer able to go to the theatre Ned could still keep in touch with production methods and new trends in scenic design. Many original models for the settings of new plays found their way to Sheldon's little stage, and these aided him in visualizing a new play as he read it. In his own work too it helped to have the background before his eyes as he wrote. This simplified the plotting of entrances and exits, arranging positions in ensemble scenes, planning stage business, and so on.

Now that his sight was gone imagination took over the function of the small stage. The backgrounds for plays were constructed from verbal descriptions, and the little model went the way of other things that belonged to a life that was past.

The visitor sitting in the easy chair by Ned's bed saw also the empty wall space over the doorway to the vestibule, toward which the bed faced. Here for many years had always hung a landscape by Willard L. Metcalf, one of that important group of American impressionists known as "The Ten." During the artist's lifetime he made a practice of leaving his latest work for a while with Sheldon, so that the space above the door held a constantly changing exhibit of Metcalf paintings. As the darkness deepened about him Sheldon carried in his mind, with grateful remembrance to the artist, the bright sunlight, the shimmering greens and yellows, the subtle distances of Metcalf's New England landscapes.

There was also a change in Sheldon's appearance. The smooth, ruddy face was as it had always been, singularly unmarked either by time or suffering. And the thick black hair, carefully groomed as ever, was beginning to show only scattered flecks of gray. But across his eyes, the clear brown eyes that had once been so striking a feature of his good looks, he now wore a narrow black silk mask, which he referred to as his "sleepy."

The mask was the subject of some debate between Sheldon and Dr. Doherty, his oculist. Determined to eliminate so far as possible the evidence of his condition, Sheldon felt that he must cover his sightless eyes. He was convinced that they would disturb people who came to see him, and he would not take Doherty's word that they looked as they always had. In the doctor's opinion this was a minor point. He felt that the eyes would be more comfortable without the pressure, however slight, of the silk band.

There were other and less obvious reasons for the mask. Since he could not conceal his condition he dramatized it. There was a suggestion of harlequinade, a symbolism of the theatre in the narrow black strip that inevitably diverted attention from the horror of blindness itself. And there was perhaps a whimsical amusement in the thought that the mask added a certain interest to his appearance, the nearest thing to a touch of vanity of which one could ever accuse him. Long years before when he had stood upon the ancient stage of the Farnese Theatre in Parma he had exclaimed to a friend, "I can see myself like some old Scapin, in high red heels and a little black mask . . . !"

Perhaps too the mask served a defensive purpose. If he could no longer look into the eyes of other people, he could equalize the disadvantage by preventing them from looking into his.

There were further touches of the theatrical in the background against which he spent his days. Helen Howe, the monologist and novelist, was taken to see Sheldon first in the early days of his blindness. Her impression gives the picture so familiar to countless others:

> Framed against the panels of a high, dark blue screen— actually put in place to keep off draughts, but with the full dramatic effect of a cyclorama—on a high slab-like pallet lay what might have been the effigy of a Crusader. A blue coverlet [sometimes a blue Cashmere shawl, sometimes a satin spread of Turkish embroidery in geometric design in varying shades of blue] reaching to the floor completely covered the figure beneath. Only showing on the pillow was his head, incapable of turning to right or left, his eyes covered under a black mask. The features were handsome and strong, and even to the very end his color was ruddy. From this uplifted altar where, in a sort of physical crucifixion, his

*body was held fast, an atmosphere of light and health
streamed out, which healed and refreshed everyone who came
within its rays.*

To the newcomer all this was somewhat awesome, perhaps even disconcerting. It was not quite like anything one
had ever seen or imagined before. The effect was so startling
that one promptly forgot that the central figure of this
rather elaborately set stage was a blind man and an invalid.
And this was exactly the effect Sheldon sought. It might
produce amazement, but this helped to dispel the uneasiness
so many people feel in the presence of the hopelessly in-
capacitated. If this was not accomplished while the visitor's
eyes took in the scene, the sound of Sheldon's big, warm
voice immediately broke down the barriers and put the
stranger at his ease.

Although he rarely spoke of his own state, he was perfectly easy in discussing blindness objectively. During the
early years of their friendship Helen Howe frequently performed her monologues for him. Like other artists she found
Sheldon an exciting audience, whose sensitivity to every
nuance was a challenge to one's finest effort. But there was
one number in her repertory that she could never bring herself to do for him. This was a sequence ending with a powerful scene between a mother and her son at his bedside in a
veterans' hospital. The point of the scene is that the mother
knows the boy has been permanently blinded, though he
does not. Sheldon had heard high praise of this particular
monologue and insisted that Miss Howe do it for him. At
length, rather fearfully, she yielded.

"There was a full minute's silence after I did it, and then
he said with great feeling, 'That is very moving. But you
mustn't *wince* when you do it. Play it to the hilt!' He had

clearly felt I was holding back because of a shrinking from playing on the nerve closest to him."

Even about his own blindness Sheldon could talk if it served to lighten the way for another. Once his friend Marion Meigs Hyde (now Mrs. William Woods), daughter of his old headmaster at the Hill School, brought to Sheldon a sixteen-year-old boy who had recently lost his sight. The youth was full of bitterness, despair, and rebellion, and his equilibrium was seriously threatened. Mrs. Hyde thought that if he could talk with Sheldon, it might help him in the difficult process of readjustment. Sheldon welcomed the boy in his usual easy, friendly fashion, and in a few moments the youngster's tension began to disappear. By prearrangement Mrs. Hyde was called to the telephone, so that the two were left alone together. The fictitious call was prolonged for half an hour, and when she returned she found the boy sitting in the big chair by Sheldon's bed, his head eagerly bent forward, a look of deep interest on his face, and a faint smile on his lips. As she softly closed the door of the room she caught Sheldon's voice in the middle of a sentence: ". . . and we have one great advantage over sighted people; no one can ever fool us with expressions or gestures they want us to see, or with remarks they want us to believe. We learn to see the person exactly as he is."

Since the beginning of his illness, and increasingly when blindness overtook him, Sheldon systematically sought and exploited every possible compensation for the things he had lost. Increased mental resources, deepened perceptions, acuter sympathy for human nature—the continued power to serve, were all factors in his acceptance of the changes which had occurred. One secret of his vitality and his poise lay in his ability to extract the maximum interest from the simplest and homeliest details of life.

On summer mornings as he lay stretched in the sun on his roof terrace, the sound of the breeze in the shrubbery and flowers so carefully tended by Mr. Ernst gave him all the pleasure of a walk through deep woods. In the winter his great blue room was full of flowers whose fragrance re-created in his mind the whole miraculous cycle of germination and growth, and the decay that precedes rebirth in nature.

In the apartment there was always a dog scampering about. For some time the ruling favorite was Trixie, the dachshund belonging to Catherine, the cook. Even as a small puppy Trixie would regularly trot into Sheldon's room as soon as he awakened in the morning, and while he had his coffee she would lap her milk. Breakfast completed, she would stand with furiously wagging tail until Mr. Ernst would lift her up onto the bed. "How is my little baby today?" Ned would inquire. And Trixie's answer would be an energetic licking of her friend's face. This operation completed, she would give a happy little sigh and curl up beside him. To one denied the warmth of human contact there was comfort in the feel of the little creature's warm softness as she lay beside him. Sheldon, dictating letters to his secretary, would frequently report that Trixie was present, "curled up across my neck" or "coiled up like a rattle-snake between my feet." The last of a series of devoted dogs was Sally, a little Boston bull whose desolation at her master's going showed that Sheldon's gift for friendship was not restricted to his human associates.

On the terrace outside the big living room pedigreed pigeons whirled and settled. Their cooing and the beating of their wings was special music to his ears. It was Henrietta Metcalf who interested Ned in pigeons and brought him his first birds, a pair of beautiful helmets. "The lady is quite young," she explained, "and she may not feel romantic yet, being shy and reserved." But Sheldon was sure everything would work out, and he was delighted when the birds immediately set up housekeeping in the model quarters he had had constructed. The birds were christened Penny and Royal (after Mrs. Metcalf's home in Connecticut), and in due time Ned wrote that "they are now setting on two eggs, which we hope will develop into Bill and Coo."

From now on the pigeons and their increasing family became a vital interest to Sheldon. Mr. Ernst brought frequent bulletins on their deportment. Royal, it seemed, was sitting on the eggs by day, and Penny by night—which to their master seemed "a fair and equitable arrangement." But when Royal began to tire of his part of the hatching job and was reported as being frequently absent from the nest and was sometimes seen in the company of other ladies on neighboring roofs, Sheldon became anxious. "He doesn't seem to take the responsibility of fatherhood very seriously."

The pigeons were a special link with the physiologist Dr. Gustav Eckstein, whom Sheldon had met through Mrs. Pat Campbell. Between the penthouse and Eckstein's laboratory at the University of Cincinnati there was a heavy exchange of letters and telegrams. These covered everything from Japanese art to the immortality of the soul, and there was nearly always a good deal about pigeons. Dr. Eckstein, an authority in several fields beside the human anatomy, was a knowing observer of birds and had written a charming biography of one called *Canary*, which was a prized fixture of Sheldon's library.

Eckstein co-operated wholeheartedly in the pigeon venture, supplying Sheldon not only with advice from his long specialized experience, but also with birds. "The homers are setting," Ned reported happily after the installation of the first arrivals from Cincinnati. "I cannot resist raising this first brood, so I promised the offspring to Cornelia Skinner's little boy, aged eleven, who has a perfect place for them down on Long Island."

It was not long before even Sheldon's hospitality was strained by the increased population of his terrace, and he too was making gifts to friends all over the country. To his niece Georgiana MacArthur he wrote:

> Yesterday we sent off seven homing pigeons, aged six weeks, to a friend in Vermont. It was rather like sending very small boys to boarding school for the first time, but their new home is a wooded island in the middle of a lake, and I am sure they will like it and be given excellent care. Meanwhile their parents are busy hatching out another brood so life goes on serenely.

The recipient of this gift was Alexander Woollcott, who had made elaborate preparations for the new arrivals. He took up the matter of pigeon raising with the utmost serious- ness, devoting himself to the birds' diet and shelter with an anxious gravity such as he rarely bestowed on mere humans. In the following weeks the Woollcott-Sheldon corre- spondence grew bulky with descriptions of breeding habits, moulting problems, roosting facilities, and nesting materials. In his detailed requests for guidance in this awesome re- sponsibility Woollcott resembled a bachelor uncle suddenly confronted with the raising of a large number of infant nephews and nieces. And Sheldon in reply gave him all the expert advice of one now in the know, or of an old master highly accomplished in the field. One letter of several typed pages related to the formula, mixing, and possible sources of ingredients for the particular mash indispensable to this breed of pigeons. Woollcott took all instructions thankfully and followed them to the letter. Soon he showed less nervousness over the new responsibility, and presently he was writing back gaily of the major and minor events in his own feathered universe.

Sheldon watched over the growing families of his birds with true concern. At hatching time he instructed Mr. Ernst to place pillows under the nests to catch any young pigeons that might fall out. With the death of Mrs. Homer, the first mortality in his colony, he was really grieved, although Eckstein quickly supplied Mr. Homer with a new mate. "It seems mysterious and terrible somehow," Sheldon wrote his friend in Cincinnati, "that her miraculous living organism should cease to be. This is equally true for every Italian and Englishman lying dead on the Egyptian sands; but Mrs. Homer was within my own small orbit. Well, the new Mrs. Homer is beautiful too, and is eating, and apparently well contented."

During the winter of 1943 the bird colony was temporarily augmented by a house guest—the Indian myna bird belonging to Sir Kenneth and Lady Lee. Ned reported the arrival to his cousin Elsa Denison Jameson:

> "A friend of mine who lunched with me yesterday brought along her Himalayan myna bird, and she loaned him to me for two days. He is the size of a blue jay, black with the black lustre of a highly polished top hat, yellow beak and feet. He says 'Hello!' 'Am I a good boy?' 'Where's Nellie?' 'Archibald is a good boy,' and 'You're a so-and-so,'—this last in a low mutter. All with uncannily perfect diction. Sally, my Boston terrier, is horrified. He said 'Where's the bow-wow?' and Sally flew under my bed. We are all fascinated."

The following day he wrote again:

> "The myna bird who has been visiting me for two days has just left to go home. He was still asking where Nellie is,

and insisting that he was a nice boy. Dr. Eckstein told me last night that there was a myna bird at the Washington Zoo, and when they were in danger of having their income reduced by Congress, the director taught the bird to say, 'Where's our appropriation?' to every senator and member of the House who took his children to see the monkeys. It worked like a charm and they got their money."

The following July, while the Lees were in Virginia, Archie made a longer visit. For six weeks the antics of Archie added a note of hilarity to life in the penthouse. Ernst Steuben relates that:

> Archie took particular delight in sitting on top of Mr. Sheldon's head, in the midst of his bushy growth of hair, which Mr. Sheldon remarked, "he presumably fancies to be the jungle of India where he hails from . . . Come down, Archie!" Mr. Sheldon would summon him. "Come down, Archibald!" "What did you say?" was Archibald's reply, and nonchalantly he would begin to whistle a little melody.

It delighted Sheldon when guests, deep in confidential talk and supposing themselves alone in the room as usual with him, were startled to hear Archie suddenly speak up for all the world like an interested third party. When he at last departed Sheldon wrote Eckstein rather wistfully, "He has such character, personality and charm . . . he was indeed a nice boy."

Still greater than his delight in birds and animals was Sheldon's joy in children. Even the youngest were welcomed. Since he was incapable of taking a child in his arms, he would have a baby or even a toddler placed on his chest that he might get the "feel" which the weight and warmth and wriggling movement of the little body gave him. This contact with small humans gave him the same sense of intense aliveness that he got from animals, and there was the added thought that all the wonderful potentialities of a man or woman were buried in the small live body, and that the miscellaneous noises—the cooing, the gurgling, the squalling might one day become the sounds of wisdom or love or poetry.

His gentleness with children, his warm reassuring voice completely prevented any fears they might have had of the rigid, black-masked figure. Vivid memories of his own happy boyhood contributed to his understanding and affection for the children who came. Much as he enjoyed the sheer animal spirits and life of the very young, he never forgot that a child is a person in his own right and deserving of respect.

One afternoon a friend of Sheldon's took her small son to pay the first of many visits to Eighty-fourth Street. The mother had carefully prepared the boy for the sight of a man lying on his bed, his eyes covered with a small black mask because he was blind. The boy was a little frightened, but she assured him that their friend was no longer suffering and that it was always fun to be with him. When the mother returned to her son, after leaving him with Sheldon for an hour, she found the child enjoying himself hugely and loath to go. On the way home, in the midst of an enthusiastic account of the visit, he broke off to exclaim, "But, Mother, you never told me he was a noble prince!"

When a three-year-old, the son of Mrs. Raymond Sheldon, with the same given name as the playwright's, was first taken to call, his mother had qualms about the possible effect of Sheldon's appearance on the shy, sensitive boy. But Sheldon could be trusted to meet such a situation. As soon as the door was opened to admit the visitors, he called out, "Hello, Ned! See what I have for you here!" The boy's eyes rested a moment on the figure of the man on his high bed, then focused with excited attention on a large, gaily wrapped package on Sheldon's chest. He immediately climbed up on a stool beside the bed and promptly opened the package which contained a glittering engine and train. Before he lost interest in pulling it around the room supper was brought in. Small Ned had his own table and chair, and at his plate were two gaudy crackers. He was enraptured. "Open both the snappers," the older Ned told him. "Put one cap on your head and one on mine, and your mother too will put one on." The party ended with the boy's introduction to the delights of ice cream, so that the whole occasion was surrounded with unforgettable glamor.

Sheldon's way with children conditioned them quickly and happily to "Uncle Ned." Often a visit included an egg hunt, or some fascinating game. Older children would be treated to cobweb parties, where a maze of string would be wound all about the big room, with small treasures at suitable points to whet one's appetite and an important reward at the end. Once with the aid of Mrs. Raymond Sheldon, a professional puppeteer, Sheldon put on a puppet party for the children of theatrical friends, including Doris Keane's little daughter Ronda.

Sometimes on sultry afternoons in midsummer when the city seemed to gasp for breath, Ned's secretary would round up a whole group of children and invite them up to the penthouse for a "hose party." Addison Metcalf, his godson, remembers these occasions as the very peak of childhood bliss. The youngsters in bathing trunks would spend an hour on the roof terrace while Mr. Ernst expertly showered them with the hose. The shouts, the sounds of delirious cavortings, the snapping hiss and splash of water would fill the air, and Ned lying in the deep blue shade of his living room before the open French doors would be oblivious to everything but the joy of the children and the memories of his own childhood summers by the cool Wisconsin lakeside. These parties, too, would culminate in lavish servings of ice cream and cake for everybody, and the children would return to grateful parents healthily exhausted, but already keyed up over the idea of the next call from "Uncle Ned."

He was in constant touch with the youngsters of his own family. Peggy and Polly Sheldon, daughters of his brother Theodore, and Edward Sheldon MacArthur and Alexander MacArthur, his sister Mary's sons, were followed in all their activities from birth on. One of the most delicately understanding of his friendships was with his sister's stepdaughter, Georgiana MacArthur.

Through the years Ned eagerly awaited every letter from his brother's household. "What a home Peggy and Polly are growing up in," he would exclaim with satisfaction. He entered eagerly into all family plans for the children, offering advice and not hesitating to voice hearty disapproval when some project ran counter to his own belief or experience. "Now I'm going to stick my neck right out," he would say, "and you can cut off my head if you feel like it! But I think . . ."

Friendship with Sheldon was usually a family affair. The children of his physician friends, Carl Binger and Henry Murray, became habitués of the penthouse like their parents. The same thing was true of Henrietta Metcalf's children. Friendship with the Basil Kings, and with others, extended over three generations. Children and grandchildren of Sheldon's friends looked upon continued association with the playwright as one of the most cherished family legacies.

Family events always had a special flavor if Sheldon took part in them. A birthday visit to Eighty-fourth Street was a far more glamorous affair than any ordinary party, though it usually included all the classic trimmings of such festivities. The son of one of Ned's younger friends, George Brewer, spent the afternoon of his sixth birthday in the blue room. Sheldon wrote Woollcott:

> Young George went off carrying eleven balloons—he left one in the shape of a cat under my bed—wind-up fire engine, a tin drummer boy who makes an infernal noise on his drum and a large chamois bag full of marbles. He was also full of ice cream. He mentioned on leaving that he would come again soon.

More solemn occasions also took on added meaning in Sheldon's presence. When two children of an old friend discovered at boarding school that they had never been christened, a circumstance that labeled them as outcasts among their smugly orthodox friends, they insisted that the situation be remedied the next vacation, and that the ceremony be performed at "Uncle Ned's" bedside.

The day before the birth of her daughter, Helen Hayes and her husband Charles MacArthur were dining with Ned. Talk naturally was of the coming event, and there was a long discussion about names for the child. After examining a wide range of possibilities, Sheldon finally said, "If it's a girl, she must be called Mary—nothing else would be right."

Before the evening was over it seemed as if the talk had speeded up the process of nature, and instead of returning home the MacArthurs went straight to the hospital. There little Mary MacArthur was born the following day.

In due time she was brought to Sheldon and he made her

acquaintance in the usual way, by having her placed upon his chest where she squirmed about happily, patting his face and pulling his hair in approved baby fashion.

Presently a christening service was held in the blue living room. Sheldon had issued the command: "Build an altar!" And under the skillful hands of Mrs. Koehler, the house-keeper, the ecclesiastical furniture was created. A table was covered with green velvet and a length of filet lace, and silver candlesticks and bowl set out. Vases filled with smilax and apple blossoms filled the room with fragrance. For Sheldon the day was made doubly happy by the presence of his sister Mary and Ruth Gordon, the baby's godmothers, and Alexander Woollcott, the beaming godfather.

The ceremony was repeated with variations when the MacArthurs' adopted son was also christened at Sheldon's bedside. The Reverend William Neely Ross of the Dutch Reformed Church in Nyack, where the MacArthurs lived, came down to officiate, and the godparents this time were Lillian Gish, Alexander Woollcott again, and Sheldon him-self. Sheldon was highly gratified by the poise and initiative shown by the principal in the ceremony. At the close of the minister's benediction little Jamie, then four years old, piped up with his own evening prayer:

> *Gentle Jesus meek and mild,*
> *Look upon a little child;*
> *Pity my simplicity,*
> *Suffer me to come to thee.*

Sheldon thereafter took great pride in pointing out this instance of precocity. To be so thoroughly on the job at his own christening could augur nothing but good for the young James MacArthur.

The same festive atmosphere which made children respond so eagerly to Sheldon's invitations colored his entertainment of adults. Most visits with Sheldon involved a meal —luncheon, tea, or dinner—on the theory that people talk better when warmed by food and drink. It was the continued wonder of Sheldon's friends that, with the rapid extinction of cooks as a species, the playwright always commanded culinary talents of a transcendental order. The food which appeared for his guests reflected the tastes of an exacting gourmet, and the wines were the choice of a connoisseur.

Sheldon's own meals were served beforehand, since he had to be fed by an attendant, and his guests ate at a small table drawn up by his bed. But one never had the embarrassed sense of eating alone before an onlooker. While the guest ate, Sheldon would talk easily, interspersing his remarks on books or people, or whatever the subject might be, with such comments as: "I hope you like lobster with Creole sauce," or, "Tell me what you think of that Châteauneuf-du-Pape. They say it doesn't travel well, but I think it's all right."

Dinner with Sheldon always had a special luster, reminiscent of a more elegant and a more leisurely age. The little table would be set with exquisite linen, with handsome silver and crystal. Sheldon in dinner jacket, with a white carnation in his buttonhole, seemed less an invalid than ever. He might have been a distinguished actor, relaxing briefly at full length before going on stage to perform an exacting role.

Sheldon's guests entered fully into the spirit of these tête-à-têtes. Women invited for dinner, though they knew they could not be seen, wore their handsomest gowns and took pains to be elegantly groomed. Once an old friend whom Sheldon had not seen in several years was asked to dine. When the invitation was issued she inquired if there was anything special she might do for Sheldon, anything she might bring him. He promptly replied, "Yes, when you come to dinner wear all your jewels." Sheldon recalled the woman's fabulous collection of diamonds and emeralds and it delighted him to think of them in his blue-room setting. The woman complied with his request, though it involved a trip to the bank and taking the jewels out of the vault where they were usually stored. When she arrived, resplendent as an Indian potentate, Sheldon made her describe minutely each item of the glittering collection.

Cornelia Otis Skinner, whose parents were old friends of Sheldon's, never forgot her first invitation to call on him.

I had just returned from a London theatrical engagement, during which I had launched my monologue show of The Wives of Henry VIII, when the telephone rang one afternoon and a voice announced the fact that it was Edward Sheldon speaking, and would I have the graciousness to come to tea with him the following Friday and bring all six of Henry's wives along with me. In my eagerness to express my graciousness I spluttered out a jargon of incoherencies and all but dropped the receiver. He talked on for a time about my family, about the theatre, about . . . I don't remember what. I was too excited to pay close heed to the conversation. I had often heard of the disarming charm that was Ned's, but I had no idea it could radiate so tangibly over the telephone. There was a quality to his voice, husky, persuasive, humorous, and deliciously masculine, that made me catch my breath. When I hung up, I realized that my cheeks were flushed and my heart was cavorting like that of a schoolgirl who has just been dated up by the local football hero. When Friday came around I fixed myself up with a manicure and a special hairdo and, although I was fully

aware of the fact that I was to call on a blind man, I dressed
in my newest and smartest frock and put on my best im-
ported gloves. I was to find out later that this was quite customary behaviour for the ladies who called on Ned. For a
date with Ned was always a date in every anticipatory feminine sense of the word. Comparing notes with Margaret Ayer
Barnes and others, I learned that whenever they dined there,
they too always wore their most becoming evening clothes.
Dinner with Ned was a charming and gala affair, which
called for charming and gala attire; and while I never knew
him to ask me what I happened to be wearing, I had the
feeling that he was pleased to hear the swish of a long skirt
or breathe a whiff of scent on a party handkerchief.

On the occasion of my first visit I was as yet unaware of
this aura. Although I had heard of the extraordinary way in
which Ned not only disregarded his illness, but was able to
make his friends disregard it, I still felt that I was going to see
him in the conventional capacity of a sick-bed caller. A little
apprehensively I walked to 35 East 84th Street, where the
doorman informed me that Mr. Sheldon was expecting me
and indicated the way to an elevator, whose operator also
informed me that Mr. Sheldon was expecting me and that
he was to take me directly up to the penthouse. There was
always a certain ceremoniousness about one's visits to Ned,
which was part of their character. Not knowing quite what
to expect, I stepped from the elevator into the tiny waiting-
room, where I stood for a few minutes feeling a little lost
and staring awkwardly at some Hogarth engravings until a
nurse appeared from somewhere and opened the double
doors that led to a warm, book-filled, ample room which was
to become so happily familiar. The light of a wood fire
danced on the bindings of countless books and the glass of
numerous framed photographs, through the long windows
the New York skyline sparkled against a paling sky, and on
the terrace outside, some of Ned's homing pigeons were
fluttering down to their sanctuaries. A table set for tea stood
before a comfortable armchair, which was drawn up beside

a large daybed in the middle of the room. And on the daybed was Ned, lying utterly motionless, but extraordinarily
alive. He was as always meticulously groomed, and the small
black mask which bound his eyes formed a dramatic contrast
to his handsome face, which was glowing and sunburned. He
was like some sort of vitally exciting King Amfortas confined
less to a bed of pain than to a classic poet's banquet couch.
And from that moment Ned's physical handicaps never, as
long as I was in his presence, occurred to me. He saw to it,
of course, that they never did . . . neither to me nor to
anyone, for I have yet to talk with anyone with whom Edward Sheldon ever discussed his malady.

Only the highest degree of organization made it possible
to keep the busy varied life of the blue room running
smoothly. But efficiency had always been one of Sheldon's
notable traits. As a small boy he had been orderly in his
habits, and at Harvard his powers of co-ordination had enabled him to do twice as much as the average student. In
his professional career he had demonstrated the same quality.
His prodigious output and full social life were possible only
because he knew so well how to eliminate waste in time
and energy and make every moment count.

The elaborate mechanism of his invalid's existence was
run in the same fashion. Even with an expert staff, it took
genuine executive ability to ensure the smooth functioning
of the Eighty-fourth Street household. Sheldon was an exacting master, and he never allowed anyone to forget that he
was the master. Members of his staff always referred to the
establishment as "we." Once in a while when Sheldon had
ordered some rare and costly delicacy for a guest, or a lavish
gift for an approaching birthday, someone would say, "But
we really oughtn't to pay so much. . . ." Sheldon would
cry out, "I'll have you remember it's *my* money, and I'll
spend it as I please!"

It was no sinecure to be attached to Sheldon's staff. He issued orders briefly and precisely, and he was uncannily aware of any lapse in the performance of duties. But if he was exacting in his demands, his appreciation of a task well done, his understanding and sympathy and his unfailing good humor took the edge off the most disagreeable chores. There were of course standing jokes in the household. Mrs. Grey, the night nurse, always tidied up meticulously when she went off duty in the early morning—and Sheldon would frequently accuse her of sweeping chicken bones and crusts under the bed. And when sounds of temper emerged from the kitchen indicating some altercation between the red-headed cook and other members of the staff, Sheldon would call out, "Leave the door open so I can enjoy the fight! I'm betting on Catherine!"

CHAPTER X

Playwrights' Playwright

WHEN Anne Parrish asked Sheldon why he stopped writing plays after 1930 he replied briefly, "You *must* see a play in rehearsal to have it right." This was true so far as it went, but it did not tell the whole story. In the first place Sheldon had already shown that he could write for the stage without going near the theatre. Two hits, *Lulu Belle* and *Dishonored Lady*, proved that his talent had not suffered in the years since he had been bedridden. Moreover, even after 1930 playwriting continued to absorb him. But his attitude toward it had changed. Before losing his sight, he still found some satisfaction in the personal rewards of authorship; after that he was only interested in what he could do to further the work of other writers.

There were dramatic examples of this generosity. Some of these leaked out, despite everything Sheldon could do to prevent it, but far more were never revealed. Professor Quinn in a note on Sheldon in *Representative American Plays* stated:

> It would be violation of confidence to record here the many instances in which Sheldon has been the unacknowledged collaborator with other playwrights or has adapted from other literature plays which have made wide popular appeal. . . . But if the truth were really known, he would

be more fully recognized not only as a playwright of original-
ity, but also as one who has inspired actors of prominence by
providing them with plays which revealed to them and the
public talents that otherwise might have been unsuspected.

No one knows the extent of his contributions to Broadway productions between 1930 and 1946. But it is safe to
say that there was no season during those years which did
not see at least one play in which he had some part, and frequently two or three. Absolute anonymity was always a
condition of any help he gave another playwright, and the
avoidance of all publicity after his illness set in was almost
a mania. But the theatre does not keep secrets as a rule, and
a good deal has come to light since Sheldon's death. There
are still writers who have hesitated to acknowledge his part
in their work. But from the number of those who have freely
and proudly admitted their debt, it is possible to see the
scope of his influence.

To playwrights, as to his fellow humans in general,
Sheldon was, as Anne Lindbergh has said, "the creative observer." With regard to his work in the theatre, he was also
"the creative listener." During Sheldon's lifetime, Barrett
Clark pointed this out. "Important as his early plays were
and much as our contemporaries of today owe to their influence, it is the man whose sympathy and enthusiasm and
advice reach out in all directions, whose mind is constantly
alert to catch the overtones of writers and actors, many of
whom carry to him their problems and their hopes—it is
this man, I say, who is in a way our ideal audience, our
sounding-board, the man of whom we may always be sure
that he is listening." And because he was always listening,
with his vast knowledge of the theatre, his mastery of dramatic technique, his sharp perception of human nature, when

he reached out a helping hand the effects were almost miraculous. Barrett Clark expressed the general attitude when he spoke of Sheldon as "this demi-god of the theatre."

Playwriting was not only an end in itself to him. Often enough it was a means to something else, even to the moral and spiritual salvation of an individual. To many a desperate fellow writer passing through a barren period in his work, to a man or woman on the threshold of alcoholism or even of suicide because of an unhappy love affair, to someone facing an apparently insoluble personal problem, he would say, "Come, let's do a play together. What about a plot like this?" And with scarcely a pause he would begin to discuss a situation, sketch in a character, throw out a bit of dialogue. To the watcher the process of his invention was infectious, especially with the radiating warmth and light of the personality behind it. It was rare indeed that something did not happen to make the destructive impulse give way to that thrilling sense of creation which Sheldon could kindle in anybody.

Much as he delighted to work with an accomplished and experienced playwright, there was an intense personal fulfillment in bringing new talents to light. The case of Margaret Ayer Barnes is conspicuous but not unique. Sheldon believed firmly that every life had drama in it, that anyone with intelligence and a normal endowment of imagination could write a play. This may have been an overoptimistic gauge of the creative powers of the average individual, yet the history of the theatre tends to confirm the theory. It may be less true today than it was twenty-five or thirty years ago, but it is still surprising how many of the plays which reach Broadway are the work of people with little or no experience of the theatre and with the most unlikely backgrounds. So far as Sheldon was concerned, the playwright's essential material was life itself, and his chances of success were in proportion to the intensity of his own emotional experiences. The writing techniques could be taught. He was not concerned with the drama as literature; that belonged in the province of high genius. He was interested first of all in workmanlike plays that entertained. His own skill in converting even trivial or hackneyed situations into actable, and salable, theatre material was so sure that he could make the veriest novice produce results.

He was a born teacher. He saw clearly what the final goal must be, yet he knew well (as so few professional teachers can ever remember) how little the beginner has to work with. No one who wanted to write was considered too embryonic. "A dramatist must start somewhere," he would say. During the sessions of playmaking his delicate tact and understanding prevented the beginner from feeling overwhelmed by a sense of inferiority to his guiding spirit. There was never any letdown in his confidence in the venture. There were always words of praise at strategic moments, a constant flow of concrete suggestions—and through it all a shining thread of humor.

A Harvard friend and poet, Norreys Jephson O'Conor, wanted to try his hand with a play. "Ned's sympathy and understanding were shown when I mentioned my aspirations; he never laughed at my fumblings, but always gave me the feeling that I might eventually succeed. I remember outlining a crude idea for a melodrama, and Ned's amused comment that there were one or two crimes that I had not included."

When one young playwright who had floundered in discouragement at last had a play accepted, Sheldon wrote, before the tryout, not merely congratulations but advice for making the most of his opportunity.

> *I am very glad you are getting a production, chiefly because it ought to reveal any faults in the play and indicate to you how they are to be remedied. I know you will make the most of this opportunity. Watch carefully, note the reaction of the audience and don't worry. Then when it is all over, quietly sit down at your typewriter and fill up all the holes. Meanwhile, don't be surprised when you discover the holes. I think they can all be plugged. . . .*

Any friend of Sheldon's who evinced the slightest interest in playwriting would be urged to go to work immediately, with Sheldon working at his side. George Brewer, a young friend with whom he was particularly congenial, once mentioned an idea that someone might make into a play. Sheldon assured him that *he* was the one to make it, and made him begin then and there. He entered into the project with all the zest and determination he would have put into a play of his own. In this particular case he was on ground poignantly familiar. The theme of Brewer's play was that of a young woman facing blindness and death. But any reminders of his own situation were lost in his complete absorption in the work.

The play reached Broadway under the title *Dark Victory*, with Tallulah Bankhead in the leading role. Its run was brief, but it was later made into a successful motion picture, thus justifying Sheldon's faith in the original idea and, more important, in his friend's talent.

No day went by when some problem relating to the theatre was not presented to him. Sometimes it was a question of production—the right star for a certain play, the best supporting actor, advice about managers and directors. But most frequent were the requests for help in playwriting.

> Could you run through this book and then tell me how
> you think it would play? . . .
> I have a play on Emily Brontë. Would you look at it and
> see if it is really any good? . . .
> Does the following scenario listen like a good drama plot
> to you? Two brothers . . .
> You once asked me why I didn't adapt some of the old
> English classics. Had you one in mind? Could you send me
> a list of any you think likely? . . .

There were endless letters of gratitude for help or advice
that had been given.

> Thank you for listening to my story. I can see now how
> it drops. . . .
> Very well, I'll get the Roughead books and read them
> for a suggested plot. . . .
> All right. As you suggest I'm making the scenario before
> tackling the job. . . .
> You're right. I do write better from character to plot
> rather than from plot to character. . . .
> Yes, you are perfectly right. As you say, the play slows up
> occasionally, and does need a great deal of cutting. . . .

And there were always letters that struck the note of
the following:

> The store of energy I took away from your talk is still
> with me. I realize that my first writing of the play had been
> done without enough discrimination. I had accepted too
> readily the things which came first to mind. Your digging into
> the soil of the play exposed its roots to me. I have all your
> notes at my elbow—notes which I took while you talked that
> memorable afternoon. . . .

Even when no concrete results were forthcoming (which
was rare), to discuss a play with Sheldon was an exhilarating
experience. His very stillness, the look of intense concentration on his face as he followed a reading gave the writer

a sense of achievement which, as many have testified, even the applause of a full theatre later on did not match. If there was a pause in the reading, Sheldon would cry out, "No, no! Don't stop there. You can have some water when we finish the act." There was no disguising his eagerness, his alert anticipation of the plot development. To the playwright seeking an opinion of the "holding" quality of his work, this spoke volumes.

But it was in the technical discussion, the actual criticism of the piece after it had been read, that the full effect of Sheldon's genius was felt. The richness of his imagination would be revealed in his notes (carried of course in his head) on undeveloped possibilities of characterization. His knowledge of stagecraft, his sense of dramatic coloring would flash out in quick suggestions for dialogue and business. Presented with the barest outline of a plot, he could sense its possibilities at once, tell if it were fundamentally sound. Any flimsiness of structure or padding, even when disguised with clever and amusing dialogue, would be mercilessly pounced upon.

Nothing so clearly showed Sheldon's mastery of his craft as his flawless sense of timing—that uncanny ability to gauge the interval between a cause and a desired effect on the stage. He owed this in part to his keen understanding of the actor's art, which so many playwrights lack. He knew that building an effect was not a matter of logic, but of cumulative emotion. How far must a situation be carried so as to produce a real tug at the heart, before it lapses into bathos? What is the point at which to end a comic scene so that it will produce a belly laugh, beyond which there will only be a nervous titter? Sheldon would continually suggest changes to quicken the movement, or to hold it back so as to take full advantage of the emotions that had been building up.

He could often visualize complete scenes more fully and more precisely than the author himself, keeping every detail sharply fixed in his photographic memory. "Now in Act II, scene 3, there is a false note. . . . Switch Mary's entrance back to scene 3 in Act I—she would be much more effective there. Why not save that 'son-of-a' exclamation for the climax of Act II where it would count for more? . . . That weak spot just before the Act II curtain needs strengthening. . . . I think the dialogue in Act I is eating up the action. . . ."

It was not only the ambitious beginner who came to him for advice and was stimulated by the play of his imagination. Cornelia Otis Skinner was already launched on a successful career as a monologist when she first met Sheldon and had revealed her ability as a dramatic writer in *The Wives of Henry VIII* and other sketches. But as her acquaintance with the playwright warmed to friendship she regularly went to him for help and advice in developing new material. She tells of "evenings of concentrated work" spent with him, of how "Ned helped me, as he did all his friends who wrote for the theatre, immeasurably with all my monologue solo dramas, to the point where it was almost a case of pure collaboration, although he would never let me give him public credit for his share in their creation. . . ."

Although he was usually content to let writers find their way to him, once in a while he would take the initiative to cultivate someone who had attracted his interest. Such was the case with Elizabeth Ginty, a Broadway figure whom for some reason or other he had never met in his physically active days in the theatre. Miss Ginty, almost a creature of

legend herself, had been David Belasco's secretary and girl-
of-all-work. There was a general idea around Times Square
that she had even written some of Belasco's best plays, although she stoutly denied this. Big-boned, big-hearted, Miss
Ginty was a woman of intense loyalties and hot dislikes. She
had a reputation for picturesque speech. "That dirthy dog!"
was the mildest epithet directed at anyone who did not see
eye to eye with Belasco, her beloved "Governor," or with
Edward Sheldon who held second place in her idolatry.

At Christmas in 1925 she received the following telegram:

> DEAR MISS GINTY: I HAVE WANTED TO MEET YOU FOR A
> VERY LONG TIME. I WONDER IF YOU WOULD COME AND EAT
> A VERY SMALL PIECE OF MINCE PIE ETC. NEXT SUNDAY AT
> HALF PAST SEVEN. MY ADDRESS IS THIRTY-FIVE EAST EIGHTY-
> FOURTH STREET. CHRISTMAS GREETINGS.
>
> EDWARD SHELDON

Miss Ginty had never forgotten the sound of Sheldon's
voice which she had once heard backstage at the Belasco
Theatre, and the invitation produced the usual effect of
such summonses. She was tremulous with expectation as she
rode up in the elevator to the penthouse, and the evening
was passed in a glow of enchantment.

Sheldon was soon the confidant in both her professional
and her domestic affairs. She was a lonely woman, and he
was glad when she finally acquired a large, handsome cat.
The animal was christened Edward Sheldon, permission
having been graciously given by the namesake. "But you
must promise to send him to Harvard," Sheldon stipulated,
to which Miss Ginty solemnly agreed. The exploits of Edward supplied the friends with a theme for continuous
discussion over several years. Plans for the Harvard educa-

tion were seriously threatened when Edward once, in a moment of heedless abandon, ripped the Ginty upholstery to pieces. His mistress then decided that he needed the discipline of a military school, a plan which Sheldon agreed to take under advisement pending possible reform on the part of the miscreant.

Next to Belasco, Sheldon came to occupy the chief place in Miss Ginty's heart. "They are my two gods," she would say with finality. Sheldon, who regretted her rugged disbelief in any deity besides Mr. Belasco or himself, had long talks with her on this subject. Life had always seemed a very chancy affair to Miss Ginty, and once when she expressed a particularly fatalistic view Sheldon burst out vehemently, "But, Elizabeth, there *must* be some pattern to your life!" When Belasco died in 1931 and the principal anchor of her existence was gone, Sheldon was the person who best understood her loss. She treasured always the telegrams he sent her at the time and during the hard months following.

> ALL MY THOUGHTS DEAR ELIZABETH. IF ANYTHING CAN COMFORT YOU IT MUST BE THE REMEMBRANCE OF HOW MUCH YOU DID FOR HIM. MEANWHILE MY DEVOTED AFFECTION. NED.

> ELIZABETH DEAR: I WOULD BE SITTING RIGHT BESIDE YOU THIS MINUTE IF I COULD MANAGE IT. MY LOVE TO YOU ALWAYS. PLEASE SLEEP TONIGHT. NED.

Sheldon kept a close ear to her comings and goings, and no circumstance of her life failed to evoke some sign of his interest. When she sought distraction after Belasco's death by moving into a new apartment Sheldon wired:

> I AM THINKING OF YOU IN YOUR NEW HOME. PLEASE DON'T GET TIRED MOVING AROUND FURNITURE. LOVE ALWAYS. NED.

On Belasco's birthday, for many years celebrated by a gathering of his friends, Ned always sent her a telegram.

The producer's death had one fortunate result for Miss Ginty; it removed the great shadow which had hidden her own talent for so long. Soon Sheldon persuaded her to let him see her work, and she made the most of his advice and criticism. Ned knew that he was dealing with no tyro, but a woman as wise in ways of the theatre as he himself. Though he treated her writing with respect, keeping always to the fore his confidence in her ability, he could be ruthless in his comment. "But, Elizabeth, this sounds like an *obituary*," he said once, referring to a bit of dialogue which the author herself rather fancied. In returning to her the draft of a play on Queen Elizabeth he wrote seven pages of detailed criticism of which the concluding paragraphs are a fair specimen:

> Scene 2, dear Elizabeth, I think you have fallen flat on your face. The only good thing is the Tillbury speech, but there is no build-up for it at all. I know to my boots that your treatment of scenes 2 and 3 just won't do. You are making such a ghastly mistake in not having Dudley dead. To hell with dates. If Schiller, Drinkwater, Shakespeare and Maxwell Anderson can take enormous historical liberties, I don't see why you can't take this tiny one. Particularly as it ruins your scene if you don't. But, if you want to be outrageously obstinate on this point—which I deeply deplore—then for God's sake get a living Dudley into the scene. . . . Give Elizabeth something to do. At present she has nothing. . . . And I know, too, that you will never be able to add anything, humanly or dramatically, to that last picture of Dudley going out and leaving Essex behind. . . . I know you could do something unforgettable and heartbreakingly beautiful in the way of a curtain. Both the scene and the play need this.

"Plaisir d'amour ne dure qu'un moment,
Chagrin d'amour . . ."

Well, there you have my impressions, dear Elizabeth. Be patient with them and with me. I look forward to Sunday evening.

Queen Elizabeth was never produced, but Elizabeth Ginty came into her own in 1939 with *Missouri Legend*, a play about Jesse James. Sheldon was fascinated with the Jekyll-Hyde personality of James, the successful outlaw who was also a pious member of the local missionary society. He supplied many details to point up the hero's character. With young José Ferrer and Lillian Gish in the leading roles, *Missouri Legend* was a vigorously original contribution to the 1939 season.

Another writing career in which Sheldon played a major part was that of Ruth Gordon. When the actress lost her first husband in 1927 Sheldon sent her a telegram in the pattern which had now become familiar to his friends:

> DEAR MISS GORDON: I AM THINKING ABOUT YOUR DAYS IN THE PRESBYTERIAN HOSPITAL IN CHICAGO AND YOUR HUSBAND'S VERY EXTRAORDINARY TENDERNESS AND DEVOTION IN TAKING CARE OF YOU. IT MAKES ME FEEL VERY SORRY FOR YOU. I HOPE SOMETIME WHEN YOU FEEL LIKE IT YOU WILL COME UP TO SEE ME. MEANWHILE MY EVERY THOUGHT AND SYMPATHY.

Two years later, when he learned that Miss Gordon, who had achieved a brilliant success as an actress, had begun to write, the general invitation became more explicit:

> DEAR MISS GORDON: WILL YOU DINE WITH ME SATURDAY THE FOURTH AT SEVEN THIRTY AND BRING YOUR COLLECTED WORKS. I NEED SOME GOOD SERIOUS READING.
>
> EDWARD SHELDON

Miss Gordon accepted the invitation and brought with her a play on which she was working. Sheldon listened intently as always, commented encouragingly, and gave the author the definite feeling that, whatever might be the fate of the work in hand, she *could* write. Fifteen years later Sheldon's faith was justified. When Miss Gordon's *Over Twenty-one* became one of the hits of the 1942 season, on the night of the opening in Detroit he wired:

> DEAREST RUTH: DISAPPOINTED NOT HEARING PLAY BUT YOU WILL READ IT TO ME LATER. LOOK FOR ME IN THE FRONT ROW TONIGHT. YOUR AFFECTIONATE NED.

Some time after this Miss Gordon had a dinner appointment with Sheldon. That evening she felt tired and out of sorts, anything but a stimulating dinner guest. As she was about to leave for Sheldon's apartment she recalled her amusement recently in rereading a girlhood diary. She thought that perhaps Ned would get a smile or two from her adolescent pinings for a theatrical career, and she took the diary along with her.

Sheldon not only smiled, he roared with laughter at Miss Gordon's picture of the emerging artistic temperament against the unsuspecting background of Wollaston, Massachusetts, most particularly at the hopeless bewilderment of Mr. and Mrs. Jones in trying to deal with the problem of a stage-struck daughter. He saw at once that here was material for a most humanly appealing play, and the public agreed with him when *Years Ago* at last opened on Broadway, with Patricia Kirkland playing Miss Gordon and Fredric March in the role of her distracted father.

Sheldon felt a special responsibility for this play, and kept at the author's elbow throughout the writing. He supplied valuable suggestions for building the character of the gymnastics teacher brought in by the parents to divert their erring daughter from the lure of the footlights, and "sew her up tight in the physical culture bag." He wrote detailed advice for intensifying the climax of the play, particularly for the girl's "outburst of defiance and protest against all the frustrations of her life—past, present and future—which ought to equal St. Joan's outburst against imprisonment in the scene of her trial." Those who saw the play will recall the effectiveness of this speech in mellowing the stern father, bringing back to him little by little his own stage-struck youth.

Writers often feel that it is dangerous to discuss their work in process. Ideas tend to slip out of focus, lose their original meaning, or evaporate entirely when subjected to the views of somebody else. Sometimes the writing impulse itself is weakened if one's story or play does not arouse immediate enthusiasm in the other person. But with Sheldon it was otherwise. Thornton Wilder's experience was that of all the writers who knew him. "With Ned you never lost a play, or tried to capture an audience, but *shared* a thing in a state of growth."

Sheldon's genius for friendship was shown by his ability to put himself completely in the position of the other person. In the case of Wilder this required little effort. From the beginning the two men spoke a common language and shared a common philosophy of life. Late one summer Wilder wrote Ned:

> September's not far off. Save an evening for me, sir, about the 7th or 8th, because through all the diversity and spotti-ness and intermittence, I need to count more and more on the fixed and constant and unshakable friends, of which rare commodity you are the Prince and high example. And it is with that kind of dependence I sign myself
>
> Your friend,
> THORNTON

Although Wilder's novel *The Bridge of San Luis Rey* had won him a Pulitzer prize, his efforts at playwriting prior to 1937 had met with indifferent success. Early that year he took a rough draft of *Our Town* to Sheldon. There was no interruption during the reading, and when it was finished there was silence—that long, almost breathless silence familiar to everyone who ever read a manuscript to Sheldon. One knew that behind the masked eyes the whole piece was being recapitulated visually, scene by scene to the final climax, and that the effect was being weighed and measured. This time the pause was unusually prolonged. When Sheldon at last spoke it was clear that Wilder's play had given him a new kind of dramatic experience for which he could find no ready expression. But it was obvious that he was greatly excited, not merely by the poignant truth of Wilder's story but by the technical ingenuity of its presentation. A day or two later he elaborated on this in a note to the author:

> . . . You broke every rule. There is no suspense, no relationship between the acts, no progress; but every seven minutes—no, every five minutes—you've supplied a new thing—some novelty—in the proceedings, which is at once a pleasure in the experience, and, at the same time, a contribution to the content of the play. Most plays progress in time, but here is a progression in depth. Let us know this town more and more!

Wilder took the manuscript to Europe with him and discussion continued by correspondence. In midsummer he wrote from Zurich:

> Dear Ned, joy of your friends:
> Yes, I took your advice, and it's all working out finely. Before we see Emily Gibbs in the Elysian Fields on the hill above Grovers Corners, New Hampshire, we have the whole second act about her wedding and what led up to it; we know a lot about her and I think we love her. . . .

The play that had "broken every rule" was one of the major dramatic works of the decade in which it appeared. It had a great popular success and marked Wilder at once as one of the country's foremost playwrights. Confident of the public's willingness to accept him on his own merits, Wilder at once began another play, even more unorthodox than *Our Town*. He wrote Sheldon in the autumn of 1941:

> Here I am in New York suddenly for broadcast rehearsals! But I'm looking forward to the time when I can ask to come and see you and combine a report to you on the English trip with a reading of Act II of The Skin of Our Teeth.

Few plays at whose emergence Sheldon had assisted moved him more deeply than *The Skin of Our Teeth*. Its theme of man's inevitable upward growth, in defiance of all natural cataclysms and falterings of the human heart, was the bedrock of his own credo. Naturally he was eager to know how producers would look upon it, and he was as apprehensive as Wilder when the first reports came in. A letter from the author in February, 1942, was not encouraging:

> . . . We begin to get reactions on the play. And to my consternation arrived word that it was "defeatist," "pacifist" and "anti-war."
>
> Apparently through New England "tightness" and dread of preachiness, I had understated or smothered all the implications that were real to me: man's spiral progress and his progression through trial and error.
>
> We sent it to X [a distinguished actor-director] for his direction, and, we hoped, his performance, and he telegraphed back, "The play is brilliant, original, profound, and very funny too, but it troubles me. Am writing." Five days have gone by and no letter has come.
>
> So I went to work and rewrote the third act, modifying also some of the bolder of the theatric novelties, and perhaps

attenuating some of the legitimate "hardness" of the *Welt-anschauung*.

I also came upon the fact that Act II, whose subject is a homage to marriage and the home . . . lacked any moment of the congenialities possible to the family situation; the children were represented as purely exasperating and the mother as nagging. So that was altered. So I hope that now there's a text that won't repel readers and auditors. . . .

Whatever misgivings Wilder may have had were wiped out in the reception of the play both in America and in Europe. Its tremendous success proved that it was not only absorbing entertainment, but that it had a message which a world in the midst of catastrophe was eager to hear. To Sheldon all this was deeply significant. *The Skin of Our Teeth* added to his friend's stature as an artist and at the same time showed that the principle in which his own life was rooted had universal meaning.

Wilder commemorated his friendship with Sheldon in *The Ides of March* which appeared in 1948. The novel, Wilder's first in a dozen years, was described by the author as "a phantasia on certain events and persons of the last days of the Roman Republic." The story is told in a series of letters from and about Julius Caesar. It presents an original and sympathetic concept of the dictator's character against a richly living background of Roman life of the times. One figure in the novel, the keeper, as it were, of Caesar's conscience, is the wise and noble Lucius Mamilius Turrinus, an invalid living in retirement on Capri. Sheldon's friends had no difficulty in recognizing the prototype of Turrinus.

The Ides of March has a dual dedication. The first part is to Lauro de Bosis, Roman poet and aviator, who was killed resisting Fascism. The second part is to

EDWARD SHELDON
who though immobile and blind
for over twenty years
was the dispenser of wisdom,
courage, and gaiety
to a large number of people

In 1928 when Jane Cowl was appearing in *The Road to Rome* she brought the author, Robert E. Sherwood, to see Sheldon. The two men were friends from that evening, and thereafter the blue room above Eighty-fourth Street was for Sherwood, as for Wilder and so many others, a proving ground for ideas and plays. Sheldon watched the younger playwright throughout the years of his growth, as he progressed from the lightly satirical *The Queen's Husband* and *Reunion in Vienna* to works like *The Petrified Forest* and *Idiot's Delight* which probed sharply at the sore spots of contemporary civilization. Alan Squier, the sensitive, defeated hero of *The Petrified Forest*, was a type Sheldon knew well. Many of his fellows had come to the penthouse for light and guidance in finding their way through the murk of moral uncertainty that had engulfed the modern world. Sheldon felt that it was not the world but the individual who was at fault, and many of Squier's lost generation found moorings again in his teaching and example. But there were plenty of others, as Sheldon sadly realized, who could only drift into oblivion like Sherwood's hero.

The night *The Petrified Forest* opened, the author dined with his chief critic. The discussion turned on the very problems treated in the play. Sherwood was so lost in the talk that he forgot all about the play which at that very moment was on trial, until at ten-thirty Sheldon reminded him that he ought to check in at the theatre to see how it was faring.

With the explosive *Idiot's Delight*, Sherwood's pessimism seemed to have found its lowest point, and he began to turn his thoughts toward the positive values in American life. While *Idiot's Delight* was still playing he wrote Sheldon:

> I'm very anxious to talk with you about the "Young Lincoln" idea, and would like to come up to see you whenever convenient. *The play is to be based on Sandburg's Prairie Years,* starting with the Rutledge Tavern in New Salem, and ending with Lincoln's departure from his home in Springfield for Washington and the Civil War and death and immortality. . . . Please let me know when I can see you.

There were many meetings over *Abe Lincoln in Illinois.* Each step of the play was submitted to Sheldon's judgment, and there was detailed discussion all along the way. Finally the completed manuscript was read aloud. Although Sheldon already knew it well, he listened with rapt attention, swept along by the steadily rising wave of feeling that culminated in the noble cadences of Lincoln's farewell speech to his Springfield neighbors. Aside from its indisputable merits as dramatic writing, *Abe Lincoln in Illinois* expressed something that was now filling Sheldon's own thoughts. Although this was in 1937—a year before Munich—he saw clearly the direction in which events were moving. He was sure that America would eventually be faced with a war for survival, and that the outcome would depend as much on the spiritual weapons at her disposal as on the guns, planes, and tanks that she had not even yet begun to think about. What moved him most profoundly in Sherwood's portrait of Lincoln was its stirring justification of the American ideal of peace and good will—stirring enough to make people want to fight for it when the time came.

The second World War brought a halt to Sherwood's visits to Eighty-fourth Street. From Broadway he moved to the White House, from playwriting to speech writing for President Roosevelt. The thousands who had filled theatres to see his plays now became millions who listened to the pungent phrases and dramatic climaxes that went out in the President's voice through the White House microphone. Ned Sheldon, whose radio during those years was tuned to every development in world affairs, was immensely proud of the role played by his friend. He was also gratified that the dramatist as such had come into his own as a public servant. Sheldon had great respect for President Roosevelt's talent as an actor, and he realized how important this had been in keeping America emotionally united during the war years. It seemed highly fitting and a mark of judgment that the President should have used the services of one of the country's major playwrights.

Perhaps indirectly Sheldon also served, through his influence on Sherwood's mind and work during the long years of their friendship. His modesty would have been affronted at the suggestion. But Sherwood himself, speaking of these years, once declared, "I always felt close to him and benefited by the thought of him, and I console myself by feeling sure that he knew it."

CHAPTER XI

Dante and Virgil

THE life of John Barrymore was a tangle of inconsistencies in which tragedy, buffoonery, recurrent marriage and divorce, opulence, bankruptcy, and great art were somehow tied together. But through it all for thirty-five years ran one clear bright strand—his friendship with Ned Sheldon. On the surface theirs was a curious and sometimes incomprehensible relationship. But it had powerful roots. No one ever stood in greater need of Sheldon's gift of human understanding than did John Barrymore; and no one ever received it in fuller measure.

As young men they had been drawn together by congenial tastes and a passionate curiosity about life. They saw the world and their own adventures in the same rich, highly colored tones. Both were romantics, but not to the same point. They were convinced that reality could be shaped pretty much to their own desires if they went about it in the right way. It was in the way they went about it that they differed.

In the first days of his prosperity Barrymore set up housekeeping in a Greenwich Village apartment which was a mélange of medieval austerity and Oriental pomp. To create a retreat from the pressures of city life he built a garden on

226

the rooftop, hauling up tons of earth for the purpose. Unfortunately the house was not a modern steel-framed structure and the roof threatened to collapse under the weight. When Barrymore discovered this he moved to other quarters, leaving the owner of the building to cope with the effects of his fantasy.

Sheldon also gave free reign to his decorative impulses in his apartment on Gramercy Park. The brilliantly plumaged macaws which briefly adorned his dining room were supposed to give a dash of "live" color. This they did, until they began to molt out of season. Ned realized then that the birds would not flourish in a purely ornamental capacity. So he found suitable homes for them elsewhere and contented himself with hanging pictures on the walls.

In his love of the picturesque, in his reliance on instinct and feeling in meeting the critical issues of life, Sheldon certainly showed his romantic nature. But he learned early how to compromise with reality. When somebody asked him why in his play *Romance* he made Cavallini and Tom Armstrong go their separate ways in the end, he exclaimed, "But they couldn't possibly have been happy together—forever! They had a beautiful dream, and no one could take that away from them. But life was something else." Ned's romanticism always had a certain aesthetic quality; it served to soften and idealize the crudities of existence without ever obscuring the basic facts. Consequently he never faced the kind of disillusionment that dogged Barrymore always. For Barrymore believed to the end that the romantic dream was valid.

Ned knew why this was. Barrymore had grown up in a world of total insecurity—emotional, financial, and moral. It was a situation all too familiar in theatrical families, but in the Drew-Barrymore ménage it was aggravated by conflicting temperaments. There was plenty of excitement in the early lives of the Barrymore children, but too little satisfaction of their emotional needs; and this affected the course of all their lives, Lionel's and Ethel's as well as John's. In the case of John the lack was critical. Underneath the mask of devil-may-care cynicism there was a tender dreamer, and behind the dreamer a lost child.

Throughout the years Sheldon's affection was Barrymore's chief anchor in normal life. He looked upon Sheldon not only as someone with whom he could share his fun, but also as one on whose understanding and unselfish interest he could always count. Though Barrymore was five years older, his attitude toward Ned was that of a son to a far-seeing and always forgiving father.

Jack's career was one of Sheldon's major preoccupations. When the two first met Barrymore was simply a talented light comedian who had taken to acting as a line of least resistance. It was the thing his family had always done. Ned knew from the outset that he had the potentialities of real greatness in him. Lionel Barrymore put this categorically in *We Barrymores:*

> The influence that made Jack dissatisfied with his performance as an amiable comedian was one man, Edward Sheldon. Ned saw, and was the first to see, the possibilities of Jack Barrymore as an interpretive dramatic actor. To understand the real depth of that perception, you must realize that, in addition to the irresponsibilities that marked all his appearances, his drinking and his other eccentricities, Jack did not then have a full rounded voice, and his diction was slovenly. But Ned Sheldon saw through to something, the real something, whatever it is, that we call genius, and he set about to develop it in Jack.

Over a period of several years a number of Barrymore's closest friends banded themselves together as "The Barrymore Board of Regents" for the purpose of protecting him both from the harpies, male and female, always ready to take advantage of his susceptible nature, and from himself. This "Board" consisted of Sheldon, Constance Collier, Arthur Hopkins, Alexander Woollcott, Robert Edmond Jones, and Jones's wife, Margaret Carrington. Along with Sheldon, Margaret Carrington was a vital agent in Barrymore's development. It was this extraordinary woman who took his harsh, rather unpleasant rasping voice and rebuilt it into a sensitive instrument capable of revealing the essential spirit of the man, and magnificently adapted to express the subtlest nuances of poetry.

Sheldon was already bedridden when Barrymore achieved the peak of his success in *Hamlet*, both in New York and London. But one can imagine that the triumph of his friend (which was also a triumph of his own intuitive judgment) helped to soften the blow of his personal tragedy. There were further triumphs, and Ned shared these too; but it was in the increasing chaos of Barrymore's domestic life that his steadying hand was most felt. Whenever he was in New York, Barrymore and his current wife were often at Ned's bedside. In California or elsewhere there were constant letters, telegrams, and telephone calls to keep Sheldon abreast of developments, usually in anticipation of his help in ironing out some problem.

In 1928 Barrymore was writing frequently about the hopelessness of his domestic life and, in the process of finding a way out of the complex maze, he made several trips to New York. Invariably his first stop was at Eighty-fourth Street. His companion on these visits was his pet monkey

Clementine, who, judging by the following communication, received the same thoughtful attention from Sheldon as did her master:

> *Dear, dear Uncle Ned:*
>
> *I enjoyed the beautiful grapes very much and ate them one at a time. I was the more grateful for them as I am rather lonely at present, my father being such a business man—though not liking same very much, as I can hear him saying things to himself in the next room which no maiden monkey should hear. I have a feeling I shall get used to it in time, and also when he is not a business man he can be very pleasant and takes me out much more, and gives me a bath with eau de cologne, though why I cannot imagine, and lets me sit on his head while he plays the self-player piano to himself and myself.*
>
> *I wish to again tender to you, dear Uncle Ned, my great obligations for your kindness in the matter of the grapes. I shall close now with much love and kisses.*
>
> *From your ever loving niece,*
CLEMENTINE BARRYMORE

There is little in Clementine's tone, which probably reflected her master's mood, to indicate that Barrymore was besieged by troubles at the moment. But this was the inevitable effect of the visits with Ned. One gets some idea of what these meant from a letter written a few days later en route to California:

> *Dear, dear Ned,*
>
> *It was too divine seeing you. I almost bought some dominoes before I got in the train so we could play in the compartment. You would love the porter. He is black as ink, rather stout—and has a gray pointed beard. He is a dead ringer for Othello, and has what you would call an old world courtesy. . . .*
>
> *It is too fantastic to think that after we had talked—oc-*

casionally about myself if I remember—that we had been
separated for more than a week—we felt just the same—like
a divine room in the top of the house where the sun always
comes in and where one went to play as a little boy when
one wanted to be alone.

You have no idea how much good it did talking to you.
The burrs fell out of my whiskers in clusters and must be all
over the floor. If the nurse steps on them ask her to throw
them into the fire. I never want to see them again. I am
afraid I read Lionel's play very badly. I was so tired I could
hardly see and he is banking so much on your liking it. I
had millions of other things to ask you, but they will keep
till the next time, as no one else but you gets them.

Diana is adorable, and the three of us will have such fun
as she grows up or gets larger, as she is quite grown up
enough as she is— We are approaching the great art centre
of Chicago—where I will post this. Ever so much love, dear
Ned. It was great.

JACK

Sheldon's friendship for John Barrymore also included
Ethel and Lionel, and John's daughter by his second marriage,
Diana. Ethel Barrymore had always been an object of Ned's
passionate admiration, both as an artist and as a person. Like
her brothers, she too looked to Sheldon for professional
advice, and in times of stress she relied on him for help and
comfort. There were occasions when she was indebted to his
practical assistance in her career as an actress, and to his
kindness and strength in helping her over the rough spots of
her personal life.

Diana Barrymore shared her father's attitude toward
Sheldon. She spoke of him as "my father confessor, my
priest." She had first been taken to Sheldon's apartment by
her mother, Michael Strange, at the moment when her
parents were about to separate. Throughout the painful

process of her growing up, made especially difficult by
the stormy background of her home life, she automatically
turned to "Uncle Ned." He saw her through her first marriage to Bramwell Fletcher and their divorce. When she
made her stage debut in *The Romantic Mr. Dickens* in 1940,
Sheldon followed the proceedings with a father's hopes and
fears, keeping the young actress's real father supplied with
all details. Barrymore was at the moment on the verge of
another matrimonal disaster, and Ned was afraid that his
own troubles might cause him to overlook this momentous
event in his daughter's life. But the day the play opened Jack
let him know that Diana was on his mind:

> DEAR NED: SENT DIANA A WIRE AND MADE ARRANGEMENTS TO
> HAVE DELIVERED TO HER A BIG RED APPLE. EVER SO MUCH LOVE.
> AM FEELING FINE. YOURS,
>
> JACK

The red apple was an old Barrymore symbol. It was a
token for good luck which members of the family always
sent each other on opening nights.

Lionel Barrymore and Sheldon had a close tie in their
affection for John. The older brother generously and gratefully recognized that Ned had succeeded where his own
efforts to steady Jack's course had often failed. Lionel also
owed much to Sheldon in his own career. He never forgot
that it was Ned who had insisted on his undertaking Colonel
Ibbetson in *Peter Ibbetson* and the part of the brutal Chiaramantese brother in *The Jest*, both magnificent portrayals.
There was a further and still more personal bond between
these two. Ned understood that acting offered but limited
scope to Lionel's gifts. He recognized the seriousness of
Lionel's work in painting and music. Though he could judge
the former only by hearsay, he knew that it was a substantial
accomplishment. But he could hear Lionel's orchestral com-

positions on the radio and through recordings, and his sound musical judgment told him they were not the works of a mere dilettante.

Lionel too brought his personal life to Sheldon's bedside. When his second wife, Irene Fenwick, died on Christmas Eve, 1936, the desolate Barrymore hurried to New York. He had only a brief visit at Eighty-fourth Street but it sufficed to bring him within sight of "the end of the tunnel," as Sheldon termed it. When he arrived in Chicago on his way back to California, Lionel telegraphed:

DEAR NED: I AM BACK TO CHICAGO AND THAT MUCH NEARER GETTING BACK TO NEW YORK. I CANNOT TELL YOU HOW SWEET AND RESTFUL AND CONSOLING IT WAS TO BE EVEN THOSE FEW HOURS WITH YOU. HOME HAS CEASED TO EXIST ANYWHERE AND NEW YORK WITH YOU IN IT IS THE BEST PLACE I KNOW. ALL MY LOVE DEAR NED. I AM JUST LIVING TO GET BACK.

LIONEL

Sheldon knew that beneath the seemingly casual attitude of the Barrymores toward each other, close ties bound the brothers and their sister Ethel, that the success or ill fortune of one deeply affected the other two. In a letter to Sheldon written in June, 1928, John Barrymore gives a rare and refreshing glimpse of a happy reunion with his older brother and sister:

Dear, dear Ned:

I don't know who it was who first invented the phrase, "I have been meaning to write to you," but it was probably Adam on one of his week-ends with Lilith.

Ethel has just left, and we had a grand family reunion. Lionel came back in time to get in on it, and I think she is ever so much happier than she was, thank Heaven! It was great that she came out here and that everything went the way it did. It was like old times with the added Cromwellian accent that we were all on the wagon, which made it all much more fun and in no way impaired the hours we kept. Ethel and I went over on the boat to Catalina before Lionel got back, which she adored. She ate enormously and slept thirteen hours, which she apparently had not done in years. She also caught a fish which we ate for dinner.

Abstemiousness and good health had given Jack a new interest in work and he was full of plans.

> *The Last of Mrs. Cheyney* (which was to have been filmed), I am glad to say, is off, Lubitsch discovering that it was difficult to make an omelette with air, so I am concentrating entirely on *The Dane in the Bowl*, which I will produce early in September; also at the Greek Theatre in Berkeley. These sylvan interludes may be the precursor of better things. Lubitsch has a fine story in mind which we will do after that anyway. The hero is something like the strange man with the dogs in *When We Dead Awaken*. A lot of it will be done in the snow, which will be fun.

The same letter also introduced a new personality into Sheldon's life, whose friendship had important effects on his thinking.

> I gave Krishnamurti a letter to you yesterday. He is a charming person but rather shy. Coming through Chicago the newspapers and a lot of absurd women strewed his path with roses and hailed him as Messiah. When he came out here, De Mille was doing *King of Kings*. He happened to be there one day, and was photographed between De Mille and Harry Warner made up as J. C., with a beard that looked like Nat Wills. Krishna was telling me the story the first time we met, and said with a perfectly good Oxford accent, "I left soon after this, as I thought three Christs on the same lot was perhaps a little too much!" He is a grand little soul and I think you will adore him.
>
> Ever so much love,
> JACK

There was a certain incongruity in the fact that Barrymore, to all intents so complete a pagan, should have brought Sheldon and the young Hindu together. Yet for all his apparent cynicism the actor could sense spiritual values in others that he had not been able to possess himself. When he met Krishnamurti he detected instantly the strong identity between the young Oriental and his old friend even though in race, background, and tradition the two men were poles apart.

Krishnamurti had just emerged from a period of isolation in his Ojai Valley retreat, his mental processes and spiritual perceptions sharpened by this self-imposed discipline. His personality and teaching soon gained him a wide following, especially when he was hailed by Annie Besant, the Theosophical leader, as a new Messiah. Krishnamurti repudiated this claim, but he was convinced of the authenticity of his own direct knowledge of the Divine. He taught that the supreme authority for belief was the individual's own insight. "No one can give us truth," he asserted, "each of us for himself must discern it."

This was precisely where Sheldon had arrived. Through another kind of isolation he too had disciplined himself to look beyond the world of everyday experience to find his true being. In the young Hindu mystic he met for the first time another creature whose life was centered like his own. Traveling different roads, both men had found truth in a realm outside the narrowly circumscribed self. Krishnamurti had found his way through the age-old traditions of Oriental thought. Sheldon had reached the goal by the lonely path of suffering.

It is not surprising that the two men found at once, and without preliminaries, that they stood on common ground. After the first meeting Krishnamurti never failed to see

Sheldon whenever he was in New York. From the invalid he gained further insight into problems he was still trying to solve, and in return he introduced his new friend to the lore of Eastern mysticism. From then on Sheldon began to read and seriously study the Upanishads, the Vedanta Sutra, and other works of Indian philosophy.

Some time after their first meeting Krishnamurti was speaking in Santa Barbara. Mary Gallagher Catlin, a friend of Sheldon's, happened to be in the audience. Krishnamurti discussed "the possibility of a person rising completely above and beyond one's physical being to a serene and lofty plane, where the pains and turmoil of one's body were non-existent." Mrs. Catlin was impressed by the speaker's next remark: "And in my life I've known only one person who has been able to accomplish this—a friend in New York." "The friend in New York" could mean only Sheldon, and after the meeting Mrs. Catlin talked with Krishnamurti about him. "I had hoped," she recalled afterward, "that he could help me understand the WHY of Ned's illness; why it had to happen to him. He said that illness itself wasn't the thing of importance; what mattered—what had the highest significance was that Ned had risen above it all; that Ned was Ned."

The friendship with Krishnamurti which Sheldon owed to Barrymore was only one instance of the latter's ability to give as well as take. There were other ways in which Barrymore brought new interests into Sheldon's life and threw light on things that he had never seen. The major development of the motion picture, for instance, had taken place after Sheldon had become immobilized. Yet he had a perfect comprehension of the medium and did a good deal of work in it, both in adapting his own plays and in helping other writers with film scenarios. Much of this understanding was gained through John Barrymore who continually supplied Sheldon with details from his own Hollywood career. In 1929 he wrote Ned a letter which might serve as a footnote to the history of the screen at the critical moment in its evolution from silence to sound:

> . . . I am leaving here (Hollywood) next Friday, the 26th. I will telephone you as soon as I get in, and would love to see you in the afternoon if you haven't any other dates. It will be grand seeing you again. Everything seems to be working out all right regarding the things I was worried about. I will tell you about it Tuesday.
> . . . Will you do something for me? (N.B. It seems to me I have asked this question before.) Will you try to think of some more movies for me, ones where the talking device might possibly be used. It seems to be coming in, and apparently now is the time for me to make a killing in it.
> Something just occurred to me. Have you read recently that thing of Anatole France, I think it is called St. Julian the Hospitaler, though I am not sure. Lionel told me about it after he had been collaborating with Haig and Haig, so he may have written some of his own stuff into it; but the idea sounds great, particularly the end of it where the leper turns into the figure of Christ. I think it would be tremendously moving and beautiful, something the other people would not or could not do. The story must be monkeyed with if it is not sufficiently Chautauqua. After he leaves his wife he could think her unfaithful to him and wander over the world with that thing in his heart. When he is a hermit the animals would all adore him, and we could work in the St. Francis motive, which I have always wanted to do in the movies, preaching à la Krishnamurti to the lions and bears and rabbits and birds around him in a circle. The children are afraid of him, but after he gets in bed with the leper and he becomes Christ, one could have strange, shrill celestial

music on the movietone and beating of wings, etc., and the Christ could be sufficiently Rotarian to tell him that happiness is only found through forgiveness. As he leaves his funny little hut and the animals, which ought to be pretty good, the children could follow him, as now he is regenerated and as beautiful as God, gauze and the camera can make him.

All this sounds a little like the "Rollo" books as I write it, but I'm sure you know what I mean. In the first part of the movie he could be a flaming, sexual, vital, sardonic creature like the young man in *Sintram and His Companions*, by *De La Motte Fouquet* [sic], which Rex Ingram always wanted to do. Anyway we will talk about it when I see you.

During the next fourteen years, through fluctuating fortunes and steady physical and mental disintegration, the calls on Sheldon were frequent. Sheldon realized what was happening. He knew that the underpinnings of Barrymore's character were too frail to maintain his accomplishment in *Hamlet* or the relative steadiness in his personal life that he had known for a few brief years during his marriage to Dolores Costello. But there were no reproaches or criticisms. He made vigorous suggestions when he thought they might be effective, and he brought pressure to bear on other friends of Jack's to help him keep his head above water. Once, learning that Barrymore was paying a surprise visit to New York, at a moment when things were going particularly badly, Sheldon alerted Woollcott to meet the actor and be with him as much as possible, to steer him away from some of his more bibulous cronies. Woollcott was fond of Barrymore and would have tried to help him under any circumstances, but a request from Ned was something like a divine order. Immersed though he was in his own feverish life, he promptly pushed everything aside and for four days kept close watch over the fugitive from Hollywood. When absolute necessity prevented him from being with Barrymore himself, he saw to it that some completely trustworthy delegate could assume the task.

When other friends of Barrymore became indignant at his vagaries and increasingly undignified behavior, Sheldon said nothing. He could even burst into laughter at the clowning, off stage as well as on, which others found offensive. But there came a time when this saddened him because he knew it for what it was—Barrymore's last defense against the fate which he had so long and so wilfully antagonized.

Through his friend's efforts at matrimony Sheldon watched hopefully. He understood Barrymore's naive belief that the legality of marriage would give the emotional security he craved—and that so long as this illusion was maintained the shaky structure of his friend's life might still stand. Even during the final and most pitiable of Barrymore's attempts to find happiness in marriage, when the brilliance of his whole early achievement as an actor was almost obliterated under a cloud of ridicule, Sheldon stood by, gravely concerned but ever-sympathetic. When Barrymore and his fourth wife (for whom the marriage had promised a shortcut to Broadway) were considering a joint appearance in a lamentable farce called *My Dear Children*, Sheldon like the rest of the theatre world was aghast. But his advice was couched in the gently tolerant tones of a parent who knows that violent opposition may precipitate the disaster he hopes to stay.

> *You were very nice to listen so patiently to my criticism of* My Dear Children. *I know just how it feels when one is enthusiastic about something to run point-blank into disagreement. But I know, too, that you wanted me to be honest and tell you exactly how it struck me. As you said, Elaine,*

we are all after the same thing. Of course, my opinion is only
that of one man, and I hope you will get others. I think that
Charlie MacArthur, Ben Hecht, Arthur Hopkins, Robert
Sherwood, Robert E. Jones, and Sidney Howard would be
glad to give their disinterested, sympathetic, and valuable
advice. While you are about it, ask them what they think
of *Macbeth* and whether they cannot suggest another classic.
To my mind there are three points against *Macbeth*—against
it, I mean, as your first production. These points are (1) the
fact that *Macbeth* has never been a popular play in America, no matter who played it; (2) the fact that no actor ever
made a great personal success or really hit the bull's-eye as
Macbeth; and (3) the danger, which Elaine was quick to
recognize, of making her first New York appearance in such
a tremendously exacting part.

What about Shaw's *Caesar and Cleopatra?* A superb play
with two magnificent parts. . . .

The *Macbeth* project was abandoned. But stronger
pressure than Sheldon could exert just then caused Barrymore to go ahead with *My Dear Children.* The play opened
on the road and had a surprising run of thirty-four weeks in
Chicago, where the Barrymore name and latest matrimonial
exploit provided enough interest to offset its shortcomings.
But Sheldon knew what the reaction would be if the play
were brought to New York, that it would deal a final blow
to Barrymore's reputation and that he probably could not
survive it. Without advancing the true reason, he argued
against continuing the play on other grounds. And at the
same time he sought to steer his friend away from the pitfall
of *Macbeth* which still enticed him.

July 18, 1939

Hello, dear Jack!

Arthur Driscoll has been very nice about keeping me informed as to your doings, and I am fairly up to date in these

matters. It is on this basis that I give you the following advice. Why not close the play, return to Hollywood, get a good agent (if you are not already tied up) and make some money? I realize your interest in the theatre and sympathize with it, as you well know, but I see no use in continuing to play *My Dear Children* when so much has to be taken out of your salary that you are losing money, instead of making it. The weekly sums to Elaine, Hotchner, etc., make it impossible for you to come out even, unless you play to very big business, and you can't very well expect to do this in Chicago in mid-summer. Do a few pictures, Jack, at the best salary obtainable, get some of these immediate debts cleared up, and then come back to the theatre with another play and without obstacles.

You telegraphed me about *Macbeth*, asking what I thought. As you know, it is my favorite play. But I doubt very much if next season is the right time to produce it. I think if you go on with the theatre, it should be in a play which has the chance of popular success. You need a popular success. This *Macbeth* has never been. I mean in the sense in which *Hamlet*, *Julius Caesar*, *The Merchant*, and *Romeo and Juliet* have been popular. Also *Macbeth* is not a part in which great actors have appeared to their advantage. Nobody ever did much with the part, except possibly MacCready.

I understand how you feel about the play, and it might be a fine idea to do it sometime on the heels of a real success. In other words, when you are in a position to indulge yourself and take a chance. But you are not in this position now, and should go after something where the money is more or less sure. At present that means pictures. Later on when your decks are cleared and your financial sky is blue, then is the time to consider a *Macbeth* production. Also I doubt very much if you are in physical shape to play such an exacting role eight times a week. You asked me what I thought, and there it is.

I wish you would cut through and out of this Chicago

engagement, head straight for California, let Lionel find you
a quiet and economical place to live, then concentrate on the
best pictures, best part, and best salary available. I hope that
Arthur Driscoll thinks the same. I need not tell you how happy
I am to think that he is your lawyer. . . . What you have
needed is a lawyer whose brains were only equalled by his in-
tegrity, and at last you have found this combination. I am
glad you saw Charlie on his way to California. He telephoned
me and said that you were looking well. He is another friend
upon whose character and common-sense you can rely.

Good luck, dear Jack. Please think over this California
plan very, very carefully. I hope so much that you will see fit
to put it through. Let me know if there is anything I can do
at this end. I wish I could go to Chicago and talk with you
for about five hours. Please consider that I am right beside
you when you read this letter.

Yours affectionately,
N<small>ED</small>

Notwithstanding the drain on his energy and his bank
account, Barrymore continued the Chicago run of *My Dear
Children*. Then, to Sheldon's secret horror, the play was
brought to New York in January, 1940. His feeling was
shared by all of Barrymore's genuine admirers. Broadway,
which usually takes such things in its stride, was frankly
shocked by the deliberate abdication of its crown prince.
Barrymore's acting was a caricature of his great art, and the
point was underscored by incidents such as that of a drunken
Hamlet appearing one night in the audience and clambering
up on the stage to confront the actor—not with the ghost of
buried Denmark, but with the specter of his own lost greatness.

The play ran until May, 1940, and when it closed John
Barrymore and Edward Sheldon parted, all unknowing, for
the last time.

My Dear Children seemed to Sheldon a betrayal of the

one sound instinct in Barrymore, his feeling for his art. Yet even this did not alter his faith in his friend's genius. There were still two years of life left to Barrymore, and they were marked by steady deterioration. But Ned's hopes for him never faltered, and though the appeals for help became fainter and more infrequent, he remained continually on the alert to lend a hand when he could be of any help.

Once during the last months, alarmed by the reports of Barrymore's condition, Sheldon telephoned their mutual friend, Charles MacArthur. "Are you doing anything today, Charlie?" he asked. MacArthur, willing to go through hell and high water for Sheldon, said that he was available for any project his friend might have in mind. "If I get you a seat on the plane for the Coast, could you take a note out to Hollywood for Jack—and would you put it in his hand?" MacArthur said that he would be ready when the plane left. On the way to the airport he stopped by Ned's apartment and picked up the ticket and the letter which Sheldon had dictated. Next morning MacArthur was in Hollywood. He telephoned Barrymore and was greeted with hilarity. Jack told him to come up to his house at once.

MacArthur found his friend in circumstances and with a companion that reflected scant credit on him—and in a woeful state of mind and body. He handed over the letter—airborne across three thousand miles by personal messenger and containing Heaven knows what words intended to hold him back from disaster. Barrymore took the envelope, studied it for a moment, frowned, wavered, and then crossed to the fireplace. With a Barrymore roll of the eyes and a lift of the famous eyebrow, he tossed the letter unread into the flames, muttering as he did so, "Oh Virgil, Virgil!" Unwilling at the end to torture himself by any last appeal from Sheldon, he could still see clearly the meaning of their whole relationship. Like Dante on the perilous way through the Inferno, he too had had his Virgil to guide him. But somehow his grasp on the steadying hand had slipped. Like the original Virgil's hero, he could see only "Griefs and avenging Cares, pale Diseases and Melancholy Age . . . Poverty and Death" closing in around him.

Yet Barrymore never lost sight of what Sheldon had meant to him. Once in a moment of deep humility and clear-sightedness he cried out, "All I want on my tombstone is, THIS GODDAMNED SON OF A BITCH KNEW NED SHELDON!"

As he lay dying Sheldon's name was on his lips. Throughout the last days Sheldon remained in constant touch with him, until finally on May 29, 1942, a wire came from Lionel.

> DEAR NED: JACK PASSED QUIETLY AWAY TONIGHT.
> HE SENT YOU HIS LOVE. ALL MINE. LIONEL.

Sheldon concealed his grief in characteristic fashion. With other close friends of the actor he devoted himself to defending him against the host of detractors whom in death, even more than in life, Barrymore had aroused. It is due to Sheldon as much as to anyone else that the shoddy details of Barrymore's personal history have been largely forgotten and that he is now best remembered for what he truly was, one of the great artists of the American stage. Arthur Hopkins made the point when he said that "nothing subsequent to his great creative era could destroy his rich period of full realization," and—more accurately—when after Sheldon's death he referred to Barrymore as "a success of the highest lustre . . . one of the beckoning stars, and in the galaxy with him is Edward Sheldon . . . his own best star. . . ."

CHAPTER XII

Broadway Roll Call

INCREASINGLY as the years passed Sheldon made every effort to avoid publicity in any form. Like his insistence that no mention be made of his help to other playwrights, this was part of his deliberate scheme to destroy the identity he once possessed and had now left behind. But once in a while something would appear to spread the legend growing up about his name. In 1941 the New York *Times* noted:

> If America has a theatrical center, it is a little known one, the New York apartment of Ned Sheldon, a man who has been an invalid for many years. To his bedside come the theatre greats, for inspiration and advice, and his informal salon is a kind of hub for the best theatre of the country.

Much as reports of this sort irritated him, there was no denying the facts as given. In his apartment the lines of every important development in the theatre crossed, and he was himself a kind of spiritual center for the lives of dozens of theatrical people. His bulging address book, kept scrupulously up to date by his secretary, read like a *Who's Who* of the theatre. Though there were hundreds of names of men and women from all walks of life, there was scarcely a page without at least half a dozen stage figures. Some of the entries were surprising. There were names which had disappeared from public sight so long before that one might have thought their possessors dead. So they may have been to the great world. But to Ned Sheldon, whose memory of the past was as keen as his awareness of the present, these people of a bygone time wore the same bright aura as in the heyday of their fame. And because of this many a tired old heart, chilled by the world's forgetfulness, found courage and a renewed sense of purpose in life after an hour or two at his bedside.

Despite his active concern with the contemporary theatre, Sheldon was unwavering in his devotion to the idols of his childhood and youth. Even at a distance he avidly pursued the later careers of Bernhardt and Duse, whose very names evoked for him all that was grandest and noblest in the history of the stage. He had the same veneration, if to a lesser degree, for the divinities nearer at hand. He had first worshiped at the shrine of Minnie Maddern Fiske as a boy in Chicago. Their close association during his young manhood when Mrs. Fiske starred in *Salvation Nell* and *The High Road* led to real friendship. Nothing ever weakened the spell she had first cast over him. Among the few mementos of his own active career on Broadway, found after his death among his effects, was the tambourine used by Mrs. Fiske in *Salvation Nell*, inscribed "My love to you, Ned," with the signature beneath—"Nell."

Maude Adams was another among the great names of his earliest theatre-going. When he was still a schoolboy he had seen her in *Romeo and Juliet* and in *Peter Pan*, in *Quality Street* and *The Little Minister*. Long afterward in New York he was one of the small circle who knew something of the real personality which her shyness and love of seclusion hid from the public. Later still, after he became ill, Miss Adams would sometimes take the initiative and come to see him—

a rare gesture on her part. Nothing had dimmed for Ned the memory of her golden past, and in old age she still radiated the otherworldly charm that had captivated the generation of his boyhood. As late as 1943 he wrote his Cambridge friend Eleanor Whidden about a telegram from Miss Adams which Ruth Gordon had read at the fiftieth anniversary celebration of the Empire Theatre:

> Do you remember the time we saw her in *The Little Minister* at the Hollis Street? She was your favorite in those days, and I did my rooting for Mrs. Fiske. Well, they were both wonderful in their way. The telegram last night revealed her qualities just as strongly as did Lady Babbie. Nobody changes.

Julia Marlowe also belonged to the generation of stars who had reached their full luster while Ned was in knee breeches. Their acquaintance dated from his Harvard days when he had called on Miss Marlowe backstage during a Boston engagement. After that they were brought together professionally in the ill-fated New Theatre venture. In Sheldon's estimate no other contemporary actress had the poetic insight and range for Shakespeare's heroines possessed by Julia Marlowe. She too came regularly to see him after he was housebound. In that matchless voice which even in old age was still full and musical, she would read to him, perform Shakespeare for him, and reminisce about the theatre. In a note to Woollcott dated June 25, 1942, Sheldon writes excitedly:

> Julia Marlowe has this moment telephoned to ask if she can come to see me next Tuesday at half-past four. This means I shall hear great poetry through what is still the most beautiful voice in the world.

That day she read Shelley to him. And as a special treat (which Ned recognized as such) she read the poems her husband E. H. Sothern had written to her—one for each of her great roles. Finally she read some of the love letters of Bernhardt and Ellen Terry, which she made sound like poems.

Though Julia Marlowe lived in hermit-like seclusion during her last years, she always kept Ned posted on her plans and whereabouts.

> I shall sail tomorrow to go to my doctor at Lausanne [she wrote in the mid-thirties]. I will look to find you on my return. Meanwhile know of my enduring affection. But if I live I will come again to recite more Shelley and Keats. . . .

And in 1941 there was an urgent note:

> . . . Do have some one send me news that all is well with you, dear friend. I say a nightly prayer for you. God bless you, dear Edward, and give you peace.
>
> Your affectionate
> JULIA

Not long before her death at eighty-five (like Maude Adams she survived Sheldon by several years) Ned's name came up in conversation with another friend. With a little lift of the head, in that proudly graceful movement familiar to so many playgoers of another generation, she gazed out of the window and murmured, "I knew Edward Sheldon . . . I used to read to him and do my plays for him. Ah, yes . . . I loved him dearly."

Sheldon naturally felt a special kinship with his own theatre contemporaries. It was through their eyes that he followed in minute detail all the changes that took place on Broadway. One member of this group was Frances Starr,

whom Ned had first seen in *The Easiest Way*. Another was
Marie Doro who appeared in *Clarice* with William Gillette
when Ned was a college student. He had become one of her
very attentive admirers after his arrival in New York, when
he had seemed to her "like a young god" destined for all
the good things of life. Miss Doro had also been an intimate
of Doris Keane's. She had seen the lovers often in the first
months of their dazzling happiness, and she had been as
shocked as the rest of the world that it should have come to
nothing. Once Marie Doro went with Ned to Atlantic City
to see a Doris Keane première, and she never forgot the expression in his eyes as he followed every movement of his
beloved, oblivious to the rest of the play. Later, in the summer
of 1913, Marie Doro and Ned met in Paris. They scoured
antique shops together in search of the pearl-studded crucifix
for Cavallini.

Florence Reed also came regularly to the penthouse through
the years. Ned had great admiration for her acting, especially
as the exotic and bawdy Mother Goddam in *Shanghai Gesture*—a part she had taken over from the aging Mrs. Leslie
Carter. Miss Reed respected Ned's own gifts profoundly,
but she maintained steadily from the earliest days of his career
that the writer was small beside his stature as a man.

Still another whose friendship counted much with Sheldon for more than thirty years was Otis Skinner, a somewhat
older contemporary. They first met when Ned joined the
Players Club in 1910, and through the years Skinner remained
the principal contact with that group. Otis Skinner and his
wife, the former Maud Durbin, were high on Ned's roster
of the elect, not only because they were pillars in upholding
the finest traditions of the stage, a matter of vital importance
to him always, but also because of their warm, generous

humanity. In this case, as in so many others, friendship with the parents was carried on through succeeding generations. Cornelia Otis Skinner and her son both had important places in the penthouse circle.

Sheldon first saw Peggy Wood when she was introduced to Broadway as a new singing star in George Ade's *The Old Town* back in 1910. Their paths crossed often in the succeeding years, but for some reason they did not actually meet until Miss Wood was playing with George Arliss in *The Merchant of Venice* in 1928. She of course knew all about him and was fully aware that "going up to see Ned" was already a tradition, a mark of certain prestige bestowed on those who had arrived on Broadway. Friends had often invited her to go with them to Eighty-fourth Street, but she had been sensitive about intruding upon the privileged circle of those linked to Sheldon by old acquaintance. Finally at Sheldon's own request, transmitted through Mrs. Winthrop Ames, she went to see him. Peggy Wood was one of those who from the first meeting felt the full impact of his wisdom. "It is not often that one is called upon to explain what one looks like, or how one thinks, and in terms of absolute honesty. I found the process good for the soul." She saw from the beginning that the thing which made talking with Sheldon a vitalizing experience was that so much of the dead weight of one's personality—the acquired manners, habits, attitudes which one carries around in the world—dropped instantly away. This was through no conscious effort. It was simply that in the high bright room above the rooftops, these things had no place. Miss Wood's explanation of why this should have been was the one which nearly everybody came back to: "In Ned there was simply more of the Divine than in most persons."

One of the many people Sheldon met at the Faversham

soirées back in 1910–11 was the exquisite young Billie Burke. Her fragile charm and wide-eyed innocence, masking a robust comedy sense and a good deal of sophistication, had brought her quick success in London as well as New York. When Ned first knew her she was playing the leading role in his friend Somerset Maugham's *Mrs. Dot.* Like every other man lucky enough to know Miss Burke, he found her irresistible, both then and for the rest of his life. Billie Burke was also taken with the young playwright, then barely out of college. Thirty years later she still had her first clear impressions of "his brilliant, glowing face with the dark hair and beautiful brown eyes, high color, and sensitive young mouth —sensitive to a degree—to humor or to any other emotion under which he was talking. Tall, lithe, slender, graceful— wonderful hands . . . exquisite taste—and oh, so wonderful to know."

In 1914 Billie Burke married Florenz Ziegfeld. When their daughter was born two years later Ned immediately wrote: "I hope Patricia grows up to like me one quarter as much as I like her mother." During the later years when the Ziegfelds lived at their Hastings-on-Hudson estate, Burkely Crest, Billie Burke regularly came to see Sheldon with great armloads of flowers, baskets of fruit, and prize garden vegetables—all arranged with consummate artistry. Though Sheldon could only appreciate these offerings from the descriptions of his attendants, they pleased him as much as if he could see them since they reflected so completely the charm of the giver.

On Patricia Ziegfeld's birthday in 1931, Sheldon wired her mother:

> BILLIE DEAR: I CANNOT REALIZE IT WAS FIFTEEN YEARS AGO. I REMEMBER HOW LOVELY YOU LOOKED THE FIRST TIME I SAW YOU AFTER PATRICIA ARRIVED LYING ON THAT LITTLE COT

BED AT THE ANSONIA AND YOU WERE SO HAPPY. MY LOVE TO
YOU TONIGHT AND ALWAYS. NED.

After Ziegfeld's death the following year Miss Burke had
some difficult times. Again and again she turned to Sheldon
for courage. When urgent necessity took her back to her
professional career she counted on him for help in finding
parts in motion pictures and the theatre. Alice Kauser,
handling a play in which Miss Burke was to appear, wrote
Sheldon:

> I hope that Billie Burke will see you Wednesday, for
> there is much that you alone can give her. She has the ut-
> most faith in your theatrical—I should say dramatic "know-
> how," a lost art these days. . . .

In 1937, when a ball was to be given in Beverly Hills in
honor of Patricia's twenty-first birthday, he wired her
mother:

> BILLIE DEAR: ALL MY THOUGHTS FOR TONIGHT. WILL YOU GIVE
> ME FIRST AND LAST WALTZES AND HAVE SUPPER WITH ME?
>
> NED

And the answer came quickly back:

> OH NED DEAR THE DANCES ARE YOURS AND I AM WEARING MY
> BLACK TULLE NET WITH ITS VELVET BODICE AND PUFF SLEEVES
> AND YOUR GARDENIAS AND I HOPE YOU WON'T MIND IF I HAVE
> ABSINTHE FRAPPE AT SUPPER WITH YOU. GARLANDS OF LOVE.
>
> BILLIE.

It was Alexander Woollcott who brought young Katharine Cornell to see Sheldon. She had just completed her first
important Broadway assignment in Clemence Dane's *A Bill
of Divorcement*. Though Sheldon had never seen her on the
stage, he recognized in the combination of warmth and controlled intensity, intelligent perception, and striking ap-

pearance all the potentialities of a great acting career. As always with actors and actresses, no matter what personal attractions they exerted for him, he judged her objectively, and he realized that Miss Cornell could attain her full stature only by the most careful selection of parts. He made it his business to keep constantly on the watch for suitable roles for her. He was delighted with her performance of Ellen Olenska in *The Age of Innocence*, but he did not feel that the part of Madeleine Grey in *Dishonored Lady* did much to advance her career. She was one of the few American actresses with the taste, background, technique, and physical equipment for the classics, and he constantly urged her to undertake Shakespeare. There were many discussions on this subject, some fairly heated. "He had no patience with my laziness," she remembers, "and he was angry that I wouldn't do Shakespeare every night." When finally in 1934 she made her Shakespearean debut as Juliet to the Romeo of Maurice Evans, Sheldon looked on the event as a personal triumph.

Much as he admired Katharine Cornell the actress, his deeper regard was for her qualities as a human being. When, during the war, she undertook a long European tour for the U.S.O. with *The Barretts of Wimpole Street*, an exploit of heroic proportions, he entered earnestly into the planning of the trip. Throughout the months that Miss Cornell moved from one army camp to another in the face of obstacles that only the most dogged determination could surmount, Sheldon followed every step of the way. When he heard that the company had landed in Italy in the middle of winter, he reproached himself for not having warned his friend and her colleagues of the cold and dampness they would have to endure.

During the last months of his life when Miss Cornell was

preparing to appear in Anouilh's *Antigone* he was satisfied
that she had a role to match her gifts. Anouilh's play did not
have the stark grandeur of Sophocles but, as he wrote their
mutual friend, Daisy Blaisdell, "The figure of Antigone is
incarnate compassion, and this ought to suit Kit perfectly in
any version."

Among the great ladies of Broadway closest to Sheldon's
heart was Helen Hayes, whom he had known long before
they became "in-laws"—through Miss Hayes's marriage to
Charles MacArthur, whose brother Alfred had married
Sheldon's sister Mary. As a girl of seventeen, Helen Hayes
was in the critical position of having behind her a career
as a child star, but with no assurance of what her future
would be. Fortunately the producer George Tyler was
sufficiently astute to perceive the real qualities of Miss Hayes's
precocious achievement, and he was determined that she
should be a great actress in every sense. He supervised her
reading, saw that she traveled, and above all made a point
of having her meet people, not only those who might advance her career, but those who would enrich her mind
and help her to gain confidence. It was her mentor Tyler
who introduced her to Sheldon. She remembered always her
fright as she stepped into the elevator to go up to the apartment. For already Sheldon's name was spoken with awe by
theatre people, and the backstage talk she had heard had
made the shy young girl dread the interview.

But Sheldon easily and quickly bridged what then seemed
the great gap between them. Those who recall the wistful
charm and simplicity of Helen Hayes as William Gillette's
daughter in *Dear Brutus* can imagine the impression she made
on Sheldon, then only thirty-four himself. From that day
on through the next thirty years the penthouse on Eighty-

fourth Street became for Helen Hayes the center from which she drew confidence and inspiration for the finest work of her career. Early in their friendship she made a practice of going over her parts in detail with Sheldon, discussing each interpretation line by line, testing effects with him, and working out technical problems. On opening nights, wherever she might be, in New York or on the road, there would always be a note or telegram of encouragement and good wishes from Ned. This was carefully pinned under her costume, close to her heart.

Sheldon applied himself to studying her parts with all the intensity of an actor whose own career was at stake. He knew every piece of stage business as well as most of the dialogue of her roles in *What Every Woman Knows*, *Coquette*, *Mary of Scotland*, and the long-running *Victoria Regina*. The same thing was true for Viola in *Twelfth Night* and Portia in *The Merchant of Venice*. He always considered these two roles ideal for her because the artist and the woman merged in complete harmony with Shakespeare's poetry. When she decided to play Portia, he attacked *The Merchant of Venice* as though he had never read or seen the play before, in order to feel it completely afresh. He pondered the whole intent of the trial scene and passed his ideas on to Miss Hayes. She considered carefully what he had to say, then told him, "The more I read the trial scene, the more I love your interpretation and believe it to be Shakespeare's."

The intimacy between Sheldon and the MacArthurs was of long standing. Ned had known Charles MacArthur when the latter was a young newspaperman in Chicago. Moreover, in 1925, he and MacArthur had collaborated on the highly successful *Lulu Belle*. In the meantime, Ned had come to know Helen Hayes. When his friend fell in love with her, he was delighted. Miss Hayes was not inclined to be swept off her feet, but Ned urged her along. In 1928 the MacArthurs were married and two years later their daughter Mary was born.

Sheldon loved all children, but for his goddaughter Mary MacArthur he had a special tenderness. Visitors to the penthouse became familiar with the sensitive, eager little face from the photographs that were always on display. There was one of a small pajama-clad figure leaning expectantly over the side of her crib and another of a little pig-tailed girl sitting on her doorstep, and still others down through the years. In 1949 three years after Sheldon's own death the lovely nineteen-year-old girl, just beginning her own stage career, was stricken with poliomyelitis and died. To countless friends of Sheldon and of the girl's parents, the first comforting thought when they heard the news was that "Mary was safe with Ned."

The producer William A. Brady and his wife Grace George were both staunch partisans of the author of *Salvation Nell* when his work first began to jar the complacent mediocrity of Broadway in the days before the first World War. Brady produced *The Boss* in 1911, and in 1929 the Bradys' son, William A. Brady, Jr., with Dwight Deere Wiman, put on *Jenny*. Six years after this young Brady met a sudden and tragic end. Sheldon wrote to Miss George, and his letter, as she afterward said, consoled her more than any other message.

> . . . There was an unconscious pride and love in his voice, or rather beneath his voice, when he spoke of you. I think that was one of the things that made me like him immediately. I was impressed by his ability, his force and all kinds

of possibilities in his nature, which I thought would be developed as life went on. That is why this cutting-off seems so tragic. What it must mean to you and to his father I cannot let myself imagine. There is nothing to be said, dear Mrs. Brady. But when I read the papers I found myself remembering the last lines of Galsworthy's Justice, "Safe with gentle Jesus." Safe and happy too.

With this letter what had been a cordial but purely social and professional relationship took on that deeper tone which sooner or later colored all Sheldon's friendships. For some months after the death of her son, Grace George shrank from appearing on the stage. Finally she was persuaded to perform on a radio broadcast. Sheldon at once sent a telegram that was carefully calculated to spur her to continue:

DEAR GRACE: IT WAS A REAL JOY YOUR BEAUTIFUL VOICE AND THAT PERFECTLY NATURAL BUT DISTINGUISHED DICTION CAME OVER FLAWLESSLY AND EXPRESSED EVERY THOUGHT EVERY SHADE OF FEELING WITH APPARENTLY NO EFFORT AT ALL. I ONLY HOPE THAT INNUMERABLE YOUNG ACTRESSES HEARD YOU AND LEARNED THE LESSON. THE CLARITY AND DELICACY AND UNERRING PRECISION OF YOUR WHOLE METHOD SEEM SO COMPLETELY IN HARMONY WITH THIS NEW MEDIUM THAT YOU OUGHT TO BROADCAST VERY VERY OFTEN. THE ENTIRE RANGE OF ENGLISH COMEDY IS AT YOUR DISPOSAL SO PLEASE GO AHEAD AND GIVE US SOME MORE WONDERFUL EVENINGS. I WISH YOU COULD HAVE HEARD IT LAST NIGHT. I REALLY THINK YOU WOULD HAVE BEEN PLEASED. YOURS AFFECTIONATELY,

NED

But even before this, Sheldon had made it his business to try to get Miss George and her husband interested in some enterprise which would bring them out from under the shadow of their loss. A few nights after young Brady's funeral he invited Miss George to dinner. He did not mention the tragedy but talked the entire evening about the theatre—and most particularly about *The Circle*, by his friend Somerset Maugham. Although written nearly fifteen years before, the play seemed as fresh as the day it first appeared, and was due for a revival. It was just the sort of thing Miss George could do to perfection.

It was difficult not to warm to Ned's eagerness. When she returned home Miss George's mood had lightened. "Ned's got an idea for both of us," she told her husband. They sat down together and found themselves seriously discussing the possibility of the revival.

Sheldon on his side did not let the matter drop. Soon afterward he invited Grace George and Tallulah Bankhead to tea. Ned chatted innocently until the talk got around to the theatre. Miss Bankhead deplored the chronic lack of good plays, especially good comedies, and most especially good comedy parts for herself.

"Why," said Sheldon with unsuspected cunning, "one of the finest comedies in the English language lies beside me on the table. I don't know why it hasn't occurred to some-one before this to put it on. I refer to Somerset Maugham's comedy *The Circle*. It's as real and true today as when it was first written. . . . Just the play for Mr. Brady and wonderful parts for both of you. Miss George would be perfect as Lady Kitty. Miss Bankhead as Elizabeth would show her versatility by playing a part diametrically the opposite to the roles she is more or less associated with." The seed thus planted took root. *The Circle* had a brilliant revival, and Miss George's portrait of the aging but unquenchable coquette, Lady Kitty, displayed all the resources of her art as a comedienne. In her absorption with the part the raw edges of her personal tragedy were healed over.

One of the few motion pictures that Sheldon ever saw was *Broken Blossoms* in the early twenties. He had been skeptical about the artistic possibilities of the screen, but the delicate performance of Lillian Gish caused him to change his opinion. Not long afterward he met Miss Gish, and from then on for more than twenty years she was one of that special circle of intimates which included the MacArthurs and Alexander Woollcott. She stood as godmother in the christening of the MacArthurs' son James. She and Woollcott also were present at Sheldon's bedside for another event, the broadcast of Edward VIII's abdication speech. All three theatre-hardened veterans were stirred by the high drama of that moment. It was Lillian Gish who called Sheldon "the pope of the theatre"—a phrase which stuck in the folklore of Broadway, because it summed up the attitude of stage people toward Sheldon's infallibility in things theatrical.

Sheldon had known Ruth Gordon as an actress long before he was aware of her talents as a writer. In 1936, acting for Edith Wharton, he had urged Miss Gordon to appear in Owen and Donald Davis's dramatization of *Ethan Frome*. Her haunting performance in that winter-bitten tragedy, followed shortly by her brilliant success in Wycherley's *Country Wife*, showed her remarkable range. Sheldon was able to judge her mature work himself when she did Nora in Thornton Wilder's version of *A Doll's House* in 1937. The play with full cast was performed in his living room.

This was but one instance of the theatre's coming literally to Sheldon when he could no longer go to the theatre. Scarcely a season passed that plays or scenes from plays current on Broadway were not given in the penthouse with Ned comprising the entire audience. Sometimes this was done in a spirit of pure generosity because of the actors' affection for Sheldon. Sometimes there was a frankly utilitarian purpose behind the exhibitions.

In 1943 Judith Anderson, a long-time friend of Sheldon's, wanted to bring Robinson Jeffers' *Tower Beyond Tragedy* to New York. She was skeptical, however, of the commercial possibilities of a modern poetic drama on the ancient theme of the House of Atreus. In order to settle the question she assembled a cast, rehearsed long and carefully, and then performed the play for Sheldon. His reaction was everything that she had hoped. He found the play "magnificent although not a bit Greek" and encouraged her to carry through the plan for a Broadway production.

The constant procession of celebrities across Sheldon's threshold naturally cast a certain glamor over the invalid himself, and heightened his reputation as a key figure in the New York theatre. But his interest was not limited to those who had achieved great success. He had a special fondness for the young, and newcomers to the stage had particular claims on him because of his passionate concern for the future of the theatre.

One young actor who caught his attention was Eliot Cabot, New England born and a Harvard man, who had also studied at Cambridge University. Cabot's family traditions, intellectual interests, and broad culture made him especially sympathetic to Sheldon, who had come to the theatre with a similar background. He knew that the life of the stage presented special problems to anyone who had grown up in the conservative, ordered world of Beacon Street and Louisburg Square, and he watched Cabot's adjustment with some anxiety. Although Cabot did not have the sharp brilliance of personality which leads to the top of the acting profession, he had sensitivity and a genuine devotion to the theatre. Sheldon's admiration for him grew as he watched the young man's persistence in the face of handicaps he could so well appreciate.

In 1936 Cabot married a dancer, Agnes Flannery. The evening before the wedding they dined with Sheldon, who tapped all the resources of his household to make the occasion festive. The following year the young couple had a son who was duly christened Edward Sheldon Cabot. Two years later Cabot died under tragic circumstances, and the welfare of his widow and child were a vital concern for the rest of Sheldon's life.

Another young actor who was often at Eighty-fourth Street was Philip Huston, who could talk about the theatre almost as indefatigably as Sheldon himself. He would frequently come up to the penthouse after an evening performance, and the two would talk until nearly morning. More than once these conversational marathons lasted through the night and into the following day until it was time for Huston to return to the theatre for a matinee.

During a Southern road tour in 1942 Huston was injured in a railway accident. Sheldon helped beguile the boredom of hospital days with long letters about the theatre, books, people, and all the things they liked to discuss together—including professional baseball. Huston always marveled at his knowledge of the game and individual players. When Urbanski heroically completed a run on a broken ankle, Ned declared, "That Urbanski has guts." Huston, who happened to know the player, told him about Sheldon and repeated the remark to him. The honest Urbanski retorted, "But he has more!"

Huston was a member of the cast which performed *Tower Beyond Tragedy* in Sheldon's living room. He also took part in other bedside productions, a reading of *Elizabeth the Queen* with Joan Crawford, and a regular performance of *Angel Street* with Judith Evelyn and Vincent Price. Huston had a special tie with Sheldon because of his series of performances as Tom Armstrong in various revivals of *Romance*—in Chicago with Eugenie Leontovitch, at the Cape Playhouse with Jane Cowl, and at the Mohawk Drama Festival with Cornelia Otis Skinner.

Young José Ferrer came to Sheldon's attention when he played the leading role in Elizabeth Ginty's *Missouri Legend*. After Ferrer's brilliant success as Iago to Paul Robeson's Othello in 1943, the producer Arthur Friend sent him to see Sheldon. Ferrer was of course familiar with Sheldon's story, but he was totally unprepared for what he saw. In the theatre people spoke of Sheldon's invalidism in rather vague terms and as something of secondary importance to his personality and his theatrical omniscience. Ferrer was shocked when he saw the still figure rigidly stretched out on the high bed with only the masked face showing above the bedclothes. Even the sound of Sheldon's voice, which usually put people immediately at ease, was disconcerting because of the difficult breathing that marked the last phase of his illness. Still more disturbing was the impression that the eyes behind the black mask could see everything that was going on. A faint, silent move of Ferrer's hand toward his pocket immediately caused Sheldon to say, "The cigarettes are there at your left." And a moment later, "Oh, you haven't a match," and presently when Ferrer had drunk the cocktail that had been handed him by an attendant, "Your glass must be filled."

But in a few moments the feeling of uneasiness disappeared in the flow of conversation. Ferrer was not given to talking about himself, but without realizing it he found himself confiding hopes and ambitions that he had mentioned to no one. He told Sheldon that he had always wanted to do *Cyrano de Bergerac*. Many people thought the play outmoded—for Broadway's tastes, at any rate. But Ferrer was convinced of its effectiveness still, as sheer theatre. Sheldon's reaction was highly encouraging. He had sensed at once Ferrer's rare combination of vigor and sensitivity, the essential qualities of Rostand's poet-musketeer. He was certain Ferrer could bring fresh intensity to the part to offset the artificialities and cumbersome period trappings of the somewhat gaudy piece. As usual, events proved him right. Ferrer's Cyrano was a brilliant blend of simple humanity and high romance, revealing the character as one of the great stage creations of all time. This was acknowledged by the critics generally, and better still by a grateful public which kept the play running for more than six months.

Sheldon's services to the theatre were as varied as the activities encompassed by that many-sided institution. His physical condition was no barrier to his usefulness or to the dependence of others on him. His work in finding parts for actors was proverbial. No one knew actors better or could judge their work more accurately than he. His intense human sympathies never interfered with his professional objectivity. His friend Joseph Williams, brother of the producer John Williams and a man whose life had been given to the theatre, remembered how Sheldon, in his earliest Broadway days, liked to sit back and watch an actor whom he might know intimately "totally without prejudice or bias." For this reason his recommendations carried great weight, and managers found that he rarely made mistakes in his suggestions for casting a play.

In the case of older actors his judgment was supported by an astonishing memory of every facet of the performances he had witnessed before he was thirty. But his estimates of players he came to know in later years were just as sound. His forecast of José Ferrer as an ideal Cyrano is only one example. He had never seen Ferrer act, had never seen Ferrer for that matter, so that his judgment was based largely on informal conversation.

His intuition of character, his appreciation of another's powers of imagination and physical capacities, were such that he seemed to have an almost supernatural knowledge of people. To those who knew him he was the perfect realization of Henry James's ideally constituted writer, the man "on whom nothing is lost." Thornton Wilder once said "Sheldon's attention to human phenomena was like a sponge." More than thirty years earlier Mrs. Fiske had said, "I don't think Ned observes at all, he just absorbs."

In his understanding of the actor Sheldon discerned plainly between potentialities for the theatre and true character. And this was what made him so indispensable to his friends of the stage. In a profession where the individual's success depends on his ability to create an illusion about himself, for this is what acting is basically, the line between real and assumed character sometimes becomes dim. Many of the problems and heartbreaks of theatre people are due to this fact. To feel that there was one person at least who clearly saw and gladly accepted one's real self for what it was worth gave more than one actor an anchor in reality.

CHAPTER XIII

Piccadilly at Eighty-fourth Street

SHELDON's predilection for Britain and the British was like a love affair which had passed through all the stages from young ecstasy to mature passion, coming finally to rest in a sober devotion. It had begun in his boyhood when Stevenson and Kipling had been his favorite reading, and the plays of Barrie and Pinero had filled his mind with English scenes and English manners. In 1906, when he at last found himself on British soil, it was as though he had walked into a story book. As with the young Henry James, England was fiction made real to him and each moment of the experience was a revelation of "its truth to Dickens and to Thackeray," and to all the dreams of romance and adventure that his reading had fed.

This feeling never wholly disappeared, though it was tempered in time by a more realistic attitude as he studied English history and institutions. The physical charm of England was deeply etched in his memory and as clear to his inward vision at the end of his life as when he first saw the green hedgerows of Surrey and the crumbling towers of Kenilworth. But what finally mattered most was his acute sense of the moral climate of England and the character of her people.

His circle of British acquaintances was broad and varied,

and his genius for friendship had the same effect with people across the Atlantic, most of whom he saw only at rare intervals, as on those who came regularly to his apartment. Despite years of separation in many cases, his British friends retained as intense an awareness of Sheldon's spirit as people who saw him constantly.

One of Ned's oldest and most ardent friendships was with Mrs. Patrick Campbell. From the time they first met at the Favershams' in 1908 to the end of Mrs. Pat's life in 1940, there was no period when either was far from the other's thoughts, or when they were not in regular communication. For more than twenty-five years of her extraordinary career, Mrs. Pat looked upon Ned as the fixed point in the flux of all human relationships. From 1914 on he was the confidant of her hopes and her despair. During the latter years of her brilliant dominance of the London stage he was her trusted adviser, and in her lonely old age he was the unfailing solace.

In the early thirties the woman who, as Desmond Mc-Carthy said, could be "so magnificently fierce, crushingly insolent . . . enchantingly mocking" had come to the end of her triumphs. Age fell suddenly upon her, and she was baffled and fearful. She came to America then in the hope of getting a second lease on her professional life. After a series of misfortunes in New York, she decided, at the age of sixty-five, to attack Hollywood. She had no difficulty in establishing herself as a personality—but not in a way calculated to advance her fortunes. As in New York, neither the legend of her name nor her superlative gifts as an actress could offset her growing reputation as a difficult person to get along with. Her *bon mots* furnished wonderful copy for the columnists, but the powers of the film capital did not find her mockery, which time had not blunted, so enchanting. In a remarkably short time she managed to antagonize practically everybody who might have been useful to her.

Ned followed her wayward course with great anxiety. He brought pressure to bear on his friends who might help her. By long-distance telephone and telegraph he counseled, cajoled, and frequently chided his cherished Stella. But the tide had set in against her and there was no turning it back. He knew, and it grieved him to know, that Mrs. Pat had reached the point every aging actress faces when she outlives her public.

He had always been completely frank with her, and she accepted his criticism and his advice with humility. In 1933 when she had managed to get a part on Broadway, Ned had talked long and seriously with her about making the most of her opportunity, above all of keeping calm when she and the director did not see eye to eye, and in general rising above the petty annoyances which were bound to occur—trying, with that consummate tact which was one of his supreme gifts, to reconcile her to the fact that she could no longer dominate her entourage as she once had done. For several days during rehearsals she did not even call Ned on the telephone, thus breaking a custom of many years' standing. Finally she wrote him a note telling him that she was trying to behave with patience as he would have her do, but she was not happy!

> . . . I nearly telephoned you, dearest Ned, to ask if I could come for an hour, but I feel it would be greedy—so many need your sympathy and understanding I must not be selfish. . . . Jack Mackail (Denis' father) used to say, "All the help we can be in this world is to be an example." You,

*my beloved friend, are the most glorious example on this
earth. God be praised for you.*

Sheldon knew better than the producers who were increasingly reluctant to give her parts, that her explosiveness
and cynical manner cloaked fears and old wounds which
had never really healed, and which under misfortune seemed
to have opened afresh. He knew the details of her unhappy
marriage to Cornwallis-West, and he knew the full measure
of her lasting grief at the death of her only son during the
first World War. He was familiar with the ups and downs
of her long and celebrated friendship with George Bernard
Shaw. The wit and lyricism which had filled their correspondence for so many years was giving way now to can-
tankerousness and gloom. (In 1937 while bowed down by
her own cares she told Ned that she had had "another letter
from Joey. I fancy I sense age and death continually in
his thoughts—it makes me unhappy.")

By 1938, after long months of wearing idleness, Mrs.
Pat seemed to have reached the end of her rope. Back in
New York she had tried frantically to get an engagement.
The final flicker of hope died when, after long weeks of
waiting, a part she had expected to get from Guthrie Mc-
Clintic failed to materialize. Then she decided to give up
and retreat to Paris, where her slender means could be
stretched farther than in America or England.

From Paris she wrote Ned a Christmas letter:

> *Beloved Ned,*
>
> *Each day I have hoped for some happy news to give you.
> Each evening I have wished that I could have come and
> sat by your bed. . . . This Christmas you will be nearest to
> my heart, for I verily believe I love you better than anyone
> in the world, and I also believe that God has made in you
> the bravest and finest man that ever lived.*

*I believe in God's patience because I have witnessed
yours. I believe in God's sympathy and understanding because I have known yours, and I believe in God's goodness
because he has spared you to us that we may see to what
unselfish and noble heights a man may attain. I wish you
knew how you help us all.*

 Christmas blessings upon you, dearest Ned.

STELLA

As the gray Paris winter settled down she began to feel
the final desolation of old age.

 *. . . Paris is wet and cold and has been for weeks and weeks.
. . . I have a nice little apartment with an open log fire,
but my heart feels like a tomb that hasn't even a corpse in
it.*

 *I long for news of you, so please write, write, write. . . .
How I wish I could see you— I shut my eyes and hear your
voice say, "Dear Stella."*

But a little later she wrote with rising spirits of a possibility of returning to the stage. Charles Morgan had spoken
of wanting to write a play for her. ". . . If he does and I
am not too old, and too ugly, and too tired to interest the
audience, I could get a maid to be here with Moonbeam,
and go to England."

Moonbeam was Mrs. Pat's white Pekingese, the inseparable companion of her later years. Ned knew that the little
dog was all that stood between his old friend and utter
loneliness. He had no criticism of the proposed extravagance
of engaging a maid solely to look after Moonbeam. Because
of quarantine regulations, she could not bring Moonbeam
with her into England, and he knew that Mrs. Pat would
never endure the thought of her pet cooped up for six
months in a quarantine station during the waiting period.
Either of them might die in the meantime without the final
solace of the other's presence. She told Ned that if things

worked out she could fly back to Paris for weekends with Moonbeam.

Meantime, the much publicized friendship with Shaw was drifting to an acrimonious end. In December, 1938, Mrs. Pat had written Shaw to tell him how dreadfully dull life was without money. Since he was making "such a mountain of gold out of *Pygmalion*" (the film version for which Shaw was being paid 20 per cent of the gross receipts), would he send her a Christmas box? After all, she reminded him, it was she who had taken the play to Beerbohm Tree back in 1913 and had "worked so valiantly for its success." Shaw's reply, as Stella relayed it to Ned, was "a very rude letter calling mine to him 'a string of lies' but alluding to his loss of memory!" Naturally Shaw refused to send the Christmas box. Furthermore, he expressed the hope that Moonbeam would live forever so that Stella would never disturb London by returning! "What a man—what a friend . . ." But the last word, as usual was Mrs. Pat's. The letter she sent back to Shaw was a "stinker," as she informed Ned, adding charitably, "I hope it won't kill him."

Mrs. Pat was really in financial straits, and as a measure of desperation she decided that she would try to publish the Shaw-Campbell correspondence. Some of this had already appeared in her autobiography in 1922, but there was a great deal of additional material which she thought could be turned to advantage. Three years before Shaw had sent back six packages of her letters to him, informing her that they constituted a valuable literary property. But the hitch was in obtaining Shaw's permission to publish his own letters, which in his present frame of mind he certainly would not give. The plan was being worked out in utmost secrecy since, as Mrs. Pat told Ned, "if it got to Shaw's ears, he might do something mean." Of course nothing could be done until his death, but as he was ten years older than she, there was a strong possibility (and an implied hope) that he would die first. She was confident that Shaw's executors would raise no obstacles to making the correspondence public. Meanwhile, a scheme was being concocted whereby she would obtain money in advance against the day when the letters would be published—a mortgage, as it were, on the correspondence. This was a matter in which Sheldon showed lively interest, but carefully refrained from offering any advice.

He was far more eager that she should have a last chance at the stage. He was as happy as Stella herself at the prospect that Charles Morgan might write a play for her. He admired Morgan for refusing to be alarmed by Mrs. Pat's temperament. He had chuckled at Morgan's reported comment: "The stage is not a platoon of decorous and disciplined girl-guides and if one wants a flame instead of a tepid hot water bottle, one must expect rehearsals to be a trifle incendiary. With all risks Mrs. Pat is a flame . . ."

That was the way Ned had always felt about her, and continued to feel. At seventy-four Mrs. Pat could still charm with a glance, she could still rouse glorious laughter with a gesture or a phrase. And in the midst of all her troubles, the generosity which had drawn Ned to her in his youth was still warm. Late in the winter of 1939 she wrote him that she longed to take a villa at Antibes "and sit among the flowers and scent of orange trees and listen to the nightingales"— but not alone. She knew two people whose lives had been shattered by grief. She would have them come to her and she would make them happy. But she felt this was an idle dream which like so many others could never come to pass

now. She was old and poor and tired, and she knew that she
had come to her last turning.

> . . . *On the ninth of this month I was 74 [this was in 1939]
> —that's a good age, Ned—ten years older than Duse when
> she passed on—one year older than my dear Sarah [Bern-
> hardt]—I'm afraid it's hopeless to think of the stage any
> more—the long rehearsals—the nightly work. . . . One can-
> not just make a valiant effort for money, it would be a fail-
> ure—I would have to believe that there was just something
> that I could say and do—and I believe—SILENCE—is the
> better way. . . .*

Yet still through the early months of 1939 there were
flashes of the old fire in her letters to Ned. But the mark of
finality was now on everything, on the Europe she had
known and loved, on her hopes for the theatre, on her steadily declining health. Even the possibility of making something from the Shaw correspondence was dwindling. The
final proposition from the publishers was an advance of five
hundred dollars in cash against future royalties—to be paid
back with interest. She was now of a mind simply to dis-
pose of the letters on the open market for what they would
bring. An offer had once been made her by a wealthy American manufacturer. Would Ned get in touch with him and
find out if he was still interested? She would let the letters go
now for fifteen hundred dollars, a good deal less than the
price she had originally been offered.

> . . . *It would ease things tremendously for me if he would
> buy them. Will you cable me if there is a chance? . . . This
> miserable want of money stalls one's energy and imagina-
> tion—makes a hateful nervous tension. It poisons me. . . .*

She missed her New York friends, particularly those
who were also close to Ned.

> . . . I would love a little letter from that most courteous
> soul on earth—that most dear man—Jack Wheelock . . .

Most of all she missed Ned himself.

> . . . I am homesick for you and your dear room, and a long,
> long talk—how you listened to me and never chided my van-
> ity and egotism—never made me feel ashamed of it. Deep
> down I need a message from you very deeply. I feel as a dog
> must feel shut up in a wooden crate with just enough air to
> breathe, knowing he is traveling a long journey by train—
> not knowing where it is going or to whom.

Ned grieved that the separation, aggravated now by the
gathering clouds of war, made it impossible for him to offer
some tangible help to ease the final months of Mrs. Pat's
life. The most he could do was to write her constantly, to
make her feel that he was always close to her in his thoughts.
To the lonely exile, feeling herself forsaken by the world,
Ned's letters were like a sustaining presence. Yet how much
she would have given to see him once more. Her last words
to him were ". . . I wish I could fly to you."

The debt was not all on one side. Mrs. Pat Campbell
had occupied a unique place in Ned's life. The wealth of
her experience, which she had shared with him over so many
years, had provided endless color and excitement. No one
had added more to Ned's delight in the human personality.
She did this not only through herself, but through the people
whom she brought to Ned—all spirits chosen with a fine
sense of what they could bring into his life and of what he
could give to them. One of the prized friendships Ned owed
to Mrs. Pat Campbell was that of Gustav Eckstein, the
physiologist and biographer. When news came of her death
in April, 1940 (Mrs. Pat had moved to Pau as the Germans
were moving on Paris), he wired Eckstein:

DEAR GUS: STELLA DIED AT PAU FRANCE. SHE WAS A GREAT HU-
MAN BEING. ONE OF THE THINGS I OWE HER IS YOUR FRIEND-
SHIP.

Constance Collier was another link with the British stage
dating from Sheldon's young manhood. Their meeting, like
so many others, had taken place under the Favershams' hos-
pitable roof in the years before the first World War. Miss
Collier was one of those who had added to the gaiety of
Ned's London visits. Like Mrs. Pat, she soon turned to
him for advice in her professional career.

After her success in *Peter Ibbetson*, which owed so much
to Ned, Constance Collier played the Queen in John Barrymore's production of *Hamlet*. After the play's record-break-
ing run in New York, it was taken to London. It was several
years before Miss Collier returned to America. During this
time she had had a serious illness, and in the midst of her
recovery she learned that Ned himself had become hopelessly afflicted. Her first reaction was one of unbelief, followed by horror. When she reached New York again her
first thought was to see Ned, but it took all her courage to
face him. In her autobiography *Harlequinade* the meeting is
described:

> . . . I stood outside his door trembling a little at the change
> I thought I should find. I did not want him to notice the
> slightest tremor. He called to me, and with the sound of his
> deep, vital voice, my fears dropped from me like a cloak. I
> had my dinner sitting happily beside him, and on the table
> was a replica of the little Victorian bouquet, with the very
> same colored flowers that I had carried the last night of
> "Peter Ibbetson". . . . Both of us had glimpsed those un-
> known shores and turned back to face life—he more vital,
> more brillant than ever before. . . . We had the gayest eve-
> ning imaginable talking over the intervening years. It was
> exactly as if we had parted a few hours before.

In *Harlequinade,* which appeared during Sheldon's own lifetime, Miss Collier risked his displeasure in frankly setting down the details of her indebtedness to him. But there was nothing else to do. As she herself said, there was no way to tell the story of her life without talking about Ned who, next to her mother, had been the strongest influence in it.

> . . . I have always gone to Ned Sheldon with my troubles and difficulties and he has solved them for me. He has been responsible for the best work I have done. He has kept my ideals and beliefs in the theatre and has given me the wisest counsel and help. . . .

As in all Ned's friendships, practical help was as conspicuous as spiritual advice. Throughout Miss Collier's career, both on the stage and in motion pictures, she made no important move without first consulting him. Among the papers left at her death in 1954 there was a letter of several pages on the subject of a screen version of *Zaza* which she was at one time considering. She had sent the script to Sheldon, and he had given it minute and merciless criticism. He told her that it had "no atmosphere," that it was "without the bite or vividness of real distinction," and that few scenes came "naturally to life." With his sure discernment of true drama as distinguished from banal theatricality he attacked the scenario writer's handling of the climactic scene:

> . . . In sequence 4 the climax is muffed. . . . When Zaza says that she has lied, has told his [Cascart's] wife nothing, and his mood of snarling denunciation has quickly shifted back to affection—then should come that outburst of fury, that sudden eruption of Vesuvius, which drives him out of the house like a hurricane and makes the audience want to stand up on its hind legs and cheer. It is a scene that has been the test of every actress who ever played the part. Nothing can take its place dramatically.

From his unfailing memory of past great performances
he illustrated the idea:

> . . . It was at this point that Mrs. Carter made herself fa-
> mous. Her superb and devastating paroxysm of rage will
> never be forgotten by anybody who saw it. Réjane did it
> differently—more the raw dumb agony of the ignorant fe-
> male animal—and Nazimova staged a complete nervous col-
> lapse. Farrar, in the opera, ended the scene with an attack
> of mycope or heart disease, which left her writhing on the
> floor. But they all, in their different ways, made it beyond
> question the climax of the play. In this version it would be
> just tame, rather conventional pathos, not the great vermilion
> splash which it ought to be. . . .

Sheldon never saw Edith Evans act, but from Ruth
Gordon's account of her performance in *The Country Wife*
in London and from other sources he was thoroughly aware
of the caliber of her work. In 1939 when Miss Evans was
briefly in the United States, Ruth Gordon brought her to
the penthouse. "Edith was at home with Ned in ten minutes," she later reported. Miss Evans saw Sheldon often in
the next few weeks and performed some of her great roles
for him, the Nurse in *Romeo and Juliet* (which she had
done on Broadway with Katharine Cornell), Millamant in
The Way of the World, Lady Fidget in *The Country Wife*.
Sheldon wrote Woollcott that her mastery of Restoration
comedy "touched perfection," and he unhesitatingly hailed
her "the finest actress in England."

When she returned home in September, 1939, after the
outbreak of war, she wrote Sheldon to thank him for the
long talks they had had, and to tell him how many of the
things he had said "remained and germinated" in her mind.
During the next years many letters and cables passed be-

tween them. In reply to one letter full of courage and breathing the tender freshness of the English spring which even war could not touch, he cabled her:

THANKS WONDERFUL LETTER SO LIKE YOU ALSO LIKE ENGLAND.
WE SHALL HAVE THAT DINNER YET. LOVE ALWAYS,

NED

Sheldon was vitally concerned over the fate of the English theatre during these difficult years, knowing how much the heroism of actors and actresses meant for the morale of London. In the spring of 1943 he wrote Miss Evans (soon to be Dame Edith Evans) of an idea that had occurred to him:

I have been reading Euripides, Sophocles, and Aeschylus —in translation, I hasten to add—for the past two weeks and find that in spite of their subject matter, they have the most uplifting, sustaining and soothing effect on me. They take one's mind away from the war while giving it something else—something very solid to bite on. I can only tell you my experience and suggest that they might have the same effect on other people, even in London. The emotional satisfaction of these plays is very great. And they are so thrillingly dramatic that one is seized and securely held by the scruff of the neck. An excellent position for any audience to occupy, especially in wartime.

I told you you ought to play only great parts. Well here are your great parts.

He pointed out that the plays had the virtues of small casts and simple settings, meeting the need of wartime austerity. Choruses could be reduced and their effectiveness greatly enhanced by a violin or cello in the background (an inescapable Sheldon touch). He recommended particularly the *Medea* of Euripides. "It is thoroughly up your street.

In it you could first throw a spell over your audience, then strangle it." He thought there were also great possibilities in the *Alcestis* ("a lovely fairy-tale—happy, serene, delicious") and the *Agamemnon* of Aeschylus.

> . . . I also recommend the *Antigone* of Sophocles, which is high, pure nobility in cream-colored marble. It is also, I suppose, the best constructed play in the world. Then as if these were not enough the *Electra* of Sophocles which contains perhaps the greatest acting role in Greek drama. . . .
>
> I shall never forget the overwhelming effect which Margaret Anglin made in this play. You could bring down the curtain on Electra's dance of triumph (knees lifted to the chin, toenails curved like a vulture's, head thrown back and frenzied laughter). Or you could have the unseen Orestes hurl out the bloody sword from inside the palace, let it fall on the steps with a clang, then pick it up and cuddle it in your arms as if you were holding a baby, swaying or murmuring an insane lullaby. Or you could do anything else which your imagination suggested, Miss Evans!

As the second wartime Christmas approached Sheldon sent a special message:

> *Dear Edith:*
> My Christmas thoughts and love go to you wherever you are. I wonder if you have any idea how vivid and how fragrant are my memories of my three wonderful Evans evenings! I can still hear the voice of Millamant and Mrs. Sullen and Lady Fidget and Rosalind and Cleopatra, and—through and beyond them—the voice of Edith Evans which has all England in it. There are undertones and overtones in that voice which help to convince me completely that your country is going to come out of this war on top. I know that you are not in the least conscious of these things, which is one reason why they are so convincing.
> Bless you, dear Edith. Some day you will come back and

act for me again, and we shall talk and talk. Meanwhile you
are never far away and you are my dear friend.

Yours ever affectionately,

NED

There were still other visitors from the British stage who, like John Gielgud, found Sheldon's apartment "a haven in the cordial but sometimes overexciting atmosphere of New York," and who counted their hours with him as one of the special rewards of a stay in America. Charles MacArthur brought Beatrice Lillie and Gertrude Lawrence to see Ned in 1924 during the run of the never-to-be-forgotten *Charlot's Revue*. Katharine Cornell introduced Maurice Evans when he played Romeo to her Juliet. Dame May Whitty and her daughter Margaret Webster were friends from Ned's early days in England. Dame May had always vivid memories of his youthful charm, but these were insignificant beside the picture of him "in those later days when he was, seemingly, in bondage, and yet with a spirit so free, a sight so clear, that to visit him was to lose many of our earthly limitations, and to find fresh courage to tackle one's problems."

Peggy Ashcroft's acquaintance with Ned was brief, but its effect was enduring. She wrote him often from England during the war and voiced the hope to which all his British friends clung tenaciously—"and such a wonderful hope it is—to sail freely over a peaceful ocean and arrive in New York, get in a taxi and drive to Eighty-fourth Street— And I will do it, I know!"

Mrs. Pat Campbell brought John Gielgud to the penthouse in 1937, and his experience was typical of those meeting Sheldon for the first time. When he sailed back to England, he wrote to say how much the visit had meant, noting how quickly they had reached "an understanding that, in any kind of gathering, or with anyone less responsive and concentrated than yourself, might have taken months to arrive at." Gielgud modestly discounted any part he himself might have had in this, but Sheldon wrote Woollcott after their first meeting that he had "sensed his [Gielgud's] fine intelligence at once."

One day in March, 1943, Ned wrote his cousin Elsa Denison Jameson:

> . . . I have a Sub-Lieutenant in the Royal Navy coming to see me this afternoon. I don't know what Sub means. I shall make no inquiries about the British Navy, but talk instead about Shakespeare. He was an actor and apparently a good one before the war.

The Sub-Lieutenant was Alec Guinness, who had achieved his first success as an actor and playwright just as war broke out. He had at once enlisted in the Royal Navy as an ordinary seaman and had worked up to his first command. He was in America now to pick up his ship. However, on arrival he discovered that the vessel would not be ready for some time; in fact, the keel had not even been laid. To fill the weeks of waiting he turned to the theatre and appeared in Terence Rattigan's RAF play *Flarepath*. The play had a short life, but for Guinness the experience was a happy break in the wartime routine, and helped to keep alive the hope that he might some day return for good to his profession.

John Gielgud, who had been one of the first to recognize Guinness' talent, sent him to Eighty-fourth Street. Sheldon welcomed the actor with that special cordiality he always had for young people of the theatre, heightened in this case because his visitor was a Britisher fighting for his country.

They had talked only for a few minutes before the older man realized that, underneath an exterior of smooth efficiency, the Sub-Lieutenant was deeply troubled. He was having a struggle to adjust to the harsh military routine, and the artist in him was revolted by the waste and horror of war. Sheldon had seen more than one young friend in this situation and his heart went out to his visitor. Yet what he gave in the course of their talks together was not sympathy to a man in an unpleasant situation, but the feeling that even so general a catastrophe as war could not stop the process of growth. The very fact that his new friend had been able to put resolutely behind him everything that had mattered most in life and throw his whole mind and all his energy into the task now required of him had an immense positive value. To perform these new duties, so alien to everything in Guinness' background, meant the development of new resources, of new strength. War might have momentarily deadening effects on the creative imagination, but if the man grew the artist must surely grow also.

As their friendship ripened Guinness felt his confusion drop away. It was like some special dispensation to have come upon Sheldon at this critical moment in his life. As he summed it up, "A great calm descended upon me in Sheldon's presence which I carried throughout the war."

After he finally sailed, Guinness kept Sheldon in touch with life in the Royal Navy. He wrote of long tense days at sea, of landings under heavy fire, of the loss of his ship on the rocky Adriatic coast. Even in the midst of fighting he cherished the dream that he would return to the theatre, a dream that Ned unceasingly fostered. From the Mediterranean in the fall of 1943 he wrote that his dramatization of *Great Expectations* was being revived by the Old Vic. "If

I were in New York, I would insist on your letting me come to bore you with its details, and to seek your advice on a hundred points."

Sheldon's British friendships were not limited to the people of the theatre. Scarcely a week went by when he was not visited by some English writer, statesman, or public figure. If, particularly during the war years, his grasp of everything that was happening in England was minute and authoritative, it was because his sources of information were authentic.

He had long been a devotee of Mrs. Belloc Lowndes, whom he considered a supreme craftsman of the horror story in which he took such hearty delight. He had read her classic *The Lodger* many times—as well as other tales which never failed to seize him "by the scruff of the neck."

Though he did not meet Mrs. Belloc Lowndes until 1935, they had been in correspondence for nearly a year before. This arose out of the celebrated plagiarism suit over *Dishonored Lady*, filed by Sheldon and Margaret Ayer Barnes against Metro-Goldwyn-Mayer, in which Mrs. Belloc Lowndes was quite innocently involved.

Four months after *Dishonored Lady* opened in New York (February 4, 1930), Mrs. Belloc Lowndes published a novel entitled *Letty Lynton*—deriving from the same source as the play, the murder trial of Madeleine Smith. For some sixteen months Metro-Goldwyn-Mayer were in negotiations with Sheldon and Mrs. Barnes for the rights to *Dishonored Lady*. During this time several treatments of the play were made both by the producers and by Sheldon, in the hope that one might pass muster with the Hays office. In 1931 the negotiations were broken off. Shortly thereafter MGM bought Mrs. Belloc Lowndes's novel and made a picture entitled *Letty Lynton*, incorporating copyrighted material

from *Dishonored Lady*. Six weeks after the film was released
Sheldon and Mrs. Barnes filed suit against the picture company. The trial was held in April 1933, but the decision was
not handed down until 1934 when Judge Woolsey found
against the authors of *Dishonored Lady*, declaring that there
was no infringement since both the play and the novel were
based on the Glasgow murder trial. However, when the
case was appealed Judge Woolsey's decision was reversed on
the grounds that the motion picture was not directly based
on the Madeleine Smith case, but on a treatment specifically
prepared for *Dishonored Lady* while the producers were
considering purchase of the play. Litigation lasted for seven
years. Finally the case went to the United States Supreme
Court which affirmed the findings of the Circuit Court of
Appeals. In 1940 final judgment was handed down, and
damages were awarded to Sheldon and Mrs. Barnes in excess
of half a million dollars. (This figure was substantially reduced by a later lawsuit with Guthrie McClintic who as
producer of the play claimed a share of the picture rights.
Even so the settlement was one of the largest ever made in
this country in a plagiarism suit.)

Sheldon followed every twist of the trial with keen attention. However, as his attorney Arthur Driscoll says, he
was not interested "in what it might produce in the way of
compensation to him, but . . . in establishing the right of
a copyright owner to protect his material." It must be said
also that he found distinct enjoyment in being mixed up in a
good fight, and that the drama of the court procedures
fascinated him.

In addition to the financial rewards there were also, and
far more precious, human ones. The trial brought Ned the
friendship of Gordon Auchincloss, the Special Master ap-
pointed by the court to determine the damages in the suit.

Through Gordon Auchincloss, Sheldon met his brother Charles, who became an especially close and useful friend later on.

The third association resulting from the suit was with Mrs. Belloc Lowndes. In the autumn of 1934 it occurred to Sheldon that he ought to acquaint the author of *Letty Lynton* with the details of the litigation, and to assure her that so far as her novel was concerned he knew that there was no question of plagiarism. This was a thoughtful gesture for which Mrs. Belloc Lowndes was grateful. The case had given her "a frightful amount of worry, as at first there was an idea of making out that I had plagiarized your play in my novel. Fortunately my story was finished three months before your play appeared."

When Mrs. Belloc Lowndes came to America in 1935, Woollcott, who was an old friend of hers, brought her at once to Sheldon. Thereafter during her visit she dined with him often—"almost every night," as she remembered afterward. They talked of the techniques of murder, of politics, of literary craftsmanship, of their mutual friend Woollcott, and the increasingly oppressive world atmosphere. She recalled listening with Ned to foreign broadcasts dealing with French and English political events and was amazed at his grasp of the intricacies of the European situation. Sheldon in turn found Mrs. Belloc Lowndes a mine of information on English and continental politics and a most astute observer of the international scene. The daughter of a French father and an Anglo-Saxon mother and the sister of Hilaire Belloc, her native shrewdness gave her a rare insight into the minds controlling world events. As Sheldon once wrote Woollcott, "I have discovered that all the things she says are going to happen really do happen. It is like the Delphic oracle with a slightly rolling French r." (Mrs. Belloc Lowndes's own

account of herself to another friend was, "I am half Fwench
and therefore a wealist.")

Mrs. Belloc Lowndes found Sheldon's own political
judgment uncannily accurate. This sprang, first of all, she
thought, from his inexhaustible interest in human nature and
his knowledge of motives. "He knew men and women of
every type and condition—in that unlike most Americans.
In fact, he was, in the true sense of the phrase, 'a citizen of
the world.'" It was his international outlook, and his far-
reaching understanding of the psychology of other peoples,
that led him to foresee early the drift of events toward
World War II. Mrs. Belloc Lowndes remembered that in
1935 he had given her "a picture of what he thought was
going to happen when Germany was put on her legs again.
. . . Everything he believed would come to pass did come
to pass—and that was at a time when both in England and
America Germany was regarded as no longer a threat to
the world. . . . Sheldon alone of my American friends
was convinced that whatever form of government Germany
chose, she would in time bring about another world war."

Aside from his qualities as a human being, Sheldon won
Mrs. Belloc Lowndes's profound respect for his critical
sense. "Your view of T. E. Lawrence," she once wrote from
England, "is far the best of any I have ever heard or read.
You have hit the truth in saying that 'his vanity is colossal,
though he had no conceit.'"

When war came Mrs. Belloc Lowndes was one of Sheldon's most faithful reporters of the British scene. She wrote
in vivid detail the effects of war on daily life, and always,
even in the midst of the deadly bombing in 1940, with perfect composure. In August of that year with the German
invasion expected, "probably tomorrow," she wrote that
she was at last leaving battered London for the country,

taking with her, as a precaution against the ordeal to come, an extra ration of tea.

Mrs. Belloc Lowndes sent another English friend, Mrs. James Carruthers, to see Sheldon. Mrs. Carruthers later wrote from war-torn England of their meeting: "It was worth crossing the Atlantic to have such an experience, and on the days when my spirit feels cold and weak, I think of your courage and patience in that high room above the city, and I take a pull at myself and am braver." Mrs. Patrick Campbell's goddaughter Stella Moore quickly learned that this was why "the first thing his English friends wanted to do on landing in the States is to get through customs, and jump in a taxi heading for East Eighty-fourth Street."

The fidelity of these friends through long years of separation was astonishing. Sheldon received letters from Lady Berkeley describing wartime activities at Berkeley Castle in Gloucester, where a "cottage hospital" for wounded soldiers had been established, and where a "working party" of some five hundred women sewed and knitted. He heard regularly from Emilie Grigsby, whose letters were filled with the colors and perfume of her beautiful garden at The Old Meadows in West Drayton where Ned had spent many happy hours in times long past.

As always, friends sent friends to see him. Miss Grigsby gave a letter of introduction to Sir Shane Leslie, cousin of Winston Churchill. Denis Mackail sent along his friends A. A. Milne and Ian Hay Beith. Milne was a little nervous when Mackail told him about Sheldon, but both men returned to England "to express gratitude—and amazement—for an unforgettable experience."

Sheldon was deeply indebted to Sir Kenneth and Lady Lee for wartime reports from England. Sir Kenneth at the outset of the war was Director of Radio Relations in the

Ministry of Information. When he became Director-General, Sheldon was satisfied that England now had a qualified "opposite number to Mr. Goebbels." Sheldon had met the Lees while they were in America before the war, and the friendship had been sealed when the Lees' Indian myna bird, Archie, became Ned's house guest for several days.

One of Sheldon's happiest expectations was realized late in his life when he at last met the long-admired author of *Greenmantle*, John Buchan, by that time Lord Tweedsmuir, Governor-General of Canada. When the Tweedsmuirs were in New York in 1934 Alice Duer Miller and Woollcott brought them to the penthouse. Sheldon and the novelist-statesman lost no time in discovering a deep spiritual kinship, not only in Sheldon's fondness for Tweedsmuir's work and his native Scotland, but in their intense mutual conviction that (as Lord Tweedsmuir put it) "the future of civilization depends more upon the stability of the United States and the British Empire . . . than upon all the effervescence of Japan and the European dictators."

When Tweedsmuir returned to Canada after his first visit to Sheldon he at once let his new friend know his feelings:

> *Dear Sheldon:*
>
> *It has been a very great privilege to meet you, by far the most valuable to me in this visit. You have given me a new view of human courage, for you have fulfilled Wordsworth's ideal of one who,*
>
> > *Born to live in company with pain*
> > *Turns the necessity to glorious gain.*
>
> *I look forward to returning to New York, principally to have the pleasure of seeing you again. Meantime we both send you our love.*
>
> > *Yours sincerely,*
> > JOHN BUCHAN

During the next five years there were frequent meetings between the Tweedsmuirs and Sheldon. This was another friendship in which children as well as parents had their place, and as the shadow of war moved closer Sheldon felt the anxiety of Lord and Lady Tweedsmuir over the future of their three sons, all facing military service. They were uppermost in his mind when in September, 1939, he heard Chamberlain's fateful pronouncement: "We are now in a state of war with Germany."

The war was five months old when in February, 1940, Sheldon received his last letter from John Buchan. Two or three weeks later came news that the Governor-General was seriously ill. During the next five days Sheldon was in close touch with Ottawa by telephone and telegraph, until the final report arrived. His sense of personal loss was heightened by the knowledge of what Buchan's death meant to his family, and how much it added to the general gloom of the picture with which they were all confronted.

Naturally the plight of Britain made Sheldon restive at his own country's position. Knowing that war was inevitable, it seemed that valuable time was being lost when the United States did not move more quickly to declare itself. "I look forward to the day," he told Alice Buchan Fairfax-Lucy, Lord Tweedsmuir's daughter, "when our two countries stand together as allies. For the sake of our country—as well as for the sake of the world—I hope it comes soon."

Almost without exception, Sheldon's British friends have testified to his effect on their morale during the harrowing years from 1940 to 1945. Lady Hilda Grenfel, national president of the British YWCA, was sent to Sheldon by her cousin Lady Tweedsmuir. This was a month before Pearl

Harbor. As she sailed for England to face the perils and destruction of the blitz, her final thought was of Sheldon:

> I hardly knew how to say goodbye yesterday. We had spoken of everything except your sufferings, which you surmount with such spiritual power that you fortify one's faith. To those who do this the world owes such a debt; and you know, don't you, how often you are a "refuge thought," as Edward Gray's wife once called it, to your friends.

To these friends in the midst of the holocaust, Sheldon was not merely a symbol but the living proof of man's power to survive whatever fate might bring. Again and again, when their ordeal was approaching the unbearable, Sheldon's friends across the Atlantic would have a sudden, acute consciousness of his presence. Often this would be followed, sometimes in a matter of hours, by a letter or cable from him. Woollcott was in England in 1941 and learned something of these manifestations of Sheldon's spirit which seemed to cut across barriers of time and space as though they did not exist. "The most improbable people would come up to me and ask after Sheldon," he told Gustav Eckstein. "One woman asked, 'How does he know just when to cable?'" Lady Tweedsmuir later spoke of "those wonderful cables which always seemed to come on the worst days of the war." There was more than an intuition of need behind them, more than sympathy for what he knew his friends were facing. His words breathed a positive sense that he was living in the most real and intense way through every shade of their experience. On V-E Day, five years after Buchan's death, Lady Tweedsmuir received a cable from him with one sentence:

I AM THINKING OF JOHN.

CHAPTER XIV

The Light on the Threshold

AFTER bodily movement ceased Sheldon seemed to live outside of time. "My day begins when my mind begins," he told "Mr. Ernst" when the orderly first took up his duties at Eighty-fourth Street. It was a very flexible day, lasting as long as Ned's interest was held by whatever emerged in reading, conversation with friends, or meditation. Released from editorial deadlines, rehearsal calls, and professional appointments, which regulated the lives of his friends, he escaped from the relentless grip of the calendar. To a great extent he also escaped the friction and harassments, the wear and tear of the competitive life that brought gray hair and lined faces to his contemporaries. It was as though the tragedy that had struck him in youth had thrown over him a mantle to protect him from the stresses that hasten age.

Everyone remarked how little his appearance changed with the years. But his youthfulness was most conspicuous in the fresh vigor of his mind and spirit. For all his knowledge of the world and the minutiae of human experience, he was always alert to the process of unfoldment. He had an eager receptivity toward life which most older people gradually lose in the hard rubbing of the world. This doubtless contributed to the exhilaration that his contemporaries felt in his presence. Ned had kept vital and untouched something of their own youth.

It was this quality also that made young people feel a special bond with him. They sought his companionship and counsel as regularly as did their elders. They were drawn not only by his charm and wisdom, but by an affinity of spirit they did not always feel even with their own parents.

His understanding of smaller children was shown in his genius for entertaining them. Before he lost the use of his hands and before blindness set in, he took active part in their games when they came to see him. Afterward his ingenuity was always at work to provide the sort of fun in which he could at least share their reactions. It is no wonder that children regarded his apartment as a kind of blue heaven presided over by an enchanted prince devoted solely to their happiness and pleasure.

Sheldon's acute sympathy for children did not prevent him from being objective about them. He was continually called upon as an interpreter of the young for distraught parents. He knew that most adults have forgotten so much of childhood that they do not recognize a typical juvenile behavior pattern when it appears. Too often when the child's conduct deviates sharply from that of the adult, the latter immediately sees a "problem." To Ned, whose memories of his own childhood were phenomenally vivid, it was often clear that what his friends considered abnormal in their offspring was simply a phase of growth.

He was deeply conscious always of the child as an individual, an intricate composite of many elements, the most important of which were not definable. He was always amazed at a parent's naïveté in expecting a child to be a simple reflection of him or herself. "I don't know what to do about Janie," wailed the mother of a fractious eight-year-old. "She isn't a bit like me at her age."

"Well," replied Ned patiently, "Janie also has a father. She might be somewhat like him."

But this was only a beginning. There was a good deal more to a child than inherited traits. Even the infant has experiences which are unique to him or her and which leave lasting marks on the personality. Yet Ned was never much concerned about how a child got to be the way he was. The main thing was to recognize the child's right to his own nature, and to respect that nature.

Ned had never met the small daughter of one of his friends, an intelligent, cultivated, and (generally speaking) practical woman. But they had talked of little Ellen a good deal. According to the mother, she seemed incapable of following the simplest conventional routine. Even at play she showed an almost perverse non-conformity. The same attitude was reflected in her school work. When Ned finally met the child he saw at once that she was intelligent beyond her years and highly imaginative. What made her a problem was the fact that neither quality had had much chance to express itself in the kind of routine her parents and teachers tried to impose on her. When he was later asked his opinion he replied, "She's a very *rapturous* little girl"—with the implication that Ellen had certain highly personal needs to be fulfilled before she could be expected to yield docilely to the demands of group living.

Ned had a special flair for the problems of adolescence. Believing absolutely in "the inalienable right of the soul to its own experience," he quickly won the confidence of his teen-age friends so that there was literally no problem they were unwilling to lay before him. They not only found him a patient listener to their troubles; his insight into their natures and his ability to speak their own language enabled him to put into words much that was bewilderingly vague in their inner turmoil. The very fact that he could express what was so often hopelessly bottled up through inarticulateness helped more than one youngster find his way through a major emotional crisis.

People always spoke of Ned as "solving" their problems for them. What he actually did was to make them learn how to solve their own problems. This was particularly the case in his dealings with young people. As one of them described the process:

> . . . You take your problem to Ned, who spreads it out before you. He is really tossing it right back at you, but he helps you analyze it. You take up each factor separately with him, consider each one, then put them all back together again. But now there is a fresh and clearer light on the old problem, and somehow it all adds up differently. What's more, in the end, it is you and not Ned who makes the final decision.

All this may suggest that Ned was simply a highly successful amateur psychiatrist. But he would have scoffed at the idea. His interest in people was not based on scientific curiosity, but on simple affection. If he was able to lighten the way for boys and girls groping through the darkness of inexperience, it was because he could still feel as they did. The great difference was that in him the feeling was filtered through the fine-meshed sieve of his wisdom, while in the young people who came to him it was mixed up with all sorts of extraneous matter that often clouded its true nature.

Perhaps above all else the thing that stands out in the memory of those who knew Ned in their youth is his infinite patience. He had long talks and furious correspondence with young George Foote, the son of his old Harvard classmate and the grandson of Basil King. He would give the most careful consideration to the thirty-page letters the boy sometimes wrote, letters filled with analyses of the world's problems and ingenious schemes for the rapid making over of humanity. When the boy's father threw up his hands over these adolescent outpourings, Ned would remind him, "After all he's old, George, and you're the younger one. You'll never be as old as he is right now."

A cousin of young Foote's, Alice Orcutt Howell, also had a place in the three-generation friendship between Sheldon and the family of Basil King. She was the daughter of Penelope King and Reginald Orcutt, a friend of Ned's Harvard days. Though Alice had grown up in the reflection of Sheldon's friendship for her parents and grandparents, she nevertheless felt early in life that she had special claims on him. "Somehow, he had that extraordinary gift of making each one of us a separate, individual niche in his heart of many mansions."

Alice Orcutt was eleven when she first met Sheldon. She was in that phase when the personality is struggling violently to be itself and resents pressures to make it into something else. Ned's instant sympathy for her situation set the seal on their friendship. At the moment Alice was immersed in writing a school play, and Ned regarded the project with utmost seriousness. In time the masterpiece was completed, neatly typed, and sent to him for criticism. He gave it the same meticulous attention he bestowed on the work of his professional playwright friends, commending the good spots, making suggestions for strengthening the weak ones, taking care to disturb nothing that was a true reflection of the girl herself.

A few years later during a tumultuously unhappy period

at boarding school while her parents were in Europe, Alice turned instinctively to Ned for help. She was utterly miserable trying to fit into an alien atmosphere. Ned seemed to know exactly what it meant, as she said later, "to feel pudgy, out of place, with no social graces, infuriated by a complete lack of being able to express the real me." Finally matters came to a climax and Alice left the school. She was desolate at the thought of her failure and her parents' disappointment. But Ned gave her the determination to make a fresh start elsewhere and profit by what she had learned. When she wrote to tell him her plans, saying that she now clearly saw her past mistakes, but that she was not going to be bowed down by the memory, he immediately telegraphed:

> ALICE DEAR: YOU ARE RIGHT THAT'S THAT SO PUT IT FIRMLY BEHIND YOU AND CONCENTRATE ON FUTURE WHICH SEEMS TO BE FULL OF BRILLIANT PROMISE. DO YOU REMEMBER LAST LINES OF LYCIDAS THE SHEPHERD ROSE AND TWITCHED HIS MANTLE BLUE TOMORROW TO FRESH WOODS AND PASTURES NEW. LET ME KNOW IF PASTURES TURN OUT TO BE CALIFORNIA. BLESS YOU DEAR ALICE I BET YOU HAVE LEARNED A LOT FROM THIS AND THAT IN ITSELF MAKES IT WORTHWHILE. NED.

Mrs. Howell adds a footnote to these memories of her teens:

> Looking back to that whole period I find I have formed the adult's contempt for such introverted and egocentric upheavals; and yet I realize even now that at that age, the young wish more than anything in the world to be taken seriously. And this Ned did. He always made me feel as if I were not mistaken, and that indeed some magic potentiality did exist within me.

Ned was always able to see the importance of details in a young person's life that most adults consider insignificant. He could share wholeheartedly in the small events that loom so large in the child's or adolescent's world. When he received painfully printed reports from his six-year-old godson Edward Sheldon Cabot in California, he answered them with a proper regard for the matters they described.

> . . . *I am glad you are being good. It is much more satisfactory in the long run than being bad. I hope the caterpillars eat lots of leaves and then shut themselves up inside the little grey houses we call cocoons. In the spring they will come out of their cocoons and turn into butterflies or big moths. You will enjoy watching this and helping them along.*

> . . . *I have just had the same kind of cough and cold you have, so I know what it is like. You will get over it though, and then we shall celebrate by having a party. Meanwhile I am sending you a book about a little girl named Alice, who followed a white rabbit into his rabbit hole and had all sorts of funny and exciting adventures. . . .*

> . . . *Congratulations on your promotion. I hope you make a good corporal and keep on obeying orders promptly and willingly. This is the first principle in a soldier's life. . . .*

Sheldon's devotion to his niece Georgiana MacArthur was shown by his eager attention to whatever was uppermost in the girl's life at the moment. He would often telegraph to comment on some single detail of a letter she had written. Such details seemed framed in special importance for her forever afterward.

> WISH I COULD HAVE SAT WITH YOU AND JAN ON THAT HAY-STACK IN THE MOONLIGHT. LOVE. UNCLE NED.

> CONGRATULATIONS ON YOUR WORK IN ENGLISH CLUB I AM SURE YOUR PROGRAM WILL BE GREAT SUCCESS. UNCLE NED.

> THANKS FOR SENDING ME POEM WHICH I THINK HAS REAL FEELING LIKE STORY AND AM SURE MARY [Sheldon's sister, Mrs. Alfred MacArthur] DID TOO. WHY NOT WRITE SOME

MORE STORIES AND POEMS AND THEN THEY COULD BE BOUND
IN A REAL COVER AND PRESENTED TO YOUR FATHER? IT WOULD
SURELY PLEASE HIM. UNCLE NED.

When his niece as a young bride wrote ecstatic descriptions of her new home he replied:

I APPROVE OF THOSE KITCHEN CURTAINS.

After the arrival of her first baby Georgiana had a return of her schoolgirl urge to write, and sent Ned some poems for comment. He wrote back:

> . . . It was sweet of you to send me the little poems, which I am returning so that you can put them away for Bob's great-grandchildren. They are touching and like you. But be careful about your rhymes. "Rain" does not in the sight of God rhyme with "come."

Although proverbially modest himself, Sheldon had never been handicapped by a lack of self-confidence. At an early age he had taken the measure of his talent and made the most of it. Yet he was deeply conscious of the delicate balance on which a young person's belief in himself often hung. He knew what little things can make or break the faith in our own powers when we are young, and he overlooked no opportunity to give a boy or girl a sense of the real value of any achievement. This was not merely a matter of praise. Ned tried to make each one feel that he had some genuine power that was his peculiar possession which, in one way or another, might lead to important accomplishment later on. He was quick to recognize creative effort, no matter how modest. Perhaps it would be nothing more than a well-written letter; but Ned had the knack of making the author feel that here was something to be chalked up high on the credit side of the balance against the failures that weigh

so heavily in the life of a sensitive boy or girl. When
Josephine Murray, the daughter of Ned's friends Dr. and
Mrs. Henry A. Murray, sent him a long letter from England describing the coronation of George VI, Ned wrote
back:

> *That was an extraordinarily interesting letter you wrote
> me about the Coronation. So interesting in fact that I sent it
> to your father and asked him to put it away in the Murray
> archives for your great-granddaughter. Think how you would
> enjoy a letter written by your great-grandmother describing
> the Coronation of Queen Victoria. . . .*

When Josephine returned to America she naturally came
to see Ned at once. He was gratified to find that the immature schoolgirl had flowered into a charming young
woman during her two years abroad. But he noted that she
had not yet overcome a certain shyness which he felt would
be an obstacle to the happiness he wanted for her. He immediately set about to remedy this. In doing so he used a
typically Sheldonian technique—making a virtue of a weakness. A few days after her return to New York she received this telegram:

> I AM ASKING MY FRIEND DR. —— TO MEET YOU TONIGHT. HE
> IS INTERNE AT ST. LUKE'S. HE IS ALSO SHY SO BE KIND TO HIM.

Sheldon's faculty for creating a genuine and lasting self-
confidence in so many young people thrown unprepared
into a cold-bloodedly competitive world sprang from his
belief in the supreme worth of the individual. Nothing was
more reassuring to the uncertain and diffident young who
went to him than the knowledge that he judged them for
what they were in themselves, that he did not hold them up
for comparison with their compeers and forebears. He was
always on the lookout for the thing that set one person off

from another, and when he found it he made the most of it. He believed that everybody had some special merit or talent, which would assure him a place in the world. It might be a modest place but in filling it to the best of his ability the individual would find happiness. For Ned getting the most out of life meant getting the most out of oneself. The thing he always insisted on when he talked of this question was that if you wanted to do a thing badly enough you would find the way to do it. But it was important to want a thing for the right reason, not mere worldly ambition or a desire to shine in the eyes of others, but because of a basic need to be fulfilled.

When Billie Burke's daughter Patricia was faced with the problem of many attractive girls who must make their own way in the world she went to see Ned. After the visit Ned wrote to reassure her anxious mother:

> Dearest Billie:
>
> Patricia has just lunched with me and we have had a good talk. She was so sweet and I was impressed, as I always am, by her calm reasonableness and common-sense. She spoke of you and of your wisdom with such loving admiration. Her whole attitude proved how right and how wonderful you have been with her.
>
> Of course I talked about work and jobs. I told her that she was the child of workers, and that she was a young woman of intelligence, vitality, and character, that she would never be happy without some kind of work which she enjoyed doing, that the ability to do something well—something which the world needed and would pay for—was the only way in which a woman could achieve security. Also I pointed out that this would raise her in the estimation of the best type of man and could only add to her equipment for marriage and mother-hood.
>
> Patricia followed everything I said with sympathetic understanding and seemed to agree with it. I think she feels—

and *I believe she is right—that the job she is looking for does not lie in the field of entertainment. But there are many other fields of human endeavor, and if she makes a careful and intelligent investigation, she ought to find the one which suits her best. She spoke of the solid satisfaction which her work in the hospital gave her. This made me feel more strongly than ever that her work should be connected with people in some healthful [sic] capacity. I suggested that she look into the New York School of Social Service and she said she would do this on her return. Incidentally it strikes me that the summer in New York may be a good idea. She evidently feels more stimulated to do something here than she does in Los Angeles. Perhaps this is a young man, but, if so, he may galvanize her in the right direction. If she discovers during the summer what kind of work really interests her, then the summer will have been well spent and she can start enthusiastically on the new road next fall.*

My love to you, dear Billie. Your visit is still like a sort of happy dream.

Your affectionate
NED

Sheldon studied the interests and language of his young friends with complete absorption and scrupulous attention to details. His first meeting with Gordon Phillips Hoover, a star athlete at the Hotchkiss School, occurred shortly after the boy had achieved fame by pitching a no-hit, no-run game between Hotchkiss and the Hill School. Ned knew nothing about baseball at the time, but the deficiency was soon remedied. He sent his secretary to the library for every available book on the subject, and in the two-day interval between the announcement of young Hoover's intended visit and his arrival at the penthouse, Ned completely mastered not only the rules and vocabulary of the game, but the personal histories, the batting averages, and the legendary exploits of every great major-league player from Ty Cobb on down, not omitting the record of his visitor who had been hailed by sports editors as "Baseball's Youngest Hero." The friendship thus begun grew in depth and warmth throughout the boy's school and college years. On a black day in 1944 word came that Gordon, then a lieutenant in the Navy, had been lost when the submarine on which he was serving struck a Japanese mine. This was a cruel blow for Ned, but his thoughts went at once to those even closer to Gordon, his mother (Kathleen O'Donnell Hoover, a friend of Ned's youth), his young wife and child. He tried to temper the loss for Gordon's wife by reminding her that love would always live so long as memory endured. In token of this belief, and of his affection for her and her husband, he sent her the original typescript of *Romance,* to be given eventually to Gordon's child.

He sought other means of making sorrow bearable for Gordon's mother. After her son's death Mrs. Hoover had thrown herself with redoubled effort into the war activities in which she was engaged. The result, after a few months, was a collapse that sent her to the hospital for a long recuperation. When she was able to see Ned again, he urged her—"forced" was Mrs. Hoover's own term—into an undertaking planned some years before but abandoned under the pressure of war work. This was a book on the opera, of which she had long been a serious student. Under Ned's goading, so sharp that Mrs. Hoover never dared come to him without producing evidence of the work's progress, the book was finished. Ned did not live to see the publication of *Makers of Opera* (in 1949), and delight in its fine critical reception. But he had his reward in the course of the writing, as he watched the grief for a vanished young life find outlet in a new act of creation.

Sheldon's enthusiasm for youth was naturally linked to

a keen interest in education. His constant alertness to new
ideas, to new trends in scholarship, made him an avid reader
of college catalogues. On the long book-piled table in his
living room there were always college newspapers and
magazines which served to keep him posted on the ideas
and the idiom of the younger generation. As a consequence
of this reading he acquired an enormous fund of information
on schools and colleges which was of great practical value
to his young friends and their parents. He could cite special
courses offered by various institutions. He knew the names
and scholarly reputations of important faculty members of
a score of universities. He knew all about the policies, the
social atmosphere, and the tuition costs of as many more. This
background of information combined with his knowledge
of the characters and needs of those asking his advice made
him a highly qualified counselor whose services were in
constand demand.

But it was not merely as an adviser that Sheldon showed
his deep interest in education. Ever since he had written
The Nigger he had been preoccupied with the problems of
the South, particularly the problems of education. In 1927
he happened to read in *The Tar Heel*, student publication of
the University of North Carolina, an account of a chapel
talk on the plight of students who were working their way
through the University. The talk had been given by Harry
F. Comer, general secretary of the university YMCA.
Sheldon was so moved by the situation described that he at
once wrote the following letter:

> *My dear Mr. Comer:*
>   *I have just read in* The Tar Heel *an article reporting a talk
> you made in chapel to the self-help students, and in this talk
> you gave some facts and figures regarding the financial plight
> of self-help students that have disturbed me deeply. In fact*

the picture has disturbed my sleep. I cannot imagine that there could be in our country so large a number of worthy boys prepared to enter college and yet so far short of the necessary means. With real embarrassment I admit that this is a side of life with which I am not well acquainted. On the contrary, I have seen too many able boys with abundant means who could not be persuaded to take advantage of educational opportunities freely offered them.

I would so like to help in this situation to some extent that I am writing to ask a favor of you, while at the same time apologizing for adding anything to what I am sure must be a terribly overcrowded schedule for you. If I knew you personally I would feel better about asking this favor.

Members of my family have established scholarship funds, and I would like very much to see some of your fine boys there at North Carolina enjoy their benefits. Will you please, therefore, select two of the most deserving boys of the upper classes and let me have their names so that I may get them in touch with these scholarships. I should like boys who come from the mountain section of your state, as a matter of sentiment, for I have visited your North Carolina mountains in the summer time and come to love that section and its people. Please select two boys who are of athletic physique—though not necessarily athletes—boys with promising records; and I would especially like them to be boys who are lovers of nature.

As you send me the names, will you kindly also give a brief biographical sketch of each boy, outlining his chief qualities of personality and character; his vocational interests; and listing his hobbies. I would like these details about the boys as a matter of personal satisfaction.

Thanking you for this personal favor, I am,

Sincerely yours,
EDWARD SHELDON

Comer's work brought him close to these students who were struggling against sometimes overwhelming odds to complete their university careers. He had shared the heart-break of more than one promising fellow who had simply not been able to meet the problem of earning a livelihood while carrying the required academic load. So Sheldon's letter was like a miraculous benison, all the more wonderful because it was so unexpected. Comer lost no time in acting on the writer's instructions, and with great care selected two candidates who met Sheldon's requirements. At the last moment one of the boys was prevented from taking advantage of the offer because of family complications. The other, Richard Slagle, from Franklin, North Carolina, became Ned's protégé not only for the remainder of his undergraduate life, but also through four years of medical school. His new and as yet unseen friend's generosity enabled young Slagle to pay back money he had received from the student loan fund and to finish his undergraduate work unhampered by the financial pressure that had weighed on his earlier years. When graduation time came there was an extra check to cover Senior Week and other special expenses. Meanwhile, an active correspondence had begun in which plans were laid for Slagle's medical training. The selection of a school was of paramount importance, and on Ned's advice the young man entered Cornell University Medical School in New York.

When Slagle arrived in New York he found that Ned had not only made arrangements for a scholarship at Cornell, but that he had taken care of the details of living accommodations as well. He had secured for Slagle and another Southern boy whom he was sponsoring a small apartment of two rooms and kitchenette, completely equipped down to a pantry stocked with staple foods. Slagle had expected to work during his spare time in order to pay at least part of his expenses, but Ned insisted from the beginning that his mind and time should be free for his work at medical school.

Throughout his years in New York, Slagle was a regular visitor at the penthouse. The warm relationship that developed was like that of father and son, and it continued so throughout Sheldon's life. Slagle graduated from Cornell with high standing, married, eventually became head of the Presbyterian Hospital in San Juan, Puerto Rico, and served as a surgeon in the Navy during World War II. Sheldon's affection followed wherever he went. There were letters of advice on the problems of group living, announcements of birthday presents on the way, admonitions not to let young Edward Sheldon Slagle get sunstroke, and reminders of home. Slagle's Carolina mountain background had a curious pull for Sheldon. It seemed to strike some response in a still unsilenced yearning for the beauties of nature that he had never forgotten and that he would never see again:

> . . . I am reading a book about the Great Smokies [he once wrote] and the western part of the state—its geology, forestry, history, inhabitants, etc. Naturally it makes me think of Dick, as that is his native country and has done so much to mold him. I hope that Lois and Ned, through their visits to Franklin, will grow up with the knowledge and love of the mountains. . . .

Ned's love of young people and his infinite compassion for their struggles did not prevent him from seeing also with the parent's eye. Although he had never had children of his own, and had not known the routine, the special pressures of family life, he was nevertheless highly sensitive to the effects of these things. Above all he understood the love of a parent for a child. In a moment of crisis involving the child of a friend, he had the same anxiety, felt the same necessity for instant action that the parent himself experienced.

Once news came over the radio of an earthquake in California with the expectation of a tidal wave. His thoughts went instantly to a friend in Connecticut whose son was in boarding school at Long Beach. Ned immediately put in a long-distance call to Hollywood. An hour later he was able to notify the frantic mother, astonished as she was anxious, that everything was all right. He had gotten in touch with John Barrymore who had immediately spoken with the police and school authorities in Long Beach. Barrymore then relayed back the information that all the children in the school were safe. They had scattered to shelter in busses just before the building collapsed.

In other ways besides an almost primitive alertness to signs of danger, he showed his awareness of what it meant to be a father or a mother. No one ever had to describe for him a parent's agony when his child's life did not work out. He understood the inevitable identification of a parent with a child. If it was natural for his friends to feel a sense of personal accomplishment in the achievement of their children, it was also natural, though tragically so, that they should assume the responsibility for their sons' or daughters' failures.

How many times he had heard at his bedside the heart-breaking cry, "Oh, Ned, what did I do wrong, to have my child turn out like this!" Sometimes it was easy enough to see what had been done wrong, in the light of common sense or traditional morality. But to point out an individual's past shortcomings was foreign to Ned's nature. That only opened the way to vain self-recrimination which, as he well knew, was almost as destructive as self-pity.

To the desperate father or mother of a wayward child, torn with grief and burdened with guilt, he tried to point out that the responsibility of a parent must be limited. If this were not so, the child would have no freedom of will and would not be a true individual. He did not pretend that inheritance or training were unimportant. But he believed that in the end the individual himself chooses his course, and no one else can be held wholly responsible for what he does. This was no easy idea to convey to a parent, rawly sensitive to his mistakes and grieving for his child. Ned could do it because he had the tact that is not a mere social grace, but is born of charity and an infinite knowledge of suffering.

Ned's sympathy in such situations was so acute that it seemed to follow the channels of a parent's own emotions. At the same time he saw things in a perspective that few parents could hope to achieve. Without specious optimism or sentimental cheerfulness he could discuss the situation and the child involved in such a way that some reasonable hope would emerge. He did not belittle the gravity of a boy's expulsion from college on the eve of graduation because of misbehavior. He saw perfectly the consequences to a young wife who had left her husband for another man. There was cause for anxiety in little Joey's chronic dishonesty. But in each case there was always more than had crossed the parent's mind. Perhaps the boy who had been dismissed from college had been waiting all his life for this lesson, its very hardness might teach him what he could not have learned in any other way. Ned may personally have known the young wife who had so casually sacrificed another's happiness and was certain that she would quickly find disillusionment in her infatuation and be wiser and more generous for the experience. As for little Joey, what he probably needed was less worry over his moral development and a great deal more loving. Not a few parents had reason to echo the sentiment of the mother who wrote Ned, "I shall never forget that night when you gave me my first hope for my bad child."

If Ned knew the boy or girl responsible for the parental heartbreak—and this was usually the case with the children of his friends—his help would have a concrete value. One mother was deeply distressed over an incipient extramarital love affair of her young war-bride daughter. The girl herself came to see Ned and of her own accord gave the matter a thorough airing. There was no doubt that she was about to go off the deep end with a man whom she had met only a short time before. Ned listened with that warm understanding he always had for lovers. He knew all about the glamor which young passion throws over its object. Nevertheless, in the course of their talk certain points came out which had not entered the girl's mind. One of these was the matter of honor, a term whose brightness has been corroded by the theory that emotional needs have a prior claim over the moral sense. As the girl talked (and it was she who did most of the talking, with Ned merely throwing out an occasional, subtly directive comment), she began to see that what she proposed was not only a betrayal of her husband overseas but of her parents, her friends, and finally of herself. She began to wonder if her present mood was that important, if it was really love after all. The day after her visit Ned wrote the girl's mother:

> M—— came to see me last night and we had a good visit. She told me about last week. I explained to her that such gusts or squalls will probably be recurrent phenomena in her life, so she must learn now to deal with them firmly and skilfully. If she takes a reef in her sails, keeps a steady hand on the tiller, and does not swerve one inch from her laid down course, she will weather all sorts of episodes and go straight on. Luckily she has a gift for loyalty, a capacity for devotion and a lot of common sense. These qualities will carry her through to success, and meanwhile she is far too clear-sighted ever to let herself be bewildered or confused. Don't worry about her.

Ned had the same respect for the private affairs of children and young people as for those of their elders. But once in awhile it was evident that an immature judgment needed correction, and Ned would prod a parent to take action. When the worldly collegiate son of one of his friends took it upon himself to initiate a fifteen-year-old cousin into the pleasures of cocktail drinking and night life, Ned summoned the boy's mother to the penthouse and told her she must take him to task. When she delayed doing this because of a reluctance to interfere in her son's private affairs, Ned wrote a kind but very firm letter pointing out the dangers of the situation and where the ultimate responsibility would lie. The mother, thoroughly alarmed, then took matters in hand herself.

Sometimes Sheldon was called upon to give the *coup de grâce* to a dying romance. One day an agitated mother called him to say that her somewhat temperamental daughter had decided to end her engagement, but that her fiancé had refused to accept his dismissal. The obstinate young man had declared pontifically that he knew what was best for the girl, and he was certain that, despite her feelings of the moment, she would eventually see that only he could make her happy.

Ned talked with the girl and discovered that beyond doubt she was no longer in love, and that there were no discernible sparks to be rekindled. Her statement about her fiancé, "He just irks me!" seemed valid enough. When Sheldon met him he too found a definitely "irkable" quality in the otherwise worthy youth. After hearing the girl's story Sheldon said, "Suppose you tell him that I have invited him for luncheon tomorrow. I think I can help him to see the light."

The luncheon was a complete success. The young man came down from his lofty perch and with ego undented ac-

cepted Ned's suggestion that a few months of "disengage-
ment" might ease the situation and help each party to gain a
better perspective. It was not inconceivable that the young
man himself would experience a change of heart. This is
exactly what happened. Before the agreed time had passed
someone else did turn up, and his erstwhile fiancée was left to
go her way rejoicing.

Sheldon's instinct was infallible in distinguishing between
an infatuation, no matter how feverish, and the emotion
which makes for lasting happiness. His own capacity for
love, which was the basis of his life, made young people trust
implicitly in his judgments of their feelings. If they found
out they were not in love after all, they gained from him a
delighted expectancy of what they had to look forward to. If
they were really in love, the thrill was heightened by talking
it over with Ned.

He believed (and this was one of the few points on which
he was positively dogmatic) that the only real tragedy of life
is the inability to love, and the unwillingness to risk all for
love when it comes along. He knew the bliss of loving and
being loved in return. But this was not what counted most in
the end. "The one who loves the more deeply is always the
one who is more deeply blessed," he wrote a girl who had
been abandoned by a man who meant everything to her.
"Even if that love cannot be returned you are blessed. The
capacity to love is what is important."

With the world again at war love took on an even greater
value in the scheme of things. "The day M—— came to me
was the day war broke," he wrote an old friend whose
daughter had just become engaged. "It was somehow comforting and reassuring to hear her talking about this new
experience. It made me feel that life goes on, evolution goes

on, in spite of wars, death, set-backs of all kinds. The war seemed the unreal, temporary, unimportant thing. M——'s happiness seemed to build toward eternity."

In the slow, but always upward-moving spiral of man's destiny love was the impelling force. No man or woman could take it lightly. "Get married!" he urged a young actor friend. "Don't be a Peter Pan all your life."

He watched with fascination the changes love brought into the lives of his friends. Nothing gave him greater happiness than to have young lovers come to see him in the early days of their happiness. Whenever a couple came to announce their engagement (and Ned was often the first to know about it), there were always festivities in the penthouse. A red-letter day of his life was that of the wedding of his cousin Elsa Denison to another cousin, John D. Jameson, which took place at his bedside.

Just as he often interpreted parents and children to each other, he gave young lovers new insights into the natures of their beloved. Agnes Cabot was astonished to hear Sheldon describe her husband to a friend far more discerningly than she could have done. Another girl wrote him shortly after her engagement, "Your wonderful letter has made me happier than I can possibly tell you. You have cast a new light for me into B——'s character."

The trust that led the young to bring their emotional problems to Sheldon prompted them to turn to him also in their deepest spiritual needs. Though he had no creed himself, he had profound respect for all creeds sincerely professed. In discussing religion with him there was never any need of preliminary exploration to find the ground he stood on. He believed that it was as natural for men to differ in their religious beliefs as in their complexions or temperaments. At the same time his own complete independence, his freedom from orthodoxy and dogma, gave reassurance to those who had been unable to find answers to their questions in traditional theologies. Ned knew that for many sensitive and intelligent young people the historical statements of faith seem often merely stereotyped patterns of words. He knew how hard it was sometimes to find a connection between a man's personal experience and the creed of his fathers. He could also sympathize with those who felt resentment at the attempts to popularize religion by reducing it to the level of a club activity, thus destroying all the beauty and mystery at the heart of true belief. To unnumbered young people seeking a firm ground for the faith they desperately needed, Sheldon was able to show the way.

During the second World War few days passed that some uniformed figure was not seen in the elevator going up to the penthouse. These young men carried a new burden on their untried shoulders. No matter how much they felt the excitement of the war, however proud they may have been of their new uniforms, few of them had not known the touch of fear as their imaginations dwelt on the idea of battle with all its implications. Whether they actually talked of their innermost misgivings (and usually they did for with Ned everything came so easily to the surface), they soon felt an easing of that pressure about the heart which comes from self-doubt. Ned did not attempt to minimize the physical facts of pain and death. He did not think that fear was anything to be ashamed of; it was, after all, a natural weapon for self-preservation. All that mattered was that it should be offset by something else. "I don't remember Ned's talking about duty," one navy flier has said, "but he made you realize that if you had a job to do, you'd be given the power to do it. Whatever other feelings you might have, when the time came this would be the thing that mattered." An ex-marine sergeant put it another way: "Ned made you feel bigger than your fears."

Ardently as Sheldon felt the issues of the war and proud as he was of his friends who fought and died, he could also sympathize with those who saw the matter in another light. One lad astonished and dismayed his conservative family, which had a tradition of military heroism, by becoming a conscientious objector. Ned's tolerance and understanding did much to ease his painful situation. Although they had long talks about his ideas, and the reading and thinking through which these had evolved, Sheldon never argued against his position. He admired the boy's courage and integrity. He gave him the feeling that he too was right in following the course of his deepest conviction, and that he would find the strength to carry him through. When the young man was transferred to the Pacific Coast, Ned sent a parting message:

HEAR FROM K——— YOU ARE GOING TO CALIFORNIA TO DO MORE FIGHTING. HOPE CHANGE WILL OFFER YOU FINER AND WIDER OPPORTUNITIES FOR HUMAN SERVICE. FEEL SURE YOU WILL MAKE THE MOST OF THEM. MY THOUGHTS AND ALL KINDS OF GOOD LUCK.

There was no pattern of logic, no organized system of ideas by which Ned helped his young friends to find moral and spiritual security. The ideas alone were not perhaps the main thing. Ned in himself supplied the evidence which made it impossible not to believe that life had a purpose and that the purpose was good. What young man or woman who ever sat beside that still, yet so intensely living figure could have had a more brutal and apparently senseless mauling from life? Yet who could not fail to see that the end had been supremely right?

CHAPTER XV

"My Hand in Yours"

To THE outsider the astonishing, perhaps slightly incredible thing was that so many people should have been on terms of such close intimacy with Sheldon, and that he should have been able to create with each of his friends the feeling of a unique bond. Most of us consider life rich when we can count on two or three people of unquestionable and unquestioning devotion. Yet Sheldon had literally dozens of such attachments, and, so far as loyalty and understanding could extend, each had the quality of the absolute.

The explanation for this lies in Sheldon's own nature and the circumstances in which he lived. Friendship is too often something to be cultivated after the responsibilities of family and work have been met. It is hard to love people without learning to know them, and this takes time. Ever since his early youth Sheldon had made time for friendship; with invalidism it became his major pursuit.

In the mid-thirties a Chicago paper reported that it was more difficult to get an appointment with Edward Sheldon than with anybody else in New York. It is true that his engagement book was usually filled for weeks in advance. Yet he could always manage to see anyone with whom there was sure to be a strong mutual interest, or whom he might be able to help. Whether a first meeting would lead to friend-

314

ship depended largely on the nature of the visitor. He made short shrift of fools and bores. This did not mean that one had to be brilliant to win his interest. But if an individual's potentiality for accomplishment was limited by a basic lack of intelligence, Ned quickly discovered it, and his door thereafter was firmly closed on that unwelcome person. This may have been Ned's special brand of cruelty. However, as he pointed out on numerous occasions, he was neither a priest nor a saint, and though he lived by giving himself to others he could only do this if people spoke his own language. To the man whose mentality, education, and background were so remote from Ned's that no solid bridge could be made between them, he simply had nothing to communicate.

He also had nothing to say to the man or woman whose moral sense was atrophied through egotism and self-interest. He had a wide toleration for human weakness in general, especially for those slips from grace resulting from sudden explosions of passion which an individual had not experienced before. But the calculated actions of complete selfishness, and the revelation of such actions on the part of those he had regarded as his friends, promptly alienated him. When a renowned English actor and director whom Ned had known and liked for years divorced his loyal wife, an old friend of Ned's also, to marry a woman of wealth and social position, his name was promptly stricken from Ned's address book.

Ned's dismissal of the merely dull and irredeemably simple-minded was gently tactful in its finality. The people on whom he turned his back with complete ruthlessness were the self-satisfied and egocentric. He knew that with them there could be no true exchange of feeling, no real understanding. They were closed to everything outside themselves, as incapable of receiving as of giving.

A famous Broadway actress had wanted to meet Sheldon for years, feeling that it was due her prestige to belong to the charmed circle of his friends. The woman was a favorite with the columnists because of her gift for outrageous and witty repartee, and a complete lack of inhibition about her personal affairs. With Sheldon she exerted herself to be entertaining. Their talk covered all sorts of subjects, but it was to be noted that she managed to relate everything to herself. Apparently the visit was a success. Sheldon was gracious and courteously responsive as always; he seemed to be highly amused by some of the actress's quips. But when she got up to leave he made no suggestion that the visit be repeated.

Not long afterward she telephoned Sheldon at two o'clock in the morning. She had heard of his habit of talking with friends at all hours of the day and night, and she had presumed on their one meeting to have a nocturnal chat with him. Sheldon was being read to when the call came. The nurse answered the telephone and gave the woman's name. Sheldon reflected briefly and then said, "Please tell her I can't be disturbed now." Some time later, she tried again to reach him with the same result. She knew then that the rebuff was definitive, though she probably never understood why. "She doesn't want a friend," Sheldon confided to his attendant. "She only wants an audience."

Sometimes Sheldon refused in advance to meet people with whom he felt instinctively that no rapport could be established. This was the case with Thomas Wolfe. In 1935 Ned wrote to Van Wyck Brooks:

> . . . I am getting on toward page 800 of Thomas Wolfe's latest, which I am reading because of Jack [Wheelock] rather than because of Wolfe. It has some fine pages of rhapsody which suggests the lyric poet, but I still don't believe he is a

*novelist. The complete imprisonment within his own ego, the
distorted way in which he senses other people, the lack of any
form, architecture or development (this keeps the books perfectly static)—all those things bother me. I should be interested to know what you think of it. Jack and Max [Maxwell
Perkins] have invested so much enthusiasm and patience in
it. I hope it ends in justifying their faith. But the author
seems too cut off, too tragically remote from his fellow men
to be understood by them as a novelist. . . .*

Not long after he finished the book (*Of Time and the
River*), Sheldon was asked if he would not like to meet
Wolfe. John Wheelock had worked with Maxwell Perkins
(another close friend of Ned's and a Harvard college-mate)
in the now famous literary midwifery that brought Wolfe to
the fore as one of the most impressive writers of the time.
Wheelock had often discussed Wolfe's personality with Sheldon, and he felt that Ned as an ardent student of human nature would enjoy meeting the novelist. When he proposed to
bring Wolfe up to the penthouse Sheldon thought for a moment and then said, "I'd rather you didn't, Jack. I shouldn't
be comfortable near an ego as big as that."

There was thus a prerequisite to friendship with Sheldon.
There must be some point, no matter how small, by which
his own outgoing spirit could find its way into that of the
other person. Only thus could he hope to achieve the understanding which gave meaning to all his human relationships.

Another factor was important in the growth of intimacy
with Sheldon. Except in the cases of very old friends, like
Wheelock and Brooks, or the Charles MacArthurs, with perhaps Woollcott and Lillian Gish—people whom he had
known so long and so well that their histories were almost a
part of his own—he never saw visitors in groups. There were

several reasons for this. In the first place it was confusing to talk with more than one person at a time. Even though he had an exceptionally acute ear, with only the ear to guide him it was difficult to follow all the tones of several voices at once, and the attempt was very fatiguing. Furthermore, it was only in seeing people alone that Ned could create that atmosphere of complete freedom essential to real communication. Finally, his interest was always in the individual himself. To project himself completely into the other person's mood, to learn the facets of his personality, required concentration, a pushing aside of everything irrelevant to the moment and to the visitor himself. Once this was achieved the air seemed charged with a feeling of mutual possession. As Dr. John Kernan put it, "When I was with Sheldon I felt that he was wholly mine." And he might have added that in the hours spent in the big blue room high above the city, he belonged entirely to Sheldon.

To speak of concentration in such a connection may suggest a certain strain. But there was no trace of this in any contact with Sheldon. Indeed the characteristic reaction of nearly everybody who ever met him was one of complete, almost unearthly release. There might be times of lively discussion about some knotty philosophical problem when the pace of Sheldon's thoughts would prove too strenuous for a less resilient mind. But Ned was quick to feel this and would at once let the talk flow back into easier channels.

Even the stranger meeting Sheldon for the first time carried away with him a new sense of freedom, a mysterious lightness. This was something Ned's friends spoke of again and again, though the attempt to define closely what they meant seemed to baffle their powers of expression. They could only say that when they were with Ned they seemed to be caught in an upward-sweeping current that defied the very drag of gravity itself. "I came away from him bouncing," said Louise Closser Hale. It was literally, to use the phrase to which everyone in the end was reduced, like walking on air.

This sensation of release from pressure owed something no doubt to the knowledge that with Sheldon nothing was expected of a person beyond being completely himself. Even a newcomer, prepared perhaps with a store of small talk such as might presumably amuse or interest a man living in close confinement, was relieved at once of any necessity to justify his presence. It was as though Ned said to him, "You are you, and I am happy to see you for that reason." He conveyed this in so easy and subtle a fashion that the shyest visitor was at once disarmed.

In the early days of transatlantic passenger flying a young Englishman who had just arrived in New York by clipper went to see Sheldon with a letter from a mutual friend. It was at once apparent to Ned that the young man had more than the traditional British reserve, that he was almost painfully self-conscious. Ned immediately steered the conversation into an apparently objective discussion of transocean flying. He seemed eager for purely factual details of the experience, and it was easy for his visitor to talk about these. Presently without realizing it the young Englishman was discussing his own reactions to the flight. He thought of course that he was simply describing an experience for a man who had never had it, could never have it. But in reality he was describing himself. Furthermore, except for an occasional reflective comment from Sheldon, the newcomer did all the talking. When the visit was over and the young man was on the way back to his hotel, he had the characteristic feeling of buoyancy which most people took away from Sheldon. Some time later

it occurred to him that with Sheldon he had really talked
about himself for perhaps the first time in his life. "I suppose
that is why," he said afterward to their mutual friend in
England, "I had such a curious sense of freedom."

Any confidence made to Ned was as sacred as it would
have been with a priest or doctor. Unless a situation involved
mutual friends, each familiar with the details, he never discussed those close to him with each other. Each existed in a
separate world of his affection and understanding. Often his
friends were acquainted with each other, but it was rare that
one person knew the details of another's relationship to
Sheldon. Knowing Ned made a special tie between them,
but beyond that one did not penetrate. Austin Strong, whose
Seventh Heaven and other plays reflected so much of Sheldon's romantic idealism, once commented on this circumstance. "Each of us who knew Ned felt that he belonged to
a secret brotherhood."

More and more as the years passed Sheldon's life was centered in what Thornton Wilder called "a sort of instrumenta-
tion, an elaborate usefulness to others." Ned not only lived
to share his possessions, his strength, and his wisdom with
those in need, but his creative energy was largely spent in
contriving means to make his giving effective. Better perhaps
than his friends, who saw him always in the light of superhuman endowments, he knew his limitations. His physical
condition seemed long ago to have lost any connection with
his real life. Yet it sometimes created almost insuperable barriers to the services he was called upon to perform. He had
constantly to exercise his ingenuity to find substitutes for the
physical resources he lacked.

Though he made no effort to spare himself, his life was
a drain also on his spiritual energies. If these appeared in-

exhaustible, it was because he constantly sought ways to replenish them through new ideas, new interests, and reflection. And he was careful not to squander them on irrelevancies.

He was also conscious of the value of time. Though he was untouched by many of the pressures that gave a feverish tempo to the lives of his friends, he knew that his hours were measured, and that he must make each moment count. Yet even in this he was thinking probably less of his own fulfillment than of the needs of others. He knew the drag on the soul of prolonged misery and unhappiness. Wherever he could lighten a burden he acted with all possible dispatch so that the sufferer might return quickly to a happier existence.

Obviously Sheldon received constant appeals for financial help. He responded to these as readily as to other signals of distress. But here the limitations were clear. They were set forth each month by the bank in black and white (and sometimes red). So this was a generosity fairly easy to regulate. On principle Ned gave whatever was needed until there was nothing left, or until the objections of his financial advisers could no longer be overruled. But he seldom let these interfere with his impulses. By the end of his life he had successfully disposed of his entire fortune. Of course a great deal of this had gone into living expenses, and no one can doubt that his manner of living was expensive. Yet even a cursory audit at the end would have shown that the bulk of his fortune in one form or another had been given away.

If there was a certain prodigality in Ned's giving—whether of time, of effort, or of money—there was no waste. Yet there was no slightest effect of calculation in his services to his friends. Every gesture had a warm spontaneity that made it precious, aside from whatever intrinsic benefits it carried. But once in a while someone whom he had carried through a difficulty would learn (usually long afterward) how well Ned had studied the problem, and how carefully he had used the resources at his disposal.

Nothing in Sheldon's giving ever indicated the least interest in any possible returns to himself. That there were returns is quite obvious. The richness of his life in varied and stimulating human companionship and the passionate devotion with which he was surrounded were the reflection of his own outgoing nature. No day passed without some tribute from those whom he had helped. Yet there were instances to show that helping others could mean loss and unpleasantness to himself.

Certain writers whom Ned assisted seemed as anxious as he to conceal the collaboration. Perhaps there were one or two cases of resentment toward him for what he had done. Though the most obdurate *amour-propre* could seldom resist the infectiousness of Ned's own humility, there were cases where pride was so wounded by the advice he had been asked to give that the individual left Ned's apartment in anger never to return. Sometimes the people involved were old friends, and their loss was doubly sad for him.

Ned had long known that the marriage of a theatrical couple, both old friends, was following a rough course. Each party had laid the whole story before him, and he saw that there were justified grievances on both sides. He had a profound regard for the sanctity of marriage, and in such cases he usually did everything possible to bring a couple together again. But this time he saw that it was hopeless. The man was in love with another woman, and Ned knew that it was no passing affair. Yet the wife refused to give him up. She went to Ned for advice, and he told her frankly that she should face the facts and retreat while she could still do so with dignity. The woman was very angry with Ned, and did not come to see him again. "I knew she would never forgive me," he told a friend who was acquainted with the whole story, "but she asked what I thought she should do and I told her the truth." Matters worked out as he predicted. The woman lost out in the end, suffering all the humiliation that might have been avoided if she had taken Ned's advice.

Such rare cases only emphasize the feeling of gratitude which Sheldon usually aroused in those he helped. Merely to know him and to understand his life created a desire to serve him. Obviously this gave him real power over his friends. Yet it must be evident that nothing was more foreign to his nature than a desire for power to increase his own importance. If he had any interest in power at all, it was only to turn it back to benefit others.

Among the people most indebted to Sheldon for material aid as well as spiritual guidance were many figures of great influence, in the theatre and elsewhere. He never hesitated to use these friends to aid others less fortunate. Yet in appealing to these powerful or wealthy individuals there was no thought of exploiting any obligation they might feel toward him. He merely counted on their devotion.

More than one successful Broadway producer had Sheldon to thank for some fortunate stroke. Perhaps Ned had found a new play destined to become a great hit. He may have doctored a poor play which would certainly have failed otherwise, but eventually made money. Maybe he had found an "angel" for some manager with a good play but no money to produce it. When he sent a young actor or actress (or perhaps an old player who had slipped out of sight through long illness or misfortune) to one of these friends with a request for a hearing, the request naturally met with immediate response. "Yet you weren't just doing Ned a favor if you gave the actor a job," Al Woods once declared. "Nine times out of ten it turned out that it was Ned who had done you the favor. The kid or the old timer may have needed the job, but Ned wouldn't have sent him around if he hadn't been good, or if there hadn't been a part he was right for."

Cases like this were so numerous that the pattern became stereotyped with repetition. The pattern also had many variants. There was the young writer with a potential best-seller whom Ned sent to a publisher in need of a best-seller at that moment. There was the woman on her uppers, suffering from a serious lung infection, for whom Ned found exactly the right specialist—a man whom Ned had helped in his struggling student days. There was the case of the city boy who had studied forestry, but had somehow become trapped in an office—and a financier friend of Ned's who had just acquired a large tract of land for a reforestation project. The combinations were endless. Sometimes it took great ingenuity to find just the right combination. But in such matters Ned was a miracle of ingenuity.

However much he may have relied on his friends to help each other, he was scrupulous never to work any imposition. When a boy whom Ned was educating fell ill, he was sent to a very old physician friend. Ned wrote the doctor a note of explanation about the boy with a reminder that the bill was to be sent to Eighty-fourth Street. The physician promptly informed him that there would be no question of a bill. Ned at once wrote back that this was a personal expense, reminding his friend that he was after all in a position to meet such expenses. Patiently the doctor replied that this was not what mattered:

> . . . It really gives me pleasure to do odd jobs for you from time to time. You must therefore try to see it from my point of view. The last thing I want to do is make it awkward for you to call on me when you need me. Supposing we leave it this way. When the job concerns you I will charge you. When it concerns one of your friends for whom you are financially responsible, you will accept my services without charge.

Neither time nor distance had any real effect on the quality of Sheldon's friendships. Those who had won his affection never left the penthouse without the positive sense that his heart and mind followed them out into the world. Even though months or years might intervene before the next meeting, and many others would see Sheldon on the same terms of intimacy, there could be no question of "out of sight, out of mind." One of the things that made Ned's friendship so meaningful was the ever-renewed assurance that he shared whatever was important in one's life, whether joy or grief, triumph or disappointment, as surely as though he were physically present.

Often a friend who had spent an afternoon or evening at the apartment on Eighty-fourth Street would find a telegram awaiting him when he reached home. The message might read:

THANKS AGAIN FOR TODAY. MY LOVE TO YOU,

or:

OUR VISIT WAS NOWHERE NEAR LONG ENOUGH,

or to some out-of-town visitor:

I ENJOYED EVERY MINUTE OF OUR VISIT. I WISH YOU LIVED IN NEW YORK.

During periods of separation there would be reminders from Ned so pertinent to the moment, so vividly evocative of his presence that the recipient felt as though he might reach out and touch him. To a friend in the midst of some harrowing ordeal there was more than the figurative or symbolic in the phrase

MY HAND IN YOURS,

so often repeated in Ned's messages. No one tried to fathom how he knew the moment of crisis. The timing of his messages seemed to demonstrate something beyond intuition. One friend remembered:

> . . . *He just read your mind as though he saw into it. Once I was in such perplexity and anxiety that I could not write it to Ned or anyone. I did not know how a certain situation would turn out for those I loved best, yet I longed for Ned's under-standing sympathy. One day I received a wire from him:*

DEAREST ——, MY HAND IS ON YOUR SHOULDER.

The very fact that he knew the moment when suffering reached its climax gave added force to whatever words a message might contain. To a friend whose mother lay slowly dying he wired:

I SHALL GO TO YOU WHENEVER YOU WANT ME. BLESS YOU BOTH. NED.

To anyone outside the situation his words might sound laconic. Yet for the recipient of the message there was always some-thing that went straight to the sources of courage. When Robert Norwood, the beloved rector of St. Bartholomew's died, Sheldon knew what the loss meant to his friend, the gallant and beautiful Mrs. Oliver Harriman. Faced with mortal illness herself, she had leaned heavily on Norwood as well as on Ned. He telegraphed her:

DON'T SHED ANY TEARS THEY WOULD ONLY BETRAY A GREAT
MAN.

To another friend sick with the disappointment and humiliation of failure he wired:

DEAR MAGNIFICENT ———, MY LOVE AND ADMIRATION.

The message had a galvanizing effect of summoning up fresh resources and new confidence.

None had better cause to remember Ned's attentiveness than friends who were ill. In these cases intuition was sharpened by his own experience. To many a friend being wheeled into an operating room the last conscious thought would be Ned's phrase

MY HAND IN YOURS

from a telegram, or a letter delivered by special messenger, a few minutes before. And the first thing to greet the patient on the grim day after the operation would be another sign from Ned, like balm laid on a universe of soreness.

TAKE IT EASY. YOU WILL FEEL MORE LIKE A HUMAN BEING
TOMORROW.

Then for perhaps a period of weeks each morning there would be the familiar yellow envelope on the hospital breakfast tray as a reminder that Ned was standing by on the long road to recovery.

During the time of convalescence his inventiveness for helping to pass the tedious hours was endless. Books, games, pictures, mechanical toys for children (and sometimes for adults)—whatever he sent was not only certain to entertain the invalid, but it invariably carried also some subtle expression of Ned's particular regard for him. To women fretting under the dull and Spartan routine of hospital living he sent gifts of delicate soap and perfume, or orchids, tributes to the feminine charm which their mirrors at the moment so cruelly belied. His letters to those hospitalized far away were full of practical advice. When Anne Parrish's mother was hospital-bound through several long hot summer months, he advised "ice-cold chicken salad" for a listless appetite. To Alexander Woollcott confined in a Boston hospital, bored and exasperated with the food, Ned suggested that he send out to the Woman's Exchange ("There's bound to be one somewhere around") for homemade soup, assuring him that one taste of something from a private kitchen would change his whole outlook on life. On this subject Woollcott wrote later to his and Ned's good friend, Dr. Gustav Eckstein:

> In hospital recently I had my first experience of being taken care of by Sheldon. There was a letter or telegram every day. It occurred to me that their chief effect on any trapped and temporarily afflicted mortal was that he had a nerve if he dared to indulge in one moment of self-pity. Indeed, afterwards, in talking to Charlie MacArthur, I started to say that Sheldon could not have seen the real restorative value of his messages, when I stopped short, remembering that it takes hardihood to say of Sheldon that he doesn't know what he is doing.

Sheldon must have realized the effectiveness of these reminders, coming as they did from one who had suffered the depths of misery himself. Yet in his concern for sick friends there was never any hint of a comparison between what he had borne and their particular plight. His whole approach was simply that of one who understood that sickness sets a man off from his fellows in a special way. He knew the isolation and loneliness of anyone prevented over a long period from taking part in the everyday life of other people, and that other desperate solitude which comes from being confined within a world of pain that no one else can share. The effect of his unceasing attention, behind which lay all that he himself had endured, and continued to endure, was to break down the barrier of isolation and impart to the sufferer some of the strength which he had gained through his own ordeal. The combination of Sheldon's example plus the fact that pain brought one into a special communion with him had a therapeutic effect of untold value in starting the process of recovery. Mary Johnston, the novelist whose long-time friendship with Sheldon was carried on mainly through correspondence, reported the case of a friend whom she had told about him. The friend was afflicted with arthritis and was forced to undergo painful, exhausting therapy. The only way he could stand this "was to think of Ned Sheldon."

In other ways his example gave strength and courage when all else failed. A friend, incurably ill, endured calmly through "the positive sense of support derived simply by holding on to the thought of Ned's heroism and cheerfulness." Mrs. Oliver Harriman, dying of cancer, continued to visit Sheldon as long as she could hide her pain from him, and in the final months was sustained by the thought of his example.

Where the possibility of recovery existed, Sheldon's reassurance and encouragement spurred the sick man or woman to exert himself by every possible means to get well. Where patience in a long convalescence was needed, a few words from Ned were often more effective than all the exhortations of physicians and nurses. When Brendan Griswold, a youth of seventeen who had been a protégé of the Shel-

don family since his childhood, was stricken with rheumatic
fever and a heart ailment, Sheldon wrote him the essence of
his own credo:

> . . . Of course I am much disappointed to learn that you
> may have to be laid up for a much slower convalescence than
> we had expected. I am still hoping, however, that it will not
> be for a really long time. But in any case, old man, all I can
> tell you is that, if you have to do it, you will learn how to do
> it. And, if you are completely yourself at the finish, then it
> will be worth all the bother and the difficulty. . . . Mean-
> while take it easy, don't worry, and keep your mind on the
> end of the tunnel. You will surely come out all right.

On rare occasions Sheldon met someone who had traveled
at least part of the road along which he had toiled. Such en-
counters brought a feeling of comforting companionship,
of shared experiences of a sort he could not get from his
normally constituted friends. A meeting which gave special
pleasure was with Eben Whittlesey, the brilliant California
lawyer. Whittlesey, also blind, had nevertheless had a successful career in his profession and like Sheldon had turned
his affliction to the achievement of a full, influential life. The
two men met only once. Whittlesey, recalling the visit
after Sheldon's death, wrote:

> . . . My one conversation with him will always be a vivid
> memory, for he made a deep impression on me by his under-
> standing and by his ability to cut through the usual amenities
> of a first encounter to speak without embarrassment of the
> things which we had most closely in common.

Even to reassure his friends in illness, Sheldon almost
never referred to his own experience of invalidism. Yet
once in a while something would occur to show that he still
felt acutely what it meant. A woman whose history he

knew intimately came to tell him that the man she loved for many years, but from whom she had been separated by fate, lay gravely ill. He had sent word through his nurse that he wanted to see her. But the move had been blocked by the man's grown children, for reasons of their own. When Sheldon heard of this he was aroused to an unusual pitch. "You must override his children," he declared sharply. "He has given you the green light through his nurse. He is powerless to do more. I know—*I know*—how utterly powerless he feels. You must, you must, get through to him."

Keenly as he felt with those in physical pain, Sheldon knew that the ultimate agony is not of the body but of the mind and heart. To countless people still living, the radiance that surrounds his name is a reflection of the healing light he cast on the sick and weary souls that were laid bare before him.

His dealings with those in spiritual anguish had no suggestion of the techniques either of the confessional or the psychiatrist's office. In fact the very word "technique" carries a connotation of routine procedure which had no place in the quiet hours of revelation by Sheldon's bedside. Even when a friend came to Eighty-fourth Street with the specific objective of "talking things over with Ned," there was no probing, however subtle or delicate, to expose the sore spot. He never invited confession, and he was completely without curiosity about the private lives of his friends. When a newspaper in reporting a divorce case published intimate letters of a man very close to him, Sheldon immediately silenced the attendant who was reading. "Those belong to C—— alone," he said. "We have no business reading them." Likewise anyone who fancied himself in the role of Casanova would get short shrift if he tried to discuss his conquests with Ned. Some people saw a streak of Puritanism in him for this reason. But the truth is simply that he hated cheapness.

On the other hand, a man or woman who came to Sheldon with a heavy burden of guilt felt no timidity about his possible reaction. There was no fear that he would be shocked or revolted by the story he would hear, no misgivings about violating some fixed and sacred attitude. Nor was there any problem as to how the subject might be approached. In the easy, gentle flow of talk it would come to light of its own accord.

Sheldon knew that the greatest suffering comes not from the wrongs done us by others, but from those we do ourselves. To friends wrestling with the torments of conscience he gave the courage to see their faults for what they were. He did this through no peremptory order to face the issue, but rather by letting the issue reveal itself bit by bit until finally it stood out whole and clear. He did not extenuate or condone an evil act, but he tried to bring it into proportion with the rest of life, so that it might be assimilated and not remain, as one friend put it, "to fester like a splinter in the soul." If atonement for a misdeed was possible it must be made at once. There must be no equivocating or going back. When it was done a man could turn his face to the light.

> . . . Now that you see, make it a clean break. Don't kid yourself about this. Don't theorize about it—don't stew about it—don't write letters about it. It's what you do about it that matters. And, above all, forgive yourself!

Ned loved to quote, "The wisdom that within us grows is absolution for our sins." Suffering had to lead eventually to a recognition of what was wrong. If the recognition was complete, a man would be so filled with loathing for the evil act that he would be incapable of repeating it. Then the soul would be purged and set to rights. How long suffering must last no man could say; and Ned would have been the last to attempt to say. But he knew that it should not go on forever. In *Salvation Nell* he had stated clearly the belief that "we leave our sins behind us," and that belief never changed. He was positive that suffering, particularly the sheer misery of guilt, could be prolonged to the point where it would outwear its purpose, stultifying the soul and becoming a block to action—even the right action for which it had prepared the way. When that moment arrived it was time to put guilt behind one and get on with the business of living. "It's what you do from now on that counts," he said again and again. If one could really profit by the lesson, then all was well. Ned had traveled a long way from the Calvinist ancestors who had brought the smell of brimstone to the Connecticut wilderness in the seventeenth century. His faith was simpler and far older than theirs. It was at least as old as Aeschylus' noble lines:

> . . . *Justice turns the scale*
> *For those to whom through pain*
> *At last comes wisdom's gain.*

No matter how black the marks a man might set against himself, Ned would always produce something to offset them. Out of his phenomenal memory for the details of a friend's life he would recall some act of generosity, some gesture of heroism, never recognized as such and probably forgotten by the friend himself, to put on the credit side of the balance. If the friend, anxious to be just and to build no illusion about himself, would protest that a collection of small acts of virtue, not even consciously performed, could scarcely compensate for the monstrous thing that now tormented him, Ned would say with a touch of sternness, "Who is to be the judge of that?"

Some of his friends thought that he went too far in his consistent emphasis on their better natures, and that he was unrealistic in refusing to see them as the weak and erring mortals they knew themselves to be. Austin Strong said, "Ned always made us think that we were better than we really were." Alexander Woollcott was of the same opinion. In a letter to Lady Colefax he described an incident which seemed pointedly to reveal this side of Sheldon. This was apropos of the Kaufman-Hart play, *The Man Who Came to Dinner*, in which the leading character, Sheridan Whiteside, is a somewhat scabrous caricature of Woollcott:

> . . . As long ago as 1934 I began the process of reading plays aloud to Ned Sheldon. I was reluctant to read *The Man Who Came to Dinner* because I thought it would sound weird with all the characters coming to him in the voice of Sheridan Whiteside. However, he insisted, and when I had finished Act I there was an appalling silence. Finally he asked, "Do you think you are like that?" I found it so embarrassing to explain to him that he saw only my best side. After all, each of us has a totally different relationship with every other person in the world.

Another episode shows even more strikingly this disposition of Sheldon's to see only what was best in his friends. A woman whom he had idealized since his young manhood was involved in a lawsuit over the payment of a surgeon's fee. She had had a serious operation and the fee was undoubtedly high, though normal under the circumstances. However, the woman contended that she had not been responsible for engaging the surgeon—that he had been called in at the instigation of a friend, another woman also a close friend of Sheldon's. Actually she believed that the surgeon was in love with this friend, and she had asked her to call him in on the case, assuming that this would make some difference in the fee. She was wrong on both counts, but she refused to accept the situation and the surgeon had been obliged to sue.

Sheldon was greatly upset by the case and asked the second woman to give him the full details. She did so, but with great reluctance, knowing Ned's feeling for the defendant. When she finished the story there was one of those "appalling silences" which Woollcott speaks of. Ned broke it at last to say very slowly and distinctly, "I do not know the person you are talking about."

Perhaps in his determination to view life and people positively, Sheldon closed his mind to certain things. But he had no illusions about human nature in general. He often spoke to Helen Howe of "the tiger and the angel" in every man, and of the eternal struggle between the two. In his theory of man's moral evolution he believed that this struggle was necessary for growth. There may have been occasions when in his first reaction to the disclosure of some unexpected bit of ugliness he seemed to draw back from the facts. Yet with time he could and did accept the revolting side of people's characters, even when the people were his friends. But in accepting what was ugly he did not change his conception of what was good and beautiful. Knowing the worst of people had no effect on his love for them.

This was what it all came back to in the end. To know Sheldon was to know the power of love. There was no time or place, no murky corner of human life that it could not penetrate. It was always there waiting like a great coiled line to be thrown out at the faintest cry of need. No one ever had to grope for it blindly. Guided by an unfathomable instinct of its own, it went unerringly to the mark.

Sheldon had long known of the solitary struggle of a beautiful actress against narcotics. They were old friends, but as the drug's hold increased she saw Ned less and less frequently. However, she was constantly on his mind, all the more so because he could find no way to help her. Late one night his telephone rang. Ned recognized the woman's voice although it was very faint and her speech was thick. She was evidently in the midst of a crisis, and something had to be done at once. He talked to her gently, reassuringly, until he was certain that he was holding her attention. After about ten minutes he told her that he would have to ring off, but that he would call her back and she must not leave the telephone in the meantime. Sheldon then tried to locate the ever-resourceful Charles MacArthur, who unfortunately could not be reached at the moment. So throughout the long night Ned held the fort alone, calling the woman regularly at half-hour intervals, and in between continuing the search for MacArthur. When he spoke with the actress he recalled happy times they had had together, details of her beauty which he so well remembered, the great parts she had played, her devoted public, and lovely scenes in Europe which had meant much to her. Knowing her passion for music, he had his nurse move the phonograph up to the telephone, and when he was too exhausted to talk he had records of her favorite compositions played for her.

It was nearly dawn when he finally located his old friend and collaborator. Charlie at once took the matter in hand and went to the woman's house. He found her unkempt, demoralized, and scarcely aware of what was happening. But she was still clutching the telephone receiver. He made her pull herself together sufficiently to make the trip with him across New York to Eighty-fourth Street. After Ned had talked with her for a few moments, he summoned a doctor. He told the woman that she must not go on alone any longer, that help was at hand and she must accept it. Later that morning, calmer and rested, she went back to her own apartment. She took with her the courage to start the hard fight again, knowing that whatever had guided her hand to dial Ned's telephone that night would see her through to the finish.

Several weeks later MacArthur was invited to the penthouse for dinner. When he arrived he found a charming young woman, beautifully gowned and impeccably groomed, sitting in the big chair by the bed. It was not until she began to speak, to thank him for what he had done, that he recognized the once wretched disheveled creature whom he had brought to Ned's apartment that harrowing night.

CHAPTER XVI

Liberation

THE decades came and went with little effect on Sheldon or his way of life. At fifty-five his vitality seemed as great as it had been at twenty-five. His mind continued to find new interests in all directions. His spirit constantly sought fresh channels of service to others. There were no stagnant moments in his full, active days. He was a happy man.

His dislike of publicity in any form, which had grown steadily ever since illness beset him, had now become a passion for self-effacement. It became a matter of urgent necessity to divest himself of everything that belonged to his purely worldly self. Even tributes of friendship and esteem, if they were linked mainly to his early fame and material success, seemed to act like dragging anchors on his spirit.

Early in 1941 certain members of the Players hatched the plan for a gala dinner in honor of Sheldon, who still retained his membership in the club and was in constant touch with it through his many friends in the group. The affair was to be an Edward Sheldon Pipe Night, with a special program of music, reminiscences of Ned's career from former theatre associates, and special tributes to Ned himself. Half a dozen celebrities of his own generation would take part. A special loudspeaker would be installed in the penthouse to bring the festivities directly to him, and the main program would be broadcast on a nation-wide radio hook-up.

338

Otis Skinner was delegated to go to Eighty-fourth Street and notify Ned of the preparations. The genial Skinner, who had long held a special place in Ned's affections, enthusiastically outlined the plan. When he had finished Sheldon expressed his gratitude for the honor, but firmly vetoed the whole idea. Skinner protested energetically, explaining that Ned could not deprive his old comrades of the pleasure of coming together with him, at least in spirit. With reluctance Sheldon finally yielded to the proposal, but only on condition that there be no publicity, above all no radio broadcast.

Even without Sheldon's active participation the evening was a great success. The Players Club was crowded. Every member who had ever known Ned made a point of being on hand, if he was within reach, and dozens of telegrams brought greetings from those too far away to attend in person. George M. Cohan wrote Ned next day that it had been "a wonderful evening—and everybody seemed terribly happy." Since Sheldon had refused to have the program relayed to the apartment, a recording of it was sent to him. But there was no report subsequently that he ever had it played back.

He showed the same unwillingness to take part in group activities of his own family. In 1929 there was a reunion in Chicago celebrating the hundreth anniversary of the birth of Ned's grandfather, Henry Strong. It was a large gathering, and it was thought that Ned would enjoy listening in on the dinner by long-distance telephone. But this plan he also coolly rejected. He was happy to be with his family, as with his friends, in his own world, but he had no interest in rejoining theirs.

As 1941 passed into 1942, Sheldon's thoughts were more and more consumed by the larger issues of the world. After Pearl Harbor and America's entry into the war his day was arranged around the broadcasts of important news commentators. He followed political and military developments with scrupulous attention, weighing and evaluating every detail. His prodigious memory became a storehouse of facts and figures by which he gauged each move of the enemy and the Allies. Though the war aroused his ardent patriotism, his judgment was never swayed by his emotions, and his friends came to rely heavily on his interpretation of events. From the outset he had a clear picture of the scope of the struggle and its probable cost to the world. He deplored the lack of preparation which made the early series of Allied losses inevitable, all the more so since he had long ago seen what would happen. ("You can't make tanks out of chewing gum," he remarked to a friend in 1938.) He knew that it must be a war to the death—but not the death of the democracies. Whatever the Western Allies lacked in equipment and military techniques would be made up in leadership and the will to win. His admiration for Franklin D. Roosevelt was limited, but he gave the President credit for being able to move quickly and to move the great unwieldy mass of Americans with him. His esteem for Churchill amounted almost to veneration. When the Prime Minister spoke, every word was weighted with the traditions, the convictions, and the record of endurance of the Anglo-Saxon peoples. Churchill's courage in the face of imminent disaster, with bombs raining from the heavens and invasion threatening, gave Sheldon a feeling of tight kinship. After one great speech Ned wired a friend:

CHURCHILL MADE ME PROUD OF THE HUMAN RACE.

Those were days when few men could live wholly within themselves. For Sheldon the war meant a greater challenge than ever to leave behind all personal interests and desires.

Yet there was nothing reckless in his attitude. With the threat of destruction at his doorstep he experienced an almost animal reflex to seek safety. At one period of the war the bombing of New York was discussed as a serious possibility. Ned knew that the danger of a direct hit on his building was slight. The real peril to a man lying blind and helpless in an exposed room with many windows was from flying glass. Sheldon accordingly called in Walter Binger, a well-known New York engineer and the brother of Dr. Carl Binger, to arrange suitable protection against this contingency. Under Binger's direction a heavy steel door was installed between the living room and Sheldon's bedroom, on the less exposed side of the house. Steel shutters, also proof against heavy blasts, were placed at the windows of this room. In the event of an alarm Sheldon's bed would be wheeled into the inner room, and the steel door and shutters would be securely bolted.

This was as far as Sheldon carried the matter, and he did not let his thoughts dwell greatly on it. But Mrs. Sheldon made further and more detailed plans (of which her son was unaware) for the event of an actual bombing. She arranged with the air-raid warden and his assistants in the apartment house that, should there be sufficient warning, they would see that Ned was carried down to the main floor at once. He would then be picked up by private ambulance and taken to a designated hospital where a room would be waiting for him. Every phase of this plan was worked out in minute detail by Mrs. Sheldon (now past eighty), with the efficiency and precision of a corps commander moving troops into battle position. To avoid any possibility of confusion or error at the critical moment, typewritten sheets of instructions with each step carefully enumerated and described were given to everybody concerned.

Even during the war years, when his mind was so greatly absorbed by military and political problems, Sheldon's interest in the lives of his friends was as keen as ever. Many of these were now carrying heavy responsibilities for the nation and stood in greater need than ever of his reassurance and wisdom. They counted on him also to take his part in the round of lesser concerns that filled their lives. The opening of a play written by a friend, or in which a friend was appearing, a wedding, the arrival of a new baby, a family reunion—whatever touched them deeply brought them also closer to Ned.

He took particular delight always in the seasonal festivities that had meant so much in his childhood. At Christmas his apartment seemed to capture more of the holiday's essential spirit than any other place in town. The great living room was decorated only with the usual garlands and wreaths of pine and holly, but it breathed a spirit of tranquil joy. Ned reveled in the odors of evergreens, and near his bed he kept a great bowl of shimmering Christmas-tree balls, their mere proximity somehow serving to fix the image of their colorful brightness on his mind.

New Year's Eve was usually spent with his household. Mr. Ernst, the housekeeper, his secretary and nurses would gather around his bed, and a bottle of champagne would be opened. When the city began its midnight clamor toasts would be drunk. Then Ned would have Mr. Ernst ceremoniously place a lighted cigarette between his lips, and he would rakishly puff away at it for a moment. He had never been a smoker, but this little ritual gave him great delight. It served to remind him and those about him that he was still very much in the world and meant to make the most of its pleasures.

He looked forward to spring with all the eagerness of a

country dweller anxious to get his planting started. He was impatient if the season came late. "I hear Mr. Ernst shoveling the snow off my roof," he wrote Elsa Jameson, "which does not sound like Mendelssohn's 'Spring Song.' " He greeted the first spring flowers with almost ecstatic pleasure, savoring their sweet freshness as do few sighted gardeners. "Your arbutus is spring itself," he wrote a friend. At Easter time the blue room was a veritable garden, though flowers were never lacking at any season. Against this background of tender new life the spiritual significance of Easter worked deep in his consciousness, especially in the last years. "I celebrated Good Friday," he wrote in 1943, "by reading the last half dozen chapters of each of the Gospels. St. Matthew and St. John are particularly fine. What a story! With that indefinable sense of reality that makes it as actual as the front page of today's *Times*."

Though the tenor of his life changed little, the years inevitably thinned the ranks of those who had brought so much into it. In September of 1933 Mrs. Cadwalader Jones died in London. She was followed in a few months by Ned's beloved college professor George Pierce Baker. Two years later Winthrop Ames and Edith Wharton, who had leaned heavily on Ned after Mrs. Jones's death, went also. The deaths of Lord Tweedsmuir, John Barrymore, and Alexander Woollcott were grievous losses. Alice Kauser, who had worked so indefatigably for his early success and continued always to watch over his professional interests, had turned to Ned like everybody else when old age bore down. The war had proved a heavy drain on her, bringing personal losses and the destruction of the whole world of her youth in Europe. Before its close she was an exhausted, broken old woman. She wrote Ned to say how feeble and ineffectual she now felt herself, and a few days later she was dead. The last year of Ned's life was darkened by the threat of further disability, and the illness and death of Doris Keane.

Communication had become increasingly hard for Sheldon, particularly with friends far away. All correspondence passed through his secretary, so that it was impossible for him to write or receive strictly private letters. He naturally relied greatly on the telephone (how greatly was indicated by his astronomical bills for long-distance calls and telegrams). But even the telephone's usefulness was limited. He could only talk with the receiver on a pillow beside his head; and this required the presence of an attendant to see that it remained in place. In the last years his friends were careful to call only when it was absolutely necessary. Conversation with members of his household and visitors was his principal link with life. When this too was threatened, it seemed as though he must surely abandon the struggle at last.

His long experience with arthritis had of course prepared him for every eventuality. He had known for a long time that his hearing might be affected. In fact the disease had already reached one ear several years before he died. So he faced the possibility that one day he would belong to what Helen Keller has called "the loneliest group of human beings on earth . . . bowed down by the twofold weight of blindness and deafness, with no hope of emerging from an utter desolation . . . in a dreadful monotony of silent days." But Sheldon could not accept this sentence without protest. When the threat became definite he made plans to learn the Morse code so that messages could be relayed to him through physical contact. This would have necessitated an attendant who was also an expert telegraphist, and he probably counted on the versatile Mr. Ernst to acquire the necessary skill. Fortunately he was spared this blow, so the plan was never put into action.

Equally serious as deafness, and somehow less expected, was the possibility that he might lose the power of speech. By the winter of 1943 it was quite evident that arthritis was beginning to stiffen his vocal chords. When the first symptoms set in he referred to the condition as "a sort of sullen laryngitis which has the same effect on me as the black cloth over the parrot's cage." From then on it became progressively more difficult for him to speak, and during the last year he could only communicate in a hoarse whisper on the outgoing breath.

To Sheldon expression was life. His brilliant articulateness in speech was far less marked in his writing, clever and forceful though much of this was. But in conversation Ned's power with words was an instrument of extraordinary sensitivity and effectiveness, and one of the factors in his immense helpfulness to others. He knew that the hardest questions can be made easier by accurate definition, and that the truism of mathematics holds also for life—a problem clearly stated is half solved. But the use of words had another, more personal, aspect for him. It was his principal source of immediate aesthetic satisfaction. The artist in him continually urged him to find forms for the thoughts, the fancies, the feelings that lay beyond the world of darkness.

Once Ned quoted Barrie's words, "I feel with Robert Louis Stevenson that the greatest beggar is he who has no words," but to possess them without the ability to speak would have meant for Sheldon anguish unthinkable. Five years before his death, when told of a man stricken with encephalitis and unable to articulate, Sheldon in an accent of almost physical pain whispered "Ah, not to be able to communicate. . . ."

It is idle to speculate on what might have happened had he lost his voice completely. But with his love of life under any condition, and his demonstrated skill in adapting himself to all circumstances, it is certain that he would have found a way to go on.

But it was not so much the prospect of what the future might still hold of bodily pain and increased deprivation that suddenly lengthened the shadows about him. Doris Keane had retired from the stage some years before and had been living quietly in England. One day toward the close of World War II when Wheelock was lunching at Eighty-fourth Street he found his host unusually preoccupied. Sheldon, suddenly aware of some need to explain his abstraction, said to his old friend, "Doris is flying the Atlantic this afternoon." He went on to say that she was ill. But he ventured no further explanation—as though he himself were not sure of the circumstances, but were fighting against a feeling that matters might be very grave.

A few weeks after this Sheldon called Carl Binger to ask his opinion on a hypothetical case of a particular kind of malignant tumor. Binger replied that if the case was as Ned had described it, there was little hope for the patient's recovery. A day or two afterward Ned sent for Wheelock. The altered tone of his greeting told Wheelock that something was wrong. Ned did not attempt preliminary explanations. He could only speak now in a rough whisper and when Wheelock leaned down to catch his words, he said, "Doris has cancer." As Wheelock tried to express his shock and offer some words of sympathy, he saw that tears had found their way from behind the black mask and were rolling down Ned's cheeks. It was the first time since his earliest boyhood that anyone had ever seen Sheldon weep.

His life really closed twice before he died, first when Doris' ailment was diagnosed, and second when her torment ended. As long as possible he talked with her daily on the telephone, and through the months he suffered for her as he had never suffered for himself. It was again the agony of "this all-endured, this nothing done" that he had gone through with other friends when illness had taken them out of his reach. But this time the experience cost more than it ever had before.

Though the majority of Sheldon's friends were not aware of it, Doris Keane's sickroom now became the focus of his thoughts and his activity. Nothing that could be done for her comfort or peace of mind was left undone. Whatever he could personally do he did; what he needed from others he unhesitatingly called for.

When Doris Keane came to America she was unaware that her illness would be fatal, and had left her daughter Ronda behind in England. Under any circumstances the restrictions of wartime travel would have made it difficult to bring the girl with her. Now, however, when it was seen that she could not live much longer, Ronda must be brought to America. The war in Europe had ended, but there was still a ban on all civilian travel across the Atlantic. However, this did not for an instant deter Sheldon from undertaking the project. Time was running fast, and it was uncertain that Doris could last even until Ronda arrived. Ned was torn between his hope that the agony would be cut short and his wish that Doris might see her daughter once more. The day before Ronda arrived he wrote to Charles Auchincloss:

> *The constant pain, opiates, etc., almost make me wish that she could die right off without waiting for Ronda to come. And yet I should like the child to have this great experience, which could only develop and enrich her for the rest of her life. Birth and love and death are great teachers, if they come and are taken in the right way.*

Charles Auchincloss, brother of Gordon Auchincloss who had figured in the Sheldon-Barnes plagiarism suit with Metro-Goldwyn-Mayer, was the man chiefly responsible for cutting through the red tape and securing permission for Ronda to make the trip across the Atlantic to her mother's bedside. Pulling every string within reach, enlisting the aid of such influential people as Mrs. Roosevelt and Lord Halifax, the British Ambassador—who impressed both the British Home and Foreign Secretaries with the urgency of the case—Auchincloss secured steamer passage for Ronda to Bermuda, and a seat on a Pan-American Airways plane from there to New York. Throughout these anxious days Sheldon was constantly at the telephone doing whatever could be done directly from the penthouse. Arrangements were made for Ronda to be rushed through customs and taken at once to the hospital where her mother lay. In the midst of the hurried preparations Ned wrote Auchincloss, whom he had met only a few months before:

> *It seems strange that I should suddenly find a friend who has helped me as much as you have. I don't know how these things happen, but anyway I am grateful.*

On November 21, 1945, after Ronda's safe arrival he wired:

DEAR CHARLIE: RONDA'S MOTHER IS VERY HAPPY. BLESS YOU FOR EVERYTHING. E.S.

And next day there was another message:

RONDA WILL BE HERE THIS AFTERNOON IF SHE CAN LEAVE
HOSPITAL AND WILL TELL US ABOUT ENGLAND. DORIS SLEEPS
MOST OF THE TIME WHICH IS MERCIFUL BUT SHE WOKE UP
WHEN RONDA CAME AND KNEW HER AND IS HAPPY. E.S.

Three days after this Auchincloss received the final word:

DORIS DIED PEACEFULLY. RONDA WAS WITH HER AND THIS WE
OWE ENTIRELY TO YOU. THANK YOU AGAIN FOR EVERYTHING
YOU DID. E.S.

For the next ten days Sheldon was inaccessible to all his
friends except Doris Keane's daughter. He could not even
bring himself to speak to his mother in the apartment below.
He sent her a note, however, expressing his thankfulness that
the long trial was at an end. This was the first and only time
any reference was made to Doris Keane between Sheldon
and his mother.

Doris Keane's ashes were brought to Eighty-fourth Street,
and for several days the small container, banked with the
fresh white violets forever associated with her in *Romance*,
remained on the table by Ned's bedside. Then Ronda, in accordance with her mother's request, took them to scatter
at sea.

Knowing Ned's reticence about Doris, friends understood
his wish to be left alone. Messages and flowers from those
who had known them both were acknowledged, but with one
exception there was no direct reference to Doris. Ten days
after her death an old friend came to see Ned, and, feeling
that he could not allow the occasion to pass without some
mention of her, murmured, "It seems impossible to believe
that Doris has gone." There was no response, and the friend,
thinking that Sheldon might not have heard, repeated the re-

mark, only to have that too drop into a well of silence. Then Sheldon spoke abruptly on some subject far removed, and the conversation continued on this topic.

Only to Charles Auchincloss, who had come late upon the scene and had been so helpful during the last weeks, did he allow himself to speak of her. The day after Doris's death Ned wrote Auchincloss:

> *Dear Charlie:*
>
> *Thank you for the red roses and the note. It was like you to think of me and send them. I wish you had known Doris. She had the kind of character you and I admire. I don't know why I say "had," because the older I grow, the more certain I seem to be that people—the essential part of them—keep on moving forward and developing when this life is over. Do you remember the little girl's question in Maeterlinck's play, "Where are the dead?" and the little boy's triumphant answer, "There are no dead." He was right. . . .*

With Doris' death the mystery of their relationship was permanently sealed. Of one thing only there can be no doubt, Ned loved her always with the love a man feels for the woman whom he regards as part of himself. Whatever may have happened to come between them and happiness together, she stayed always at the center of his life. Nothing could ever alter that fact, death least of all.

After the brief period of isolation Ned's friends came again to the penthouse. They were happy, for his sake rather than their own, that he should be able to show the same warm concern for them and their affairs as always. But his face, so impervious to all that had gone before, now showed indelible marks of sorrow and anxiety. Only the people who had known him longest understood how much Doris Keane's illness and death had cost him. With sinking hearts they realized that the will to live had begun to falter.

Before the year 1945 had closed his attendants felt that some intimation of the finish had come to him. Perhaps it was because throughout the winter an oxygen tent became increasingly necessary to ease his labored breathing. He began to show now the effort which talking cost him. He hated his friends to have to strain to hear him, and he pushed himself to enunciate clearly through his ragged whisper. But at the end of a visit he was exhausted.

He became unusually contemplative. He still wanted to be read to, but his selections were mainly old familiar things— Emerson's *Essays*, Kipling, Stevenson, Archibald Marshall, whose Trollopean Squire Clinton series brought back the fresh green countryside of England—and always his beloved John Buchan.

He returned also to a book he had encountered late in life, through Lady Tweedsmuir. This was *The Human Situation* of W. MacNeille Dixon, which had originally formed the Gifford Lectures for 1935–37 at the University of Glasgow. The work dealt with man's destiny in this world and beyond, and had been described by the New York *Times* as "perhaps the most important book of its kind which the Twentieth Century has yet produced." To Sheldon it was momentous in a way that no book had been since Basil King's *Conquest of Fear*. He read it and reread it, and sent copies to friends whom he was sure would also read and think about it. The last paragraph of Dixon's work might have been a summation of everything that Ned's inward vision had taught him to believe:

> *As in the darkness, in the organism not yet born, the eye is formed to correspond to things invisible, and thus with confidence anticipates a world to come, so the soul's faculties, for love, for pity, for joy, for admiration, for achievement correspond to a reality which exists and is by them foretold.*

The soul does not provide itself with a passport for an imaginary country, and cannot vibrate to a note unsounded in the universe. . . .

The very last words of all described the principle which had guided his life:

. . . in so far as we may, we should practice immortality, and omit no effort to live in accordance with the best that is in us.

Ned's faith had been a growth wholly independent of established doctrine and traditional creeds. He had read the Bible as he had read the Upanishads and the Koran, for the beauty of its poetry and for its insight into human nature. It had never conveyed to him that high sense of mystical assurance that makes it a bulwark of faith for most people who have grown up in the Judeo-Christian tradition. He must have pondered the teachings and the personality of Jesus, but he never referred to them except indirectly. He looked upon both the Old and New Testaments as symbolic and allegorical statements, with fragmentary historical foundations, of man's striving toward moral perfection and his yearning for immortality. It was not until near the end of his life that Christianity took on for him a deeply personal reality. Three times during the last two months he asked to have the Gospel of St. John read to him.

He still made every effort within the limits of his fading strength to keep in touch with his friends. He clung with eager tenacity to those whom he had known longest. Van Wyck and Eleanor Brooks, Jack and Phyllis Wheelock—all four often dined together with him. There was special comfort in having them near him and in hearing their talk float about his bed. Sometimes he would be merely a silent listener to the conversation, but the constant play of expression across his face showed with what intentness he followed every word.

To the end his heart and life were also open to newcomers. Charles Auchincloss was a new friend whose regular Friday visits were high points in the week's routine. In the last year of his life he met Anne Morrow Lindbergh whose *North to the Orient* and *Listen, the Wind* had thrilled him with the poetry of flying. Mrs. Lindbergh's memories of their friendship reveal the vitality which Sheldon, blind and now almost voiceless, could still pour into an attachment for a kindred spirit. To Sheldon this new relationship brought fresh human warmth and intellectual excitement like a rising note of brightness to offset the gathering shadows.

On February 4, 1946, Ned was sixty. To celebrate the day Henrietta Metcalf brought her four-year-old grandson Michael Harris to see him. There was the same happy response Ned always had for children when Michael sat on his bed, patted his face, and sang "Happy Birthday" to him. In a gay but scarcely audible whisper Ned repeated the chorus with the child.

If he had become quieter and more reflective, his humor could still flash out with all the old boyish love of easy fooling. Friends not only received words of comfort and cheer in the stream of telegrams that flowed from the penthouse. There would be enthusiastic messages of congratulations or personal advice carrying the signatures of famous (or infamous) characters of history. To a man who had emerged successfully from a breach of promise suit came cheery greetings signed "Henry VIII." An actor who had just landed a juicy Hollywood contract received comradely good wishes from "Al Capone."

There was no slackening of his interest in the theatre.

He followed avidly the reviews of all the new plays. He continued as always to advise playwright and actor friends. He missed no detail in the preparations for Ruth Gordon's *Years Ago*, and was elated at its success. In early March, 1946, Broadway was brought to his bedside for the last time when Katharine Cornell came with plans for the production of Anouilh's *Antigone*.

Ned wrote to their mutual friend Daisy Blaisdell:

> Kit came and read her *Antigone* to me and you can imagine how much I enjoyed it. I thought she was wonderful. I always knew it was her part. The play is interesting with its Paris 1943 implications, but as I told Kit Sophocles is simpler and greater. She agreed with me. . . . I hope *Antigone* will have a good run here. Evidently Kit loves doing it, and so, whatever happens, she will have no regrets.

He continued as always to follow political developments, and his grasp of the movement of current history was as sound and as comprehensive as ever. In March, Van Wyck and Eleanor Brooks dined with him and the talk was largely of international affairs. When they left, Ned immediately wrote a note to apologize for having dwelt so long on Russia. He had spent six hours earlier in the day listening to a UN assembly, and his mind was impregnated with the subject. It continued to preoccupy him. He foresaw a long and tense rivalry between Russia and the West, a wearing period of fretful stalemate which he feared could only lead to another war. In a letter to a new British friend, Sir John Greenly, he stressed his belief in the necessity of a complete merging of British and American interests to meet the Russian threat.

> Perhaps the Russians still believe that it is "they or we." There is a great deal to that, as all believers in world federation admit. But I don't want it to be One World, Russian

style. I believe that the alliance we spoke of would be the best protection against that eventuality. A stout net in case the UNO trapeze breaks. When it broke before there was no such net, and as a result we all crashed to the ground.

I don't suppose that war—if it comes—will come in our lifetime. But I am not so sure about what your sons and grandsons will have to face. The worst of it is that war will not be really necessary, not really unavoidable. Our two countries, working together, could keep it from happening, just as we could have kept it from happening last time. I think that your country sees this more plainly than mine does. Well, God help us all. Only we—I mean Americans—ought to help ourselves far more than we are doing. We could.

His mind still moved agilely from world problems to the homely details of everyday life. In mid-March, Marion Meigs Hyde, daughter of his old headmaster at the Hill School, dined with him. Ned was full of amused recollections of his boyhood. He laughed heartily at one or two thoroughly undignified incidents of his time at the Hill School, reminisced affectionately of staff and pupils, described in vivid detail familiar haunts of the campus and countryside. He recited all the landmarks of a favorite Sunday afternoon tramp along a meandering brook, chuckling at the recollection of its euphonious name—"Sproogle's Run."

Late in March, Jack Wheelock saw him, all unknowingly for the last time. Before he left, Ned asked Wheelock to read one of his poems, a lyric called "Silence," which had become a special favorite in late months. With the eight lines of this poem Wheelock said his last good night:

> There is a mystery too deep for words;
> The silence of the dead comes nearer to it,
> Being wisest in the end. What word shall hold
> The sorrow sitting at the heart of things,

The majesty and patience of the truth!
Silence will serve; it is an older tongue:
The empty room, the moonlight on the wall,
Speak for the unreturning traveller.

The last week was characteristic. On Wednesday, Ned had a visit with Anne Parrish who later wrote: "I think the last words I heard him speak, five days before he died, held the essence of what made him such a friend: 'Are you all right?' Was *I* all right!"

By Thursday, Miss Schrampf remarked that Ned's breathing had become quite shallow, though there was no other noticeable symptom of trouble. On Friday, however, he realized that he was not himself and regretfully notified Auchincloss that he would have to forego their usual visit because of a stomach upset.

Throughout the weekend some member of his household read to him continuously. The reading was only interrupted by the Sunday afternoon broadcast of the New York Philharmonic. The program gave him special delight because it included the *Partita* of his old friend Lionel Barrymore. Sunday night he could not go to sleep and listened to his night nurse read chapter after chapter from Archibald Marshall's *Sir Henry*.

Monday, April 1, dawned fresh and cloudless, packed with the promise of spring. The nurse was still reading, and Sheldon interrupted to inquire, "What time is it now?" She told him, "It's six o'clock, Mr. Sheldon." He murmured, "It's been a long night, hasn't it!"

An hour later the night nurse left. The housekeeper was in the kitchen and Mr. Ernst was due for duty. Suddenly Ned was seized with a sharp paroxysm of pain. He asked the housekeeper to call the orderly at once. When Mr. Ernst came running to the bedside Ned cried out to him, "Lift me up and hold me firmly—I'm going." There was only a brief moment of struggle, and the slender thread was snapped.

The last telegrams went out to friends across the country and abroad. Many, like Ruth Draper, were incredulous at the news. "Somehow," she wrote his sister, "I never thought he might die; he seemed so a part of the things that never die— the things by which one lives, believes in, clings to as secure and beautiful forever."

As his friends entered the blue room for the last time, singly as always, there was only the silence to tell that he had gone. But the absence of that warm, bright "Here you are at last!" struck like a blow as one moved across the threshold toward the bed.

Nothing else was changed. He lay as he always had— with the high blue screen behind the bed, and the silk coverlet drawn up to his chest. His face was the same, still ruddy, with the black mask in place. There was a faint, relaxed smile on his lips.

After the first sharp pang of realization, there could be no mourning for him. No one who sat by him now, knowing the power of his life, could help but feel that this was the final step of his liberation, which had begun so long before. No one could begrudge him that.

At St. James Episcopal Church, down Madison Avenue a dozen blocks away, the hundreds of Ned's friends gathered for the last time with him. Then, over the road he had traveled twenty-five years before, he was taken back West to the scene of his happy boyhood summers at Lake Geneva, Wisconsin.

He was buried in the little cemetery on Oak Hill, a few miles from his grandfather's house, where other members of his family lay. Some years before, a great boulder that had once stood at the edge of Henry Strong's lawn had been moved to the cemetery. The stone had been a fixture in the childhood of the Sheldon children and their cousins. It had been the center of Indian war dances, the fort in the wilderness, the magic refuge from all the evil pursuers of childhood. This was the marker for the end of Ned's journey.

INDEX

Index